Pronounced for

C000203487

Early Scots Law Tales

Pronounced for Doom
Early Scots Law Tales

Edited by

John P Grant

Professor of Law at Lewis & Clark Law School,
Portland, Oregon, and
Professor Emeritus of International Law at
Glasgow University, Scotland

Elaine E Sutherland

Professor of Child and Family Law at
Stirling University, Scotland, and
Professor of Law at Lewis & Clark Law School,
Portland, Oregon

Avizandum Publishing Ltd
Edinburgh
2013

Published by

Avizandum Publishing Ltd
25 Candlemaker Row
Edinburgh EH1 2QG

First published 2013

ISBN   978-1-904968-65-8

British Library Cataloguing in Publication Data

A catalogue entry for this book is available from the British Library

Typeset by Etica Press Ltd, Malvern, Worcs

Printed and bound by Martin's the Printers, Berwick-upon-Tweed

Contents

Contributors

Lesley-Anne Barnes Macfarlane is a lecturer in law at Edinburgh Napier University. Her principal research and teaching interests are in the fields of Scots private law and child and family law and she has contributed to various academic and professional journals on these subjects. Her former experience as a solicitor, court welfare reporter, *curator ad litem* and lawyer-mediator inform her current research. Her recent publications include "Contributory Negligence and the Child" 2010 JR 195 and " 'Dear Judge, I am writing to you because I think it's pathetic': Re A-H (Children)" (2009) 13 EdinLR 528.

David L Carey Miller is Emeritus Professor of Property Law at the University of Aberdeen and a Senior Associate Research Fellow, Institute of Advanced Legal Studies, London. A corporeal moveable property specialist, he has a special interest in title to cultural property and has lectured on the St Ninian's Isle treasure case at home and abroad. Appointed to Aberdeen in 1971 after work under T B Smith in Edinburgh in the 1960s, David Carey Miller's more recent publications include two property chapters in the 13th edition of *Gloag and Henderson, The Law of Scotland* (2012) and "Lawyer for All Time" in Andrew Burrows, David Johnston and Reinhard Zimmermann (eds), *Judge and Jurist: Essays in Memory of Lord Rodger of Earlsferry* (2013).

Clare Connelly is an advocate and was formerly a senior lecturer in law at the University of Glasgow. Her recent publications include *Criminal Law* (5th edn, 2013) and she is currently writing a book on *Sexual Offences and Scots Law*.

Douglas J Cusine was in private practice from 1969 to 1974 and a member of the Council of the Law Society of Scotland from 1988 to 1999. He was Professor of Conveyancing and Professional Practice of Law at the University of Aberdeen from 1990 until 1999, and a sheriff of Grampian, Highland and Islands based at Aberdeen from 2000 until 2011. Among his publications is his co-authored (with Roderick Paisley) *Servitudes and Rights of Way* (1998).

John P Grant is Emeritus Professor of International Law in the University of Glasgow and Professor of Law at Lewis & Clark Law School, Portland, Oregon. His publications span his academic career from *Independence and Devolution: The Legal Implications for Scotland* (1976) to the *Encyclopaedic Dictionary of International Law* (with Craig Barker, 3rd edn, 2009). He was a co-editor of *Scots Law Tales*, published in 2010, to which he contributed "Not our Finest Hour: The Lockerbie Trial".

William W McBryde is Emeritus Professor of Commercial Law in the University of Edinburgh. Among his publications is *The Law of Contract* (3rd edn, 2007). Sometime Van der Grinten Professor of Commercial Law, University of Nijmegen, the Netherlands and visiting Professor L'Université de Paris V René Descartes.

Claire McDiarmid is a senior lecturer at the University of Strathclyde in Glasgow. She teaches in the area of criminal law and has particular research interests in the law of homicide and in childhood and crime (in which she co-ordinates and teaches a masters level class). She publishes regularly in both fields as also, more generally, on the criminal law of Scotland. She is the author of *Childhood and Crime* (2007) and *Criminal Law Essentials* (2nd edn, 2010) and co-author, with Professor Pamela Ferguson, of *Scots Criminal Law: A Critical Analysis* (2009).

Anne MacKenzie is a Children's Reporter based in Aberdeenshire. She graduated from Edinburgh University with a BA in French in 1977 and an LLB in 1979 and, after an apprenticeship with an Edinburgh court firm, qualified as a solicitor in 1981. Her LLM by research was awarded by Aberdeen University in 1995. Anne has a lively interest in family history and has researched extensively for family and friends. In 2012 she gained a Post-Graduate Certificate in Family and Local History by distance learning from Dundee University.

Sheila A M McLean was the first holder of the IBA Chair of Law and Ethics in Medicine at Glasgow University. She has been a vice-chairman of UNESCO's International Bioethics Committee and remains a member of that Committee, and has acted as a consultant/adviser to the World Health Organisation, the Council of Europe,

UNESCO and a number of individual states. She was founding Chairperson of the Scottish Criminal Cases Review Commission, and has chaired a number of governmental committees. She currently chairs the National Donation Strategy Group established by the Human Fertilisation and Embryology Authority. She has been principal investigator on a number of research grants and has authored or co-authored some 10 books and edited a further 14.

Hector MacQueen is a Scottish Law Commissioner and Professor of Private Law at the University of Edinburgh. His research interests include contract law, intellectual property and legal history, and his recent work has included several pieces on the development of intellectual property in Scotland after 1707.

Kathleen Marshall was Scotland's first Commissioner for Children and Young People, holding office for a five-year term from April 2004 with a remit to promote and safeguard the rights of children and young people in Scotland. She is a qualified solicitor and child law consultant, and was Director of the Scottish Child Law Centre from 1989 to 1994. She chaired the Edinburgh Inquiry into Abuse and Protection of Children in Care, which reported in February 1999. Her consultancy work has addressed a wide range of children's rights issues, for example, in relation to support for children and families, child protection, health, education, youth justice and the court system.

Kenneth McK Norrie is Professor of Law at the University of Strathclyde. His primary research interests include family law (with particular reference to families based around same-sex couples), private international law, and delict (with particular reference to defamation and privacy). He has acted as adviser to committees of the Scottish Parliament in relation to family law, adoption and children's hearings, and served on a Scottish Government Working Group on No-Fault Liability for Medical Injuries. His major publications include *Parent and Child* (3rd edn, 2013), *Defamation and Related Actions in Scots Law* (1995), *100 Cases that Every Scots Law Student Needs to Know* (2nd edn, 2010) and *Professor Norrie's Commentaries on Family Law* (2012).

Elspeth Reid is Professor in Law at the University of Edinburgh where her teaching responsibilities are in the area of private and comparative law, and she has published extensively in Scotland and abroad on these themes. Her recent publications include books on *Personal Bar* (with J Blackie, 2006), *Confidentiality, Personality and Privacy in Scots Law* (2010), *Product Liability in South Africa* (with Max Loubser, 2012), and *Private Law and Human Rights: Bringing Rights Home in Scotland and South Africa* (edited with Danie Visser, 2013). She is series editor of the *Edinburgh Studies in Law* monographs published by Edinburgh University Press and is also a member of the editorial boards of the *Edinburgh Law Review* and of the *European Journal of Comparative Law and Governance*. She is a Fellow of the Royal Society of Edinburgh and a qualified solicitor.

Robert S Shiels is a graduate of the Universities of Dundee and Glasgow. He qualified as a solicitor in Scotland in 1979 and has since worked mainly, but not exclusively, as a public prosecutor. He has written extensively on various aspects of Scots law, particularly in the area of criminal law, with books published on controlled drugs and offensive weapons. More recently, he has followed an interest in legal history, particularly in the modern era beginning in the Victorian period.

Elaine E Sutherland is Professor of Child and Family Law at the Law School, University of Stirling, Scotland, and Professor at Lewis & Clark Law School, Portland, Oregon, spending six months of the year researching, writing and teaching at each. She has lectured on child and family law around the world. She serves on the Family Law Committee of the Law Society of Scotland and participates in the law reform process through regular independent responses to consultation papers from government and other bodies. The author of some 90 articles and book chapters, she contributes the chapter on Scotland to the annual publication, *International Survey of Family Law*. Her books include *Child and Family Law* (2nd edn, 2008), *Family Law* (2nd edn, 2008), *Children's Rights in Scotland* (with Cleland, 3rd edn, 2009), *Scots Law Tales* (with Grant, 2010), *Law Making and the Scottish Parliament: The Early Years* (with Goodall, Little and Davidson, 2011) and *The Future of Child and Family Law: International Predictions* (2012).

Preface

"Pronounced for doom" were the final words uttered from the bench when a Scottish court imposed a death sentence. Although only one of the stories in this volume resulted in a pronouncement for doom, the phrase has an iconic and distinctively Scottish place in legal history and literature. It seemed apt, therefore, as the title of this collection of tales from the Scottish courts before 1900.

There is a long tradition in Scotland of publications telling the story of major court cases. The doyen of this literary phenomenon was William Roughead who, in the 82 years of his life (and right up to his death in 1952), published some 38 books and countless articles, telling the tale of important cases. Other authors confined themselves to a specific case that particularly aroused their interest and there are references to numerous such works in the individual chapters in this volume.

When we edited *Scots Law Tales*, published in 2010, we intended that each chapter should tell the human story behind a leading Scottish case: that the tales should be as much, if not more, about the people involved in the case in the context of their time and place as a legal analysis of the case itself. Our belief was that there are readers – law students and potential law students, lawyers in practice, at leisure and in retirement, and those non-lawyers who are fascinated by the law and its workings – who would enjoy in-depth and rounded accounts of these cases. The enthusiastic response to the volume proved our conviction to be accurate. It was in the course of working on that volume that we were reminded of just how many early cases, decided before the 20th century, involved absolutely fascinating people and events, and we determined to edit a volume of tales on these cases in the future.

After consulting colleagues and friends, we identified fourteen early cases that met the criteria – fascinating facts, events or personalities, sometimes all three. We then identified expert authors for these cases and gave them a simple mandate: pen a readable chapter on the case, drawing out the personalities involved, the events leading up to and after the case, what the court decided and why, and the role that the case played in the development of its area of law – and do all this in whatever length is appropriate, but no more than 6,000 words. We suggested minimal footnoting, which one author took to mean four and another to mean 90. We then applied some light-touch editing to the manuscripts submitted; and the result is this volume, *Pronounced for Doom: Early Scots Law Tales.*

While the fourteen tales were chosen principally for their inherent interest, they are not without legal significance. *Harvey v Harvey* is an early recognition of the participation rights of children, a major tenet of contemporary child law. The modern law on the effect of error on contract owes much to *Sword v Sinclair*. *Udny v Udny* is still authority in the law relating to domicile. The modern Scots law on real conditions is based, in part at least, on the decision in *Taylors of Aberdeen v Coutts*. The High Court of Justiciary had no difficulty in using the insanity defence in the *Kinloch* case, despite its novelty at the time. The criteria used in *Beaton v Ivory* to hold a public official liable for excess of authority have stood the test of time. *Hinton v Donaldson* is a seminal authority in the development of copyright law.

There is even a contemporary resonance to those cases that were decided on their particular, and sometimes peculiar, facts and circumstances. In the post-9/11 era, it is perhaps no surprise to learn that, when a state thinks its security is threatened, as it clearly did by Thomas Muir's calls for representative government, justice can be one of the first casualties. There being nothing new under the sun, it is unsurprising that the incompetents who ran the City of Glasgow Bank into oblivion should suffer only slightly greater sanction than those who brought about the financial crisis of 2007–2008. It is reassuring to know that the public was as concerned in the 18th century about the affairs of the high-born Lady Jane Douglas and in the 19th century about the doings of the not-so-high-born Madeleine Smith and Theresa Yelverton as it would be today. *Woods and Pirie v Cumming Gordon* demonstrates that courts can hear and see in witnesses what they want to hear and see; and that the unpalatable can always be avoided and justice achieved. The judicial and subsequent adventures of Theresa Yelverton illustrate the legal and social importance of marriage and the changing role of women in the 19th century. Deacon William Brodie's fate is a cautionary tale against excessive hubris.

It has to be admitted that, of the principal characters in our tales, the women fare better than do the men. The men range from a naïve tea merchant, John Sword, through the woefully incompetent directors of the City of Glasgow Bank; a ruthlessly-determined publisher, Alexander Donaldson; a shallow and inept racing man, John Udny; a devious, philandering father, William Harvey; a hedonistic and hapless thief, William Brodie; a tyrannical sheriff, William Ivory to a homicidally insane minor aristocrat, Gordon Kinloch. Only the principled and brave Thomas Muir can truly be described as a hero. Even the minor male characters are less than appealing. The Earl of Douglas, the brother of Lady Jane Douglas, was parsimonious and mean-spirited; and Pierre Emile L'Angelier, beau of Madeleine Smith, and Major Charles Yelverton were both cads.

The principal women, on the other hand, present in a much better light. Lady Jane Douglas remained indomitable in the face of a miserable brother and a feckless husband. Jane Pirie and Marianne Woods bravely sought to protect their little school in court in the knowledge that their sexuality would become a matter of issue, as it very graphically did. Madeleine Smith was free-spirited and strong-willed before, during and after her legal difficulties over the death of her lover. That proto-feminist Theresa Yelverton rose above her legal travails and the publicity surrounding them to emerge an independent and successful woman.

Our immense gratitude goes to the contributors of the various chapters who confessed to being drawn into their cases and the surrounding personalities and context to an extent that sometimes surprised even them, something reflected in the enthusiasm and diligence with which they discharged their task. Our thanks go, of course, to Margaret Cherry of Avizandum Publishing whose faith in the project was a prerequisite to its coming to fruition and with whom it has been, as ever, a pleasure to work.

John P Grant
Elaine E Sutherland
Edinburgh
October 2013

Pronounced for Doom:
Deacon William Brodie

John P Grant

The Lord Justice-Clerk and Lords Commissioners of Justiciary, having considered the verdict of assize, dated and returned this twenty-eighth day of August, against the said William Brodie and George Smith, Pannels, whereby the assize all in one voice find them guilty of the crime libeled; the said Lords in respect of the said verdict decern and adjudge the said William Brodie and George Smith to be carried from the bar back to the Tolbooth of Edinburgh, therein to be detained till Wednesday, the first day of October next, and upon that day to be taken furth of the said Tolbooth to the place fixed upon by the magistrates of Edinburgh as a common place of execution, and then and there, betwixt the hours of two and four o'clock afternoon to be hanged by the necks, by the hands of the Common Executioner, upon a Gibbet, until they be dead; and ordain all their moveable goods and gear to be escheat and inbrought to His Majesty's use: which is pronounced for doom.

Thus was the fate of Deacon William Brodie and his co-accused, George Smith, pronounced by Lord Justice-Clerk Braxfield at the High Court of Justiciary in the early afternoon of Thursday 29 August 1788. Edinburgh society in the late 1780s had been reduced to a state of near panic by a spate of audacious house- and shop-breakings and was amazed that one of the men charged, and ultimately convicted, of breaking into the Excise House in the spring of 1788 was none other than a substantial citizen and well-regarded cabinet maker, an elected deacon of his craft and a former town councillor. The question asked, then and now, was what took Brodie from a respected pillar of Edinburgh society by day to carousing, gambling thief by night. How and why did an educated and successful craftsman enjoying wealth and esteem in the community come to end his days on the gallows?

William Brodie's story fascinated writers from the very beginning. On 5 September 1788, seven days after Brodie was convicted and sentenced, William Creech, a juror at the trial and a printer, published the first account of the trial, drawing on his attendance as a juror and the formal record of the proceedings. A day later, Aeneas Morrison, co-accused George Smith's solicitor, published another account, including more details of Brodie's life than appeared in the Creech publication. The Deacon, who apparently read all the accounts of his trial while awaiting execution, was reported to have considered the Morrison version the best.[1]

Robert Louis Stevenson was so enthralled by Brodie's good-by-day and bad-by-night life that, along with William Henley, he wrote a melodrama, *Deacon Brodie; or the Double Life*, dramatising the events surrounding the Excise House break-in up to Brodie's arrest.[2] The Brodie story is generally accepted as Stevenson's inspiration for *The Strange Case of Dr Jekyll and Mr Hyde*, first published in 1886.[3] The writer and historian Peter Mackenzie thought the story worthy of retelling at length in 1890.[4] The redoubtable William Roughead, chronicler of so many famous Scottish trials, revived interest in Brodie with the inclusion of the *Trial of Deacon Brodie* in the *Notable Scottish Trials* series in 1906; his account of the trial is drawn from Creech and Morrison and is accompanied by an insightful introduction.[5] In the style of a novel, Dick Donovan, an eccentric and prolific English

1 Before Creech published his revised and expanded edition on 3 October 1788, two days after the execution of Brodie and Smith, two other accounts of the trial had appeared. Both published on 15 September 1788, these accounts by A Robertson and J Stewart were nothing more than pirated versions of Creech's original. In an application for interdict to prevent the publication of the Robertson and Stewart books brought by Creech, Lord Dreghorn declared both books gross piracies but declined to grant interdict because Creech had not entered his volume at Stationers' Hall and received the appropriate certificate prior to publication, as required by the Statute of Anne (c 19) of 1710.
2 The play opened at the Prince's Theatre in London on 2 July 1884, with Henley's untalented brother as Brodie, and was performed again in Montreal on 26 September 1887; it was first printed and published in 1888.
3 Programme notes for a production of *Dr Jekyll and Mr Hyde* at Cleveland Play House in 2003 (written by the true crime writer Albert Borowicz, reproduced in 29 *Legal Studies Journal* 759 (2005)) record that, as a child, Stevenson had in his night nursery a bookcase and chest of drawers made by Deacon Brodie and that his devoted nurse, Alison Cunningham, told him stories of old Edinburgh, including that of Deacon Brodie. The same programme notes fancifully suggest that Stevenson intended *Dr Jekyll and Mr Hyde* as a parody on hypocrisy in Victorian Edinburgh or as a rueful reflection on his own rather dissolute youth.
4 *Old Reminiscences of Glasgow and the West of Scotland* (1890), vol 2, chap XIV.
5 A second edition was published in 1914 and a third in 1921, this last as part of the *Notable British Trials* series.

author, published *Deacon Brodie: Or Behind the Mask* in 1901;[6] F E Smith (the Earl of Birkenhead), a former Lord Chancellor, included an account of the Brodie trial in his *Famous Trials in History* (1926) and *Famous Trials* (1930); in 1975, Forbes Bramble, an English architect and writer, published the novel *The Strange Case of Deacon Brodie*; and, in 1977, the journalist John S Gibson published *Deacon Brodie: Father to Jekyll and Hyde*. Billy Connelly starred as Brodie in a TV movie in 1997. There is a famous *Deacon Brodie's Tavern* in Edinburgh's Royal Mile; and, less explicably, a *Deacon Brodie's* bar on West 46th Street in New York City and a *Deacon Brodie's Restaurant and Bar* in Butler, Alabama (population 1,952).

THE EXCISE HOUSE JOB

Towards the end of the 18th century, the general Excise Office for Scotland was located in an unattractive former dwelling-house in Chessel's Court in Edinburgh's Canongate. Employing a cashier, a deputy solicitor and several clerks, it transacted much business and, occasionally, had on hand large sums of money. It opened at 10 in the morning and closed at 8 in the evening, with a watchman coming on duty two hours later. At a little after 8 pm on Wednesday, 5 March 1788, the outer door and the chief cashier's passage door were opened with keys or picklocks, his inner door was broken open and his room entered. The deputy solicitor, James Bonar, returning to retrieve something from his office, noticed that the outer door was unlocked, but assumed that the clerks were still at work; he retrieved what he had come for and left, not realising that there were intruders in the building. The intruders remained in the chief cashier's office for about 45 minutes, ransacking his desk; and they made off with £16, as it happens missing £1,600 in two hidden drawers. The break-in and theft were discovered the following morning when the clerks turned up for work. Not wanting to put the citizenry in a state of fear and alarm, the authorities were determined to keep this audacious crime from the public as long as possible, particularly as it seemed like yet another in a recent spate of burglaries and shop-breakings. Nonetheless, by the Friday, two days later, the Excise House job was the talk of the town.

6 Dick Donovan's real name, according to himself, was Joyce Emmerson Preston Muddock, though his birth record shows it as the more prosaic James Edward Muddock; his *nom de plume*, Dick Donovan, was the central character, a Glasgow detective, in 184 of his stories.

For the Excise House job, the Brodie gang had four members. Its leader, William Brodie, was described by William Roughead as a "macaroni", a term used at the time for an effeminate dandy – indeed, the term dandy emerged later to connote a more muscular form of macaroni. Brodie was no macaroni, though he was, by the standards of Edinburgh at the time, certainly a dandy. According to the advertisement in the *Edinburgh Courant* of 12 March 1788, offering a reward of £200 for information leading to his arrest and conviction, Brodie was short, at 5'4", broad at the shoulders and narrow at the hips, with a sallow complexion, black hair drawn back into a ponytail and frizzed at the sides, and dark brown eyes. The advertisement drew particular attention to his affected speech[7] and his long-strided, swaggering style of walking. The description of his dress was typical of how Brodie outfitted himself as an important and respected burger: a black coat, waistcoat, breeches and stockings, with leather silver-buckled shoes.

Brodie was, at that time, 48 years old. He was born on 28 September 1741 to Francis and Cecil Brodie and was the eldest of eleven children of that marriage, most of whom died in infancy, only William and his sisters Jean, who looked after the family home after the death of her mother Cecil in 1777, and Jacobina, known as Jamie, surviving into adulthood. Francis Brodie had established a lucrative business as a wright (cabinet-maker) to such an extent that he had acquired a handsome house, "a mansion" according to Roughead, off the High Street and had secured election as the deacon of his guild and as a member of Edinburgh Council. Francis was a well-kent and well-respected citizen; the wynd in which his home was located was named Brodie's Close in recognition of his eminence.

While little is recorded of William's childhood, it is clear that he was educated to a standard befitting his family's status, and he was apprenticed in his father's business. By the time of his father's death in 1782, William had taken over the business which, under his tutelage, continued to prosper. Like his father, he too became Deacon of the Incorporation of Wrights and a member of the Council, the latter furnishing father and son with a substantial amount of city business.

---

7 According to Walter Geike, *Etchings Illustrative of Scottish Character and Scenery* (1885), p 117, Brodie affected "a particular motion with his mouth and lips when he speaks, which he does full and slow, his mouth being commonly open at the time, and his tongue doubling up, as it were, shows itself towards the roof of his mouth".

Commenting on attitudes and behaviour in late 18th-century Edinburgh, Roughead suggests that "the social customs of the time were not conducive to steadiness and sobriety among the youthful citizens". William Brodie embraced the prevailing social customs with great enthusiasm. Like many of his fellow crafts and trades colleagues, he repaired at close of business at 8 pm to one of the innumerable taverns for some intensive drinking. When the drum of the town guard announced the closing of the city's gates at 10 pm – and when the respectable set off for their homes and beds – a more resolute group, William among them, sought further recreation. That recreation, euphemistically termed "gentlemanly vices", tended to be of a dubious nature: cock-fighting, cards and dice, all activities in which gambling was a major component. William was a devotee of cock-fighting, regularly attending the mains (competitions) at Michael Henderson's seedy "stables" in the Grassmarket; he even kept a fighting cock of his own at his yard. For cards and dice, he frequented James Clerk's disreputable tavern at the top of Fleshmarket Close, known for its select company of sharpers and their dupes, William being in the former group. He was a member of one, and certainly not the most prestigious, of the many convivial societies that flourished in Edinburgh in the 18th century. The Cape Club was formally constituted in 1764 to support a militia to defend Scotland, but its nightly meetings, at the time William was a member, centred on the social rather than the political or philosophical. While the Cape Club had some eminent members, among them the poet Robert Fergusson and the painters Alexander Runciman and Henry Raeburn, William Brodie used the club to further his business and drinking interests.

Despite this hectic work and convivial schedule, the bachelor Brodie found time for two mistresses.[8] His favourite was Anne Grant, a domestic servant originally from the north-east of Scotland, whom he maintained with their three children in an apartment in Cant's Close. While on the run after the Excise House job, he wrote to William Henderson of cock-pit fame, invoking God's "infinite goodness [to] stir up some friendly aid for their support". He maintained his other mistress, Jane (or Jeannie) Watt, in an apartment in Libberton's Wynd, in the Grassmarket near his home. Described by the Lord Advocate at trial as "a woman of an abandoned character", and by Brodie himself as "a devil", she nonetheless provided him with an alibi, testifying in

8 John S Gibson, *Deacon Brodie: Father to Jekyll and Hyde* (1977), p 31, suggests two other mistresses, Lucy Lockit and Polly Peachum.

court that he had spent the entire evening and night of the Excise House job with her.

William Brodie's principal accomplice, and co-accused at trial, was George Smith, who owned a less-than-thriving grocer's business in the Cowgate. He is depicted in *Kay's Originals* as a tall, burly man with a protruding forehead.[9] Born in Berkshire, Smith and his wife Mary travelled the land by horse and cart as hawkers before he moved to Edinburgh in July 1786. He initially resided at Michael Henderson's tavern in the Grassmarket, where he was assured of bad company. He was unwell for a considerable period, necessitating a summons for his wife to join him and the sale of all his goods, including his horse. No stranger to dishonest methods of earning a living, he met Brodie who, according to a later declaration he made to the sheriff, suggested "that several things could be done in this place if prudently managed to great advantage".[10] While at Clerk's tavern and gambling house in Fleshmarket Close, Smith met Andrew Ainslie and John Brown, the final two members of what was to become the Brodie gang.

Andrew Ainslie was designed in the Crown list of witnesses at trial as "sometime shoemaker in Edinburgh", but he was better known for his addiction to dicing and the company of cheats. John Brown, alias Humphrey Moore, was, like George Smith, an Englishman. He was a noted sharper and had been convicted of theft at the Old Bailey in 1784, for which he was sentenced to transportation for seven years. He had somehow evaded justice and found his way to Edinburgh.

The Excise House job was the culmination of the gang's criminal endeavours. It was their biggest job and, as it happens, their last. All their previous criminal activities had been on a smaller scale. According to George Smith, in August 1787, Brodie, Smith and Ainslie picked the locks of John Carnegie's grocery business in Leith and made off

9 The portraits of John Kay, the caricaturist and engraver, were collected and published after his death as *A series of original portraits and caricature etchings by the late John Kay, with biographical sketches and illustrative anecdotes* (1838). Number CVI in the series, titled "George Smith and Deacon William Brodie", depicts and gives an account of the first "interview" between the two.

10 This statement appears in George Smith's second declaration. In all, he made four declarations before the sheriff, on 8 March, 10 March, 19 March and 17 July 1788. In the first, Smith made no admissions; in the second, he made "a clean breast", admitting the involvement of Brodie, Brown, Ainslie and himself in the Excise House and other jobs; in the third, he admitted that a number of articles he was shown had been used in the Excise House and other jobs; and in the fourth, he admitted that a brace of pistols belonging to Deacon Brodie was used in the Excise House job.

with 3½ cwt of fine black tea. In November 1787, at Brodie's instigation, Smith and John Brown used a false key to enter the University library and steal the mace. A month later, Smith and Ainslie sprung the lock of John Tapp's house in Parliament Close above his goldsmith's shop; while Brown distracted the owner downstairs, they stole 18 guineas and some items of personal jewellery. In January 1788, again at Brodie's instigation, Smith and Ainslie broke into the shop of Inglis, Horner & Company in the High Street and stole a large assortment of valuable goods, including silks and cambrics (white, plain-weave, linen cloth). Much of the stolen property was dispatched to Chesterfield to be fenced by an acquaintance of Smith.

These are only some of the depredations ascribed to the Brodie gang, although its members were never convicted of any of these crimes. There were other burglaries, shop- and house-breakings from the summer of 1787 until the Excise House job in March of 1788, although it is difficult to find convincing evidence that the Brodie gang was responsible for them. Nonetheless, they all created a near-panic reaction among the citizens of Edinburgh.

Deacon Brodie became fascinated by the possibility of pulling off a big job at the Excise House in Chessel's Court. He was already familiar with the business transacted and the money held there through the work undertaken by him and his staff on the building. On occasions, he accompanied a friend from Stirling to conduct business at the Excise House. On the pretence of inquiring about his Stirling friend, Brodie and Smith went to the Excise House where Brodie distracted the staff while Smith took a putty impression of the outer door key, conveniently left hanging on a peg on the wall. Ainslie was dispatched to scout the activities at closing time; he discovered that the outer door was locked at 8 pm and that no night watchman arrived till 10 pm. As was their practice, Smith and Brown tried the false key on the outer door and it worked, but the inner door to the cashier's office, they realised, would need to be broken open. To that end, Brown and Ainslie were dispatched to Duddingston to steal the coulter of a plough, thought by Smith to be a suitable implement to overcome the resistance of the inner door. All four met at Smith's house the night before the break-in to finalise plans, Brodie bringing his father's wig as part of Smith's disguise and a rope to be used for escape through a rear window if necessary. They agreed that, if interrupted by the watchman, they would secure him and personate smugglers seeking to retrieve confiscated property.

On Wednesday, 5 March 1788, Deacon Brodie attended to his business in the morning. Between 2 and 3 in the afternoon, he went to Smith's house with some picklocks, false keys, a chisel, a whistle to sound the alarm and a spur to be left at the scene to persuade investigators that the perpetrators had come by horse and were not local. He then went home and was in the company of his aunt, two sisters and brother-in-law for the rest of the afternoon and evening, ending at 8 pm. The Deacon then changed into an old-fashioned dark suit and light coat; armed with a cocked hat, lantern and two pistols, he set out for Smith's. Two more brace of pistols were distributed to Smith and Brown, the coulter was retrieved from its hiding place, crepe masks were made ready and the foursome set out. Ainslie was stationed outside the Excise House; he was to use the ivory whistle to alert the others to any danger. Brodie was to remain behind the outer door to pass on any warning from Ainslie. Smith and Brown were to break down the cashier's inner door with the coulter and ransack his office.

All went well ... initially. Ainslie took up his position behind the wall surrounding the Excise House. Smith and Brown opened the outer door to the building with the duplicate key, used curling tongs to open the cashier's outer door and broke open the inner door with the coulter and a crowbar. Finally, Brodie arrived to take up his position behind the building's outer door. The job began to unravel when John Bonar briefly returned to the Excise House, alarming Brodie to such an extent that he walked past the deputy solicitor in the entranceway and fled for home and a change of clothes, whence to the arms of Jeannie Watt. Ainslie, confused by the arrival of Bonar, the departure of Brodie, followed quickly by the departure of Bonar, none distinguishable in the feeble light of the court, took fright, blew the warning three blasts of the whistle and fled to Smith's house. With no relay to pass on the alarm, Smith and Brown continued their plunder, eventually leaving for Smith's house in the Cowgate, upset at their meagre haul and at the disappearance of their two colleagues.

Every day since late January of that year, the three Edinburgh newspapers had carried advertisements offering £150 and a free pardon for the identity of the culprits in the Inglis, Horner & Company shop-breaking and other jobs. With transportation already hanging over him and disgusted with the cowardice of two of his fellow gang members, John Brown decided to take advantage of the offer (hoping it would include his earlier conviction in England) and approached the authorities with the full story of the Excise House job. At this time, he did not mention Brodie's involvement, no doubt hoping to blackmail him later. On the Saturday, Ainslie and Smith and his wife and maid-servant were arrested. Realising that the writing was writ large on the wall, Brodie left Edinburgh the following morning for London. When Ainslie and Smith learned of Brodie's flight, each made a declaration incriminating the Deacon. The authorities then searched Brodie's premises where they found buried pistols, false keys, picklocks and a case with putty for key impressions. On Monday, 10 March, the Edinburgh papers carried an advertisement offering a £200 reward for the apprehension of "William Brodie, a considerable house carpenter, and burgess of the city of Edinburgh".

Brodie arrived in London on 12 March and stayed with a friend, apparently within 500 yards of Bow Street, until 23 March when he boarded the sloop *Endeavour* as John Dixon and had the vessel make the journey to Leith via the port of Flushing in the Netherlands. Brodie then made his way to Amsterdam, where, still as John Dixon, he remained until he was tracked down and apprehended at the end of June. After extradition from the Netherlands, he was brought back to London and ultimately, on 17 July, to Edinburgh, where he was committed to the Tolbooth. He remained there till his trial 41 days later and his execution 35 days after that.

SPEEDY JUSTICE AND SWIFT EXECUTION

It is an understatement to describe the trial as speedy: it was completed in just over 28 hours, with both Brodie and Smith convicted and sentenced to death. At 9 am on Wednesday, 27 August 1788, the trial began before a bench of five judges, presided over by the daunting and ill-tempered Lord Justice-Clerk, Lord Braxfield, and a jury of fifteen, including the "bookseller" William Creech. The prosecution team was led by the Lord Advocate himself, the talented but dull Ilay Campbell, a year later appointed Lord President with the judicial title of Lord Succoth. He was assisted by the Solicitor General, Robert Dundas, an amiable and generous man who was to become Lord Advocate in succession to Campbell and ultimately, under the title Lord Melville, Chief Baron of the Exchequer in Scotland. The defence team was no less formidable. Brodie was represented by the Dean of Faculty, Henry Erskine, whose legal career, sadly, progressed no further, principally because of his tolerant political views in an intolerant political age. Henry, Lord Cockburn later described him as "the brightest luminary at our bar".[11] Counsel for George Smith was

11 Henry C Cockburn, *Life of Lord Jeffrey* (1852), p 91.

John Clerk, with a mere three years' experience as an advocate, who went on, in part for his confrontation with Lord Braxfield at the trial, to become so successful that it was said that he was at one time handling half of the court's business; he was later elevated to the bench as Lord Eldin.

For the whole of the trial, even when the Lord Justice-Clerk charged the jury at 4.30 the following morning, the court was, according to Aeneas Morrison's account, "uncommonly crowded, notwithstanding the fees of admission were raised as high as three, four or five shillings". It had become the practice of the doorkeepers to charge for admission to high-profile trials – and none was more high-profile than this – and for those charged to demand value for money. So, when there were threats from the bench to clear sections of the court, the result was "noise and tumult".

The most damaging evidence against Brodie and Smith was the testimony of Andrew Ainslie and John Brown, both protected by immunity on condition that they spoke the truth. Objection was taken on behalf of Brodie that, while the evidence of a *socius criminis* was generally admissible, their evidence was not because the sheriff had offered them their lives in return for turning King's evidence against Brodie. These objections were repelled on the basis that the sheriff, as an "inferior officer", had no authority to make any such deal, though the court was at pains to emphasise that the credibility of Ainslie and Brown was diminished by their admitted involvement in the crime. Further objection was taken to Brown's admissibility as a witness, because of his theft conviction in England (albeit he had a royal pardon) and his later banishment from Stirlingshire for theft. With some sophistication of thought on the part of the judges, these objections were also repelled. The court accepted that, while a royal pardon would not make a witness admissible under Scots law, the effect of a pardon under English law was to make the grantee a "new man" and admissible as a witness; and the court considered that the consequence of an English pardon should be accepted in Scotland as matter of *comitas*. Brown's banishment order was not such as to make him inadmissible, emanating, as it did, only from justices of the peace, an "inferior Court".

Brodie's flight to London and then the Netherlands, three days after the Excise House break-in and a day after the arrest of Smith and Ainslie, did not help him. Even less did it help that, in an unsigned scroll written while on board the *Endeavour* and found in one of his trunks, he admitted: "I shall ever repent keeping such company [Smith and Brown], and whatever they may alledge, I had no hand in any of their depredations, excepting the last fatal one, ... but I doubt not but all will be laid to my charge."

In his defence, it was argued that he had an alibi for the entire afternoon and evening of 5 March. His brother-in-law, Mathew Sheriff, testified that he had been in Brodie's company from just before 3 pm "until within a few minutes of eight o'clock". Jeannie Watt testified that Brodie arrived at her house "just at the time the eight o'clock bell was ringing" and remained there until the following morning. This evidence was corroborated by Watt's servant, Peggy Giles, who said that he arrived at 8 pm, also recalling hearing the tolling of the eight o'clock bell, and by a neighbour, Helen Wallace, who testified that she saw Brodie leave Watt's house just before 9 the following morning. In his final submissions, the Lord Advocate considered the testimony of Sheriff, himself an "unexceptionable witness", irrelevant as the break-in had occurred after 8 pm. While he accepted that Brodie may well have left Watt's house the following morning, he doubted the credibility of Brodie's mistress and her faithful servant as to his time of arrival. If Watt and Giles were to be believed, he questioned whether the bell they recall hearing was from the Tron Church at 8 pm or from Magdalen Chapel at 10 pm. In any event, he said, their testimony "amounts to a fabrication of the whole other evidence".

During the final submissions, the most extraordinary exchange occurred between Lord Braxfield and John Clerk, counsel for George Smith.[12] Conscious of the damning testimony of Brown and Ainslie, Clerk, describing the pair as "two corbies or infernal scoundrels", "infamous characters", "vagabonds" and "nefarious witnesses", stated that their testimony should never have been admitted. This drew from Braxfield a warning about his "indecent behaviour". Undeterred, Clerk told the jury that, as the masters of fact and law, they should disregard the evidence of Brown and Ainslie. To Braxfield's response that the jury were not the masters of the law – and to great applause – Clerk retorted, "That I deny." When Braxfield accused Clerk of talking nonsense, Clerk threatened that "You had better not snub me in that way." When it was pointed out to Clerk that Brown had received a royal pardon, Clerk – to further applause – asked: "Can His Majesty make a tainted scoundrel an honest man"? When the royal pardon was then described by the Lord Advocate as "the brightest jewel in His Majesty's Crown", Clerk to yet further applause

12 After Roughead's account of the trial was published, the exchange between Braxfield and Clerk was recorded in the *Law Times* and reproduced in the *Canadian Law Times*: (1907) 27 *Can L Times* 732.

– commented: "I hope His Majesty's Crown will never be contaminated by any villains around it." Clerk then reverted to his contention that the jury were masters of fact and law, drawing a severe rebuke from Braxfield: his remarks were "a very gross indignity, deserving of the severest reprobation". While, by this time, Braxfield had clearly had enough of Clerk's argument, Clerk had likewise had enough of Braxfield himself. Clerk offered to sit down if instructed, Braxfield invited him to go on, Clerk repeated his contention that the jury were masters of fact and law and Braxfield cautioned him to beware. Clerk exploded: "I have met with no politeness from the Court. You have interrupted me, you have snubbed me rather too often, my Lord, in the line of my defence."

Clerk told the court that he would speak no more unless he was allowed to maintain his defence and sat down. Lord Braxfield, taking Clerk at his word, called upon the Dean of Faculty to address the jury, and, on the Dean declining to speak, prepared to instruct the jury. John Clerk leapt to his feet and – to uproar in the courtroom – declaimed: "Hang my client, if you daur, my Lord, without hearing me in his defence." Such was the pandemonium that the judges retired to the robing room. On their return, tempers had cooled: Braxfield meekly invited Clerk to proceed with his speech and Clerk meekly complied, only mentioning briefly and without emphasis Ainslie and Brown's tainted testimony and the jury being masters of fact and law. William Roughead had no hesitation in putting the blame for this unseemly exchange on Clerk, "whose contention was as bad in law as were his manners in taste, [but who] was treated throughout by Braxfield with a leniency and forbearance far exceeding his deserts".[13]

Lord Braxfield's charge to the jury was hardly a model of impartiality. He began by lamenting the fall from grace of a man from a good family: "This unhappy situation seems to have arisen from a habitude of indulging vices which are too prevalent and fashionable, but it affords a striking example of the ruin which follows in their train." Acknowledging that the credibility of the damning testimony of Ainslie and Brown rested with the jury and that they should reject it if they found anything "unnatural or contradictory" in it, Braxfield boldly stated that "there is nothing in it unnatural or contradictory".

---

13 William Roughead, 'With Braxfield on the Bench' (1918) 30 JR 14 at 16. In *Old Reminiscences of Glasgow and the West of Scotland*, pp 99–106, Peter Mackenzie recounts the exchange with relish, praising Clerk's courage, while admitting that Clerk's contentions "had no proper place in jurisprudence, and no foundation in law".

Brodie's flight to Flushing and Amsterdam, Braxfield said, "affords a strong presumption of guilt". He dismissed Brodie's alibi defence: his brother-in-law was but a single witness, he was related to Brodie and, in any event, the break-in did not occur till after 8; Jeannie Watt and her maid were, Braxfield suggested, probably mistaken as to the time of his arrival. Lest the jury be unclear as to their duty, Braxfield concluded his charge with these words: "Upon the whole, gentlemen, taking all the circumstances of this case together, I can have no doubt in my own mind that Mr Brodie was present at the breaking into the Excise Office; and as to the other man. Smith, as I have already said, there can be still less doubt as to him."

The jury not only understood their duty, but performed it in a timely and exemplary fashion. At 1 pm on Thursday 29 August, the jury returned a unanimous guilty verdict against both accused. After an unsuccessful last-ditch effort by Brodie's counsel to arrest the judgment on the ground that, while the indictment alleged that the pair broke into "a house" used as an Excise Office, there was in fact more than one house in Chessel's Court so used, the court "pronounced for doom" the sentence on Brodie and Smith. That sentence was carried out on 1 October 1788.

BUT WHY?

In addressing the jury on Brodie's bad associations and dubious divertisements, Henry Erskine, for Brodie, quoted from the popular tragedy *Douglas*:[14]

> The needy man, who has known better days,
> One whom distress has spited at the world
> Is he whom tempting fiends would pitch upon
> To do such deeds, as makes the prosperous men
> Lift up their hands and wonder who could do them.

Claiming that his "client was no such man", he explained that Brodie had, along with many other respectable men of his generation, yielded himself to idleness and dissipation that, in turn, led to gambling and shady company. Accordingly, he called upon the jury to examine the evidence "with the nicest accuracy" so as to avoid convicting Brodie for what he was and not for what he had allegedly done.

---

14 "Douglas: A Tragedy", Act III. The play was written by the Scottish minister, historian and playwright John Home and published in 1874.

With two mistresses and their households to support in addition to his own grand home and a penchant for gambling, Brodie had an expensive lifestyle. Yet, he had certainly not completely exhausted his father's £10,000 legacy and his business was successful. He himself, on his voyage on the *Endeavour*, drew up an account of his financial affairs, showing a balance in his favour of £1,800, including the rents from four properties he owned in Edinburgh. He had no reason to exaggerate his financial situation, as he was using this account as the basis for ingathering funds for his planned final escape to Charleston, South Carolina. While he was clearly constantly in need of money, money alone hardly furnishes the motivation for his actions.

Apart from drink, and plenty of it, William Brodie took no potion freeing him of his conscience and releasing his basest instincts, as did Dr Henry Jekyll. Nor is there any evidence that he suffered from multiple personality (or any other) disorder. From all accounts, whether as day-time stalwart of Edinburgh society or night-time carouser, gambler and thief, Brodie maintained the same demeanour and speech, retaining his wit and humour, remaining constant in his double life.

William Roughead explained Brodie's aberrant behaviour as "mere boyish exuberance and as a protest against the Calvinistic smugness of his set", reflecting his "whole-hearted devotion to the life romantic".[15] Peter Mackenzie, in his otherwise excellent account of the Brodie saga, offered no single explanation for the Deacon's behaviour. He did, however, lament that he was addicted "to gambling, was a great dog and cock fighter, and always in ploys of that description, which were then too frequent, we are sorry to remark, in some parts of the old city".[16] John S Gibson remarked on Brodie's "infatuation with the excitement of the bloodletting at the cockpit".[17] Perhaps, Henry Mackenzie, that canny and well-connected novelist and historian, had it right when he said of Brodie: "There is a strange profligate sort of pleasure in villainy for its own sake."[18] Henley and Stevenson, in their feeble melodrama, have Brodie saying of one house-breaking, "blackguardly as it was, I enjoyed the doing".[19]

15 Roughead, "With Braxfield on the Bench", at p 14.
16 Mackenzie, *Old Reminiscences of Glasgow and the West of Scotland*, p 63.
17 *Deacon Brodie: Father to Jekyll and Hyde,* p 31.
18 Henry Mackenzie, "Manners and Customs of Edinburgh", in Harold W Thompson (ed), *The Anecdotes and Egotisms of Henry Mackenzie 1775–1831* (1927), p 70.
19 *Deacon Brodie, or the Double Life*, Tableau III, Scene I.

Why else, one might ask, would William Brodie, before setting out on the ill-fated raid on the Excise House, sing these words from the *Beggars Opera*[20] to his three companions?

> Let us take the road;
> Hark! I hear the sound of coaches!
> The hour of attack approaches;
> To your arms, brave boys, and load.
> See the ball I hold;
> Let the chemists toil like asses
> Our fire their fire surpasses,
> And turns our lead to gold.

Why else, one might also ask, would Brodie reply to the commiserations of a friend as he mounted the scaffold?

> It is *fortune de la guerre*.

---

20 John Gay's *Beggars' Opera*, originally written in 1724, and with music by Johann Christoph Pepusch, was a particular favourite with Brodie.

A Victorian Father's Feet of Clay: Harvey v Harvey

Kathleen Marshall

FAMILY BACKGROUND

One might assume that respectable Victorians took great care over the marriages of their gently nurtured daughters, so how did it happen that the life and happiness of young Rachel Chambers Hunter were placed in the hands of William Harvey?

Rachel was 18 years old when she married William on 13 February 1842, in the parish of Foveran, 11 miles north of Aberdeen. Her home was Tillery House, built by her great-grandfather, a retired planter from the southern USA. It had been substantially extended and modified into a Greek-revival mansion by her father, William Chambers Hunter. A photograph from 1850, thought to be of Rachel, portrays her as a slim, dark-haired, thoughtful-looking young woman.[1]

William Harvey was 25 years old at the time of the marriage, described by a witness in the subsequent court proceedings as "a middle sized man with large, full, blue eyes, and of a genteel appearance". His family home was Kinnettles House, near Forfar. It had been built by William's father in the grounds of a substantial estate which he had purchased with funds inherited from his uncle, who had been a planter and merchant in the West Indies. On the face of it, William and Rachel were a good match in terms of age, fortune, family background and geography. If William's significant character flaws had already begun to emerge, they appear to have been contained within the confines of his family.

---

1 Details of the family histories of the protagonists have been drawn from birth, death and marriage records, censuses and genealogy websites, which will not be individually referenced in this chapter. Information additional to that included in the report of the court proceedings was obtained from the *Session Papers* of the Faculty of Advocates, accessed through the National Library of Scotland.

William's father had died in 1830. Kinnettles was inherited by an older son, John Inglis Harvey, but William's mother, Angelica, continued to live there until her death in 1860. The younger children of the family had inherited other portions of their father's estate. William had been well provided for, with lands at Monecht. He was also tenant of a well-staffed farm at Rothmaise, the home to which he brought his young bride.

Four children were born to them, but two died in infancy. The survivors, John, born in 1844, and Rachel, born in 1845, were the focus of the 1860 custody proceedings, *Harvey v Harvey*,[2] that were to become a leading case in terms of children's rights to resist inappropriate parental control.

SCANDAL AND TRAGEDY

One of the children who did not survive was a son born on 17 April 1847, and named William Chambers after his maternal grandfather. His mother was very ill prior to the birth. She slept downstairs, tended by Mrs Sarah Rennie or Gibb, a midwife who later testified to the goings-on upstairs, where William Harvey, the baby's father, was ensconced in a bedroom next door to that of his wife's visiting sister, Agnes. She was then aged 19 or 20 and therefore a minor in terms of Victorian law. They seemed to spend a lot of time going into and out of each other's rooms but, at the time, kindly Sarah had been inclined to assume that they were just updating each other on Rachel's health. Nevertheless, she observed, "It appeared to me that Mrs Harvey received very little attention from either her husband or her sister during the time that I was in the house. They were very seldom in her company, and constantly together, both in and out of the house." In particular, she noted, they spent a great deal of time together the night the baby was born.

It was later alleged that this was the period during which William Harvey first seduced his wife's sister, thus committing the capital crime of incest, as then defined.

The subsequent elopement of William and Agnes is well documented. In November 1847, on the pretence of visiting relatives in Forfar, Agnes accompanied William to a lodging-house in Portland Street, Southampton, where they passed several days and nights in the same room as husband and wife. The intention was that they

2 (1860) 22 D 1198.

would go abroad. This seems to have been abandoned for, on 22 November, they took a train north, alighting at Tweedmouth Station (Berwick-upon-Tweed) at nine o'clock in the evening.

Unfortunately for them, as they sauntered arm-in-arm along the platform, they were confronted by Mr Alexander Thom, Agnes's maternal uncle, who happened to have been on the same train and who had been apprised of the situation by Agnes's father. He took her by the hand and said she must come along with him. She and William resisted. A scuffle took place. A policeman was called and the whole company resorted to the office of the Justice of the Peace. William jumped in immediately, informing the justice that he had been assaulted by Mr Thom. Mr Thom then narrated the background to the incident. William and Agnes admitted the facts but disputed Mr Thom's right to custody of Agnes as he had no authority from her father to take her. He insisted that he did indeed have such authority as she was his niece and under age. A rural office, late at night, was clearly not the time or place for closely reasoned arguments. Whatever the rights or wrongs of Mr Thom's claim, the magistrate, no doubt suitably scandalised, handed Agnes into the charge of her uncle and threatened William with detention should he interfere further. Agnes was returned to her family in Aberdeen and William fled to the north of France, fearing prosecution for incest.

Unsurprisingly, in January 1848, divorce proceedings were instituted by Rachel against her husband, with the summons served edictally upon William who was now in Canada at the home of his brother. On 9 February, he wrote to his wife, expressing his enduring love for her and asking for forgiveness and reconciliation, which he considered to be "the happiest course for all". He asked for the divorce proceedings to be suspended, and signed off as "Your miserable and repentant husband". The proceedings were not suspended. Decree of divorce was pronounced on 6 June 1848. William arrived back in Scotland on the following day.

William continued to try to correspond with Rachel, sending letters through a number of intermediaries. In January 1850, he sought custody of the children in the sheriff court. While these proceedings were underway, he wrote to Rachel, insisting that he was acting from the purest motives of love and regard for her and the children, and describing his "superhuman efforts" to obtain a house to accommodate them.

In summer 1850, he raised four further actions in the sheriff court: three were actions of count and reckoning against: his mother (as executrix of his father's estate); his brother (as a trustee to whom he had conveyed his whole estate with a view to settlement of William's debts); and the trustees of his ante-nuptial contract, who were paying interest on the trust funds to Rachel, on the grounds that the divorce rendered William, as the guilty party, dead in the eyes of the law. The fourth action William raised that summer was for reduction of the decree of divorce.

He lost all of these actions and a decree for expenses in relation to one of them saw him removed, in September 1850, to a debtors' prison in Dundee. He remained there until 9 October 1851, having come to a settlement with his creditors, involving the granting of a disposition *omnium bonorum,* with a view to settling his debts of £1,700.

In March 1852, William set off for Australia. Rachel married Dr Keith Jopp and they went to India, leaving the children in the care of her parents at their town residence in Albyn Place, Aberdeen.

At this point, William seems to have given up on Rachel, so he turned his attention back to Agnes. March 1853 saw the beginning of correspondence with her father in which William professed to love Agnes "with my whole soul". He enclosed letters for Agnes asking her to join him in Australia, with the children if possible. One may well imagine the stunned response of Agnes's father, who refused to have any contact or correspondence with William, sending any necessary replies through William's brother.

William returned to Scotland for a visit in 1854 and stayed with his mother at Kinnettles. The children, now aged 10 and 8, visited him there. It was meant to be a short visit, but it was later alleged that William tried to reassert control over their lives. Certainly, his correspondence from then on shows him trying to embed the idea that it was he who had entrusted his children to the care of their maternal grandparents on the understanding that he was still the one with the authority to make the decisions.

He left for Australia again in March 1855, returning to Scotland in September 1859. He asked that his children visit him again. His daughter, now almost 14 and aware of the history of their family, refused by letter in the curtest of terms. His son John, aged 15, was eventually persuaded to go. He arrived at Kinnettles on 5 October and fled on 10 October. The 1860 court report notes that "from some conversation he [John] had with the petitioner [his father, William], he became uncomfortable and alarmed, and consequently he escaped secretly from the house about midnight". He walked five miles to Forfar from where he caught the early morning train back to his grandparents in Aberdeen. He subsequently refused to have any contact with his father.

For William, it was time to assert the paternal authority to which he felt entitled by law. He petitioned the Court of Session for access to and custody of his children.

COURT OF SESSION 1860

It is interesting to compare the facts recited in William's petition and later submissions with the answers of the respondents (his children, their mother, stepfather and grandfather) and the supporting documents.

William presented himself as a merchant in Melbourne, Australia, a man of means with promising business and investment interests in that country. He had been unfairly treated, having been divorced by his wife while he was out of the country. It was alleged that he had "accidentally heard that an action of divorce had been raised against him ... but the said action was never intimated to him ... the statements made in that action were *ex parte* and of a fictitious nature". His subsequent attempt to have the decree of divorce reduced had been dismissed as being out of time, having been submitted more than a year and a day after it was issued. He said he had been prevented from pursuing the matter before that date due to lack of funds. Moreover, no-one had ever told him that he had lost the custody of his children. He had resumed actual custody on his return to Scotland in 1854 and entrusted them to their grandparents when he left again for Australia, under conditions communicated to the grandparents in writing. He had also made provision for the children's maintenance and education whilst in their grandparents' care. The children were entirely dependent upon him for their aliment and education and had no other means of support. The correspondence he had had with his children while he was abroad showed the affection with which they had regarded him. The fact that they had turned against him was due to the improper interference of his former wife and her family.

The Hunter family presented quite a different picture. The divorce was proof of William's adultery with his wife's sister, which he had at times admitted. Papers were produced to show that William was well aware that the divorce was in process. While William had tried to reassert parental control and impose conditions, this had been rejected by the grandfather through an intermediary. William's brother gave evidence that he had given a letter to William to that effect, which William denied ever seeing. The children had been encouraged to write to their father while he was abroad, and had done so dutifully, but now that they were older and aware of the family history, they wanted nothing to do with him. The respondents' answers to William's petition continue:

> Beside the annoyance which the petitioner has caused by these judicial proceedings, he has taken repeated, and indeed frequent, opportunities, by his personal conduct, to annoy the respondent, his former wife, and her family .... Among other proceedings, he, on two different occasions, intruded into the house of Tillery, where the respondent, Mrs Hunter or Jopp, was residing with her children as the guests of the respondent, her father, Mr Hunter. On the second of these occasions, which occurred during Mr Hunter's absence, he made a forcible entry into the house, accompanied by two other persons and insisted on searching the rooms, and afterwards the grounds around the house. On this occasion, although required to leave the house by the servants, and certain of the neighbours who were called in, he refused for a considerable time to do so, and stated that "he and the parties with him were armed, and prepared to resist any force that might be used towards them".

As for William's supposed wealth and position:

> The petitioner ... has no settled business, or income, or means of support – is utterly bankrupt – and is unable to maintain and provide for or to educate his children. He has been obliged to leave Kinnettles House, where for a time, he resided last year with his mother, and he has no establishment, or settled residence, or home. Although well connected, and formerly associating with persons of position and influence and education, his former friends now refuse to hold intercourse with him, or to meet him as formerly.

A letter was produced from William's mother, banning him from returning to Kinnettles and assuring him that she would take action to prevent him from ever doing so. William had sent as a response, "As to my return to Kinnettles, believe me, that is a matter in which I will entirely use my own discretion." William did not contest the claim that, since the date of the divorce, he had contributed nothing towards the support of his children, who had been maintained entirely by their mother and grandfather.

The court appointed a curator *ad litem* for the children "for the purpose both of protecting their interests, and of ascertaining and securing that they were not acting under any undue influence, but were expressing their own feelings and convictions in opposing the wishes of their father".[3] The curator reported back to the court:

3 This is how the purpose of the appointment was explained by the Lord Justice-Clerk at p 1207.

The curator, in the special circumstances of this case, desires to add, that, since his appointment, he has had interviews in his own house with each of the minor respondents separately, and without any of their relations or friends being present; and from these interviews, he has been satisfied, that it is clearly his duty to concur with them in opposing the present application. They have stated to him their earnest desire and determination to use every means to induce the Court to refuse the present petition. The curator is satisfied that this is the expression of their own individual views and feelings, and that they are not acting under the control and influence of others.

The content of this report led William to drop his claim of undue influence.

THE SCOTTISH LEGAL CONTEXT

The principles of Scottish law were, and to some extent still are, derived from the law of ancient Rome, mediated by the efforts of significant legal authorities such as Stair.[4] Rome had recognised a virtually unchallengeable power of the male head of a family, known as the *patria potestas*. At one time, it allowed him to exercise the same control over his descendants as he had over his slaves – even to the extent of putting his children to death. Thankfully, Scotland's "reception" of Roman law was more moderate, but the concept of the predominant rights of the father remained.

Children had a different status depending on whether they had attained puberty, a threshold fixed in the law of Scotland at 12 for girls and 14 for boys. Under that age, they were categorised as "pupils", with no legal capacity. On attaining puberty, they were classified as "minors" and able to make some personal decisions on their own and to participate in other legal transactions with the consent of their guardians, known as "curators". Minors could, for example, get married without consent and choose their own place of residence. The child's father was their natural curator, but other persons could be appointed, for example on the father's death. The law of Scotland followed that of Rome in averring that the power of the father, rooted in his *patria potestas*, was more extensive than that of other curators. On one view, regardless of the minor's right to choose his residence, a father could exercise a right of custody beyond puberty. He might

4 Sir James Dalrymple, Viscount Stair, wrote the highly influential *Institutions of the Law of Scotland* (1681).

lose this right if he had already allowed the child to live an independent life, so that the child was to be regarded as "forisfamiliated" or emancipated.

THE LEGAL ARGUMENTS

William staked his legal claim on the firm rock of his *patria potestas*, supported by significant legal authorities such as Stair. "A father", William argued, "did not lose his legal right to the custody of his children when they reached puberty, unless the children were forisfamiliated". Indeed, it would be dangerous to hold that, on reaching puberty, children were entitled to do as they wished, "unrestrained by parental control". He distinguished his case from earlier ones in which the court had found it proper to interfere with the legal rights of fathers or other curators. In some, the claim being resisted was not that of the natural father, but of other guardians, whose traditional, legal status was not so high.[5] In others, interference had been justified by the fact that the father's character was such that living with him would be dangerous to the lives or injurious to the morals of his children.[6] This did not apply in his case. He was innocent of the charge of adultery. His attempt to challenge the divorce decree had been dismissed on purely technical grounds. Even if the charges were true, it did not follow that he should pay for his offence by being denied the custody of his children or even access to them. There was no proof that his character was now to be regarded as bad.

The respondents took issue with William's legal analysis, arguing that a father's control over his children entirely ceased at puberty. They challenged his reliance on Stair, acknowledging that Stair favoured the extension of paternal authority at least till the child reached majority. However, they argued:

> [N]o writer of so early a date as Stair could be regarded as an authority on a question of personal liberty. It could not be doubted that our law was now more in favour of freedom, and that Stair's doctrines as to the absolute nature of the father's power, founded on the doctrines of the

5 For example, *Graham v Graham* (1780) Mor 8934, a case involving a 12-year-old girl whose father was dead. The Court of Session decided that, as a minor child, she was "mistress of her own person" and entitled to move abroad to live with her mother and second husband, in defiance of the wishes of guardians appointed by her late father.
6 The 1860 court report cites a number of cases in support of this proposition.

Roman law, would not now be received. No other writer stated a father's powers in terms so absolute as Stair; and there was no authority for holding that the father had a right to compel his child to reside with him after puberty.

Further, the respondents argued that the children *had* been forisfamiliated, given that they had been supported entirely by their mother's relations, and the grandfather had expressly refuted any claims by William to impose any conditions on their care. The respondents also referred to the issue of "character". They recalled the history of the incestuous adultery and divorce and the proof that William had consistently lied about his knowledge of events and about his own behaviour. Although he now professed innocence, his letters implied admission of his guilt.

> No doubt could be entertained as to the fact; nor was there any indication that the petitioner was convinced of the magnitude of the crime or that his character had improved. On the contrary, the proposals to his wife in the letter of 23 January 1850, and more especially those to her sister, showed that his character was still such that the children could not be committed to his charge without the greatest danger of injury to their feelings and their characters. Further, in consequence of his conduct, he was shunned by his relatives and previous acquaintances, so that to compel his children to reside with him would be to deprive them of the society of all their friends and relatives. Such had been held in England sufficient grounds for refusing applications by a father for the custody of his children, even when the children were pupils.

THE OPINION OF THE COURT

The opinion of the court was delivered by Lord Justice-Clerk Inglis. Noting that the facts of the case were "very peculiar", he indicated his intention to analyse the relevant law before applying it to the situation before him. William, he said, had contended that:

> [H]e had an absolute and uncontrollable right to regulate the place of residence of his children, and to require them to remain under his own personal custody and care, unless it can be shown that this is inconsistent with their personal safety, or would be clearly productive of moral contamination. The respondents, on the other hand, have maintained that a *minor pubes* is entitled in law to choose his own place of residence, unless he require his father to maintain him; and, at all

events, that the character and conduct of the petitioner are such as to disqualify him for the performance of his parental duty to these children, and to debar him from urging his present claim.

The court sided with the respondents in distinguishing the status of the minor from that of the pupil child: "The absolute legal incapacity of a pupil is such, that jurists have not inaptly styled the father's power over a child of these tender years as a right of dominion. But in puberty, legal incapacity has come to an end."

The court explained that minor children had power to act, in all cases, with the consent of their curators and in some cases without that consent. A minor child was entitled to choose his place of residence without the consent of his curators, or even against their advice. However, the opinion continued:

> No doubt, this liberty is more abridged during the lifetime of the father, from the greater respect which the law pays to his original and undelegated authority; and the Court have no desire to give countenance to a doctrine, which should enable any girl on attaining the age of twelve, if possessed of independent fortune, to desert the paternal mansion, and fix her own present residence, and thereby probably her future fate and course of life, in defiance of all parental control. But even during the father's life there are some legal acts which the minor may perform effectually, without the father's consent or knowledge, which indicate a recognition by the law of a power of rational choice, on the part of the minor, of a very high character.

The court acknowledged that, in earlier times, Scots law had followed more closely the earlier Roman law model of virtually complete paternal authority. However, even Stair had conceded some limits, in cases where fathers had refused to maintain their children or acted "unnaturally" towards them. It would, the court said, be difficult, if not impossible, to define precisely what those limits were in relation to a minor child, but it was possible and appropriate to set out "four practical propositions":

(1) That the control to which a *minor pubes* is subjected, does not proceed on any notion of his incapacity to exercise a rational judgment or choice, but rather arises, on the one hand, from a consideration of the reverence and obedience to parents which the law of nature and the Divine law enjoin, and, on the other hand, from a regard to the inexperience and immaturity of judgment on the part of the child, which require friendly and affectionate counsel and aid.

(2) That the power of a father, at this age, is conferred not as a right of dominion, or even as a privilege for the father's own benefit or pleasure,

but merely, or at least mainly, for the benefit, guidance and comfort of
the child.

(3) That, therefore, the father's authority and right of control may at this
age of the child be easily lost, either by an apparent intention to
abandon it and leave the child to his own guidance, or by circumstances
or conduct showing the father's inability or unwillingness to discharge
rightly the parental duty towards his child.

(4) That in all questions as to the loss of the parental control during
puberty from any of these causes, the wishes and feelings of the child
himself are entitled to a degree of weight corresponding to the amount
of intelligence and right feeling which he may exhibit.

Applying these propositions to the case before them, the court noted
that the children were asking no maintenance from their father. Since
the divorce, he had neither contributed to their maintenance nor, in
the court's view, had he attempted to assert paternal authority, other
than through the abortive petition to the sheriff in 1850. The children
were currently receiving affectionate care and comfort and appropriate
education at the hands of their grandparents. The court was scathing
in their comparison with what was on offer from their father:

> [T]heir father, who demands their restoration to his custody ... has
> been guilty of the capital crime of incest. This is a great family crime,
> which necessarily makes him an outlaw from that family which he has
> so grievously injured, and is sufficient to justify any measure which
> the Court may think necessary for the protection of the children,
> however much they may trench on the legal authority of the father.
> With this guilt attaching to him, and apparently, from his conduct and
> letters, unconscious of the enormity and incapable of understanding
> the true nature of his crime, he is the most unfitting and unsafe person
> that could well be found, for the guardianship and control of a boy and
> girl of fifteen and fourteen years of age. The petitioner, therefore, is in
> our opinion personally disqualified for the exercise of the right, and the
> performance of the duty, of a father to his minor children. But the claim,
> if it could have been otherwise supported, is materially weakened, if
> indeed his right be not altogether lost, by his abandonment of his
> children to the care of others for a period of twelve years, during which
> he has neither exercised his paternal authority nor contributed anything
> to their maintenance and education. When to all this is added the strong
> and unbiased expression of feeling on the part of the children themselves
> against intercourse with their father, the Court has no difficulty in
> refusing the petitioner's demand for the custody of his children. And if
> the children be, in the circumstances, entitled, for the reasons now
> explained, to be held as emancipated from paternal control, it is
> impossible to see on what grounds the petitioner can assert his right to

thrust his society on his children, or, as he expresses it, to obtain access to them, against their wishes. The petition will therefore be refused, with expenses.

THE SIGNIFICANCE OF THE HARVEY CASE

Most of the 19th-century case law on the custody of children, both before and after *Harvey*, was about pupil children. *Harvey* was significant in that it led the court to set out a thoughtful and authoritative exposition of the law relating to the custody of minor children. In doing so, the court sought to reconcile opposing legal opinions of the weighty academics cited by the parties, through the articulation of "practical propositions" rather than any rigid conclusions. In taking this course, the court may be vulnerable to an accusation of having side-stepped the critical legal issues. Certainly, an influential 1906 book on the law of parent and child took the view that "[t]his matter was considered, though not decided, in the case of *Harvey*".[7] But the subsequent legal history of the case shows that it has been influential nonetheless, so this may have been a wise evasion.

As the Victorian era progressed, *Harvey* was cited in academic literature and case reports as authority for:

- the general legal capacity of minors;[8]
- the curatory of girls;[9]
- the preconditions for forisfamiliation;[10]
- the discretion available to the court as regards custody of a minor;[11] and
- the extent to which a minor's wishes should prevail against the wishes of her father.[12]

The core considerations of many of these cases have been rendered obsolete by the sweeping changes to the concepts of pupil and minor introduced by the Age of Legal Capacity (Scotland) Act 1991.

7 *Fraser on Parent and Child* (3rd edn by J Clark, 1906), p 74.
8 *Hill v City of Glasgow Bank* (1879) 7 R 68, in which Lord President Inglis quoted his own opinion in *Harvey*.
9 Fraser, *Parent and Child*, p 451.
10 Fraser, *Parent and Child*, p 454.
11 *Flannigan v Inspector of Bothwell* (1892) 19 R 909. Interestingly, the party citing *Harvey* was arguing for a decision that would have gone against the wishes of the minor child, whose views ultimately prevailed.
12 *Fisher v Edgar* (1894) 21 R 59.

Nevertheless, *Harvey* has still been referred to in more recent years. The 1992 Scottish Law Commission Report on Family Law[13] cited it five times, as a case pre-figuring some of the most important principles of the 1989 UN Convention on the Rights of the Child. *Harvey* alone is cited as authority for what "is already recognised in Scots law" in relation to the parental responsibility "to provide appropriate direction and guidance in those areas of life where the child has considerable scope for independent action". It is also cited as support for the proposition that parental power to control the child's residence and upbringing diminishes as the child's actual capacity increases. These insights were incorporated into the Children (Scotland) Act 1995, which remains the foundation for Scottish family law in relation to children.

And still, in 2013, *Harvey* could be cited in a textbook on parent and child in relation to the concept of child abandonment.[14] *Harvey* is also the earliest case cited in relation to the significance of the child's views;[15] another concept that is central to the UN Convention and the 1995 Act. It could be argued that the way was paved for reception of the UN Convention by the established regard in Scotland to the case of *Harvey*, for minor children at least.

Given the court's repugnance towards William Harvey, one almost wishes that there had been a pupil child involved as well. It seems likely that the court would have refused the petition for custody even of a younger child on the ground of possible contamination of morals due to William's character. That might have introduced a more humane note into some later cases where very young children were taken from their mothers and handed over to reckless, adulterous, criminal and altogether disreputable fathers on the basis of their overweening "rights".[16]

HOW IT ALL ENDED

Of course, the story of the Harvey family did not cease with the court's refusal of William's petition for custody. Sadly, things did not turn

---

13 Scottish Law Commission. *Report on Family Law* (Scot Law Com No 135, 1992), in footnotes to paras 2.4, 2.12, 2.30 (twice) and 5.24.
14 K McK Norrie, *Law Relating to Parent and Child in Scotland* (3rd edn, 2013), at paras 21.01 and 6.22.
15 Norrie, *Law Relating to Parent and Child in Scotland,* para 9.43.
16 For example, *Steuart v Steuart* (1870) 8 M 821; *Symington v Symington* (1875) 2 R (HL) 41; *Rintoul v Rintoul* (1898) 1 F 22; *AC v BC* (1902) 5 F 108.

out well for most of them. William's former wife seems to have fared best. She and Dr Jopp returned to Scotland and had several children. She died in Aberdeen on 1 March 1892, of heart failure, possibly related to her chronic rheumatism, pre-deceasing her second husband by seven years. She was 68 years old.

Of the children who were the focus of the court case, we know that John, who had made the dramatic midnight escape from his father's family home, died before reaching majority. Rachel junior married Charles Grey Spittal, an advocate, who later served as sheriff substitute in Wick and Selkirk. They had two children. However, the 1891 census identifies Rachel as an inmate in the Royal Asylum, Aberdeen. She was then 46 years old. She remained there until her death in 1917 at the age of 71.

Agnes, who had run off to Southampton with William Harvey, ended up getting married and spending most of her life there, in circumstances somewhat reduced from her previous country house existence. In 1859, she married an office worker, Thomas Stothard Blay. She was 32 years old and he was 24. They lived in what appears to have been a respectable neighbourhood and had at least six children. She died in 1901. Was she belatedly and cheaply married off as soiled goods approaching their sell-by date? Or did she find love and happiness at last in unexpected social circumstances?

As for William, he continued his career of litigation. In 1872, he hit the heights of the House of Lords in a case against the trustees of his ante-nuptial contract with Rachel, still arguing that the interest on the funds should be paid to him.[17] He lost. He also sought to reduce the "disposition *omnium bonorum*" which had been his passport out of Dundee jail in 1851, on the basis that it had been executed "in a dark and dirty dungeon", a description the otherwise sober Lords professed to find rather amusing.[18] Needless to say, he lost that case too, the Lords observing that the case was "too clear for argument", "vexatious", and "an instance of great pertinacity in litigation, which we must regret very much".

Deprived of his *patria potestas* and his worldly goods, William eventually took up residence in a lodging house in Pitt Street, Edinburgh, where he lived as a "retired farmer" in the company of clerks, mechanics and visiting nursemaids.[19] He died in May 1904,

17 *Harvey v Farquhar* (1872) No 3, 10 M (HL) 26.
18 *Harvey v Ligertwood* (1872) No 4, 10 M (HL) 33.
19 Details from the 1901 census.

aged 85, of cerebral haemorrhage, bequeathing nothing more than this surprising legacy of a pertinacious litigant.

The Chests of Bargain Tea: Sword v Sinclair

William W McBryde

It was the summer of 1770 when the ship the *Sir Laurence* under Captain James Hunter was sailing up the Forth towards the harbour of Borrowstouness, or, in abbreviation, Bo'ness, as we would now say – the town on the ness or point of landing projecting into the water. Captain Hunter had sailed from the Black Boy Wharf in London. This was a regular journey. Two ships alternated: the *Sir Laurence* and her sister ship the *Duchess of Hamilton*. While one was heading for Bo'ness, the other would be sailing to London. So, once a fortnight, one of the ships would be ready to sail at either port. Advertised as carrying goods for Glasgow and Paisley, the vessels also carried cargo for Greenock, Port Glasgow, Ayr, Irvine, Kilmarnock and Hamilton and adjacent places. Captain Hunter had sailed about 15 June. He would land his cargo and return to London around 8 August. Then back to Bo'ness in September except, as it happened, another master had to take command in his place on that and subsequent voyages that year. Anyone wanting goods to be carried could contact Captain Hunter at the Edinburgh Coffee House in London or William Laurie, the grocer, in Glasgow who had recently moved his shop to opposite the Guard.[1]

Amongst the cargo of the *Sir Laurence* in June 1770 were three chests of Bohea tea bound for Messrs Robert and Alexander Sinclair in Greenock, but going via Gilbert Hamilton in Glasgow.[2] The tea, which was to make legal history, had had a long journey. It had come from the foothills of the rugged peaks of the Bohea Mountains in the great black tea country of Fukein (or Fujian) Province in China. Bohea

---

1 The *Glasgow Journals* of 1769 and 1770 have the shipping advertisements which give the details. There were other ships on a ten-day rota.

2 The details are in an appendix to the original petition in the case to be found in the collection of papers preserved in the Faculty of Advocates Library: Arniston, vol 104, no 7 (1770–1771); Ilay Campbell, vol 21, 6 and 7.

(pronounced "Bo-hee" or "Bo-hay") was named after the Chinese pronunciation of the Wuyi mountain range. Over 50 years previously, Alexander Pope in *The Rape of the Lock* could rhyme "bohea" with "way".[3] The other obvious rhyme was in his *Epistle to Mrs Teresa Blount*[4] about the solitary Mrs Blount, separated from her husband:

> She went from opera, park, assembly, play,
> To morning-walks, and prayers three hours a-day
> To part her time 'twixt reading and bohea,
> To muse, and spill her solitary tea.

The comfort of tea, combined with its disputed health benefits, resulted in a great expansion of tea drinking in the 18th century. It would be another century before Robert Fortune would trace the origins of Bohea tea to the market at Tsong-gan-hein[5] where, in large tea-hongs, the black teas were sorted and packed for export and taken by coolies over the rough tracks to Canton or Shanghai.[6]

The East India Company had the monopoly of importing the tea by sea to England round the Cape of Good Hope, and this tea had been bought in their sales at India House in Leadenhall Street, London, a site now occupied by the Lloyd's Building. David Mitchell had purchased the tea on the orders of the Greenock merchants. The journey from London to Bo'ness was the last sea journey for these three chests, unless from Greenock it went across the Atlantic to the North American Colonies. The tea would be very old by the time it reached there. Waiting for the *Sir Laurence* and other ships' cargoes at Bo'ness were up to 50 carters who every day went to Glasgow. The east coast route by sea from London was preferred for transport of cargo owing to the weather, length and difficulties of the west coast journey.

Bo'ness, the principal port on the Forth at the time, was not the happiest place. The decision had been made to build the Forth and Clyde canal from the mouth of the Carron,[7] a few miles upstream,

---

3 Canto IV lines 156–157. The poem was published in 1712 and revised in 1714.
4 Written after the Coronation of George 1 in 1714.
5 This might be what is now usually called Tong Mu.
6 Robert Fortune, *A Journey to the Tea Countries of China, including Sung-Lo and the Bohea Hills* (1852).
7 Later called Grange Burn Mouth or Grangemouth. Sir Lawrence Dundas started the building of a village and quay in 1777 and this port began to challenge Bo'ness; Leith expanded with the building of the New Town of Edinburgh in the later part of the century: Henry Hamilton, *An Economic History of Scotland in the 18th Century* (1963), pp 214–215 and pp 286–287.

and not from the historic port of Bo'ness, for reasons not all could understand. In 1770, about seven miles of the canal had already been built, although the construction was soon to run into technical and financial problems with major delays and headaches. It was the largest construction project until then undertaken in Scotland and was not completed for another 20 years – over budget and over time. Any canal was a threat to the carters and the route of this canal had caused protests from the merchants of Bo'ness. There was much disappointment, justifiable as it turned out, because Bo'ness harbour was eventually to enter a period of decline.[8]

At every stage in its journey, the tea had earned money for someone: the shipping, the cartage, the wharfage, the casing in the three chests and the deals made by sellers and buyers with their commissions – even, for these three chests, "candle money" of one shilling in London. As the auction began in India House, a one-inch-long candle was lighted. The lot of three, or six, chests went to the last man to bid before the candle flickered out, but then he had to pay for the candle![9]

Above all, there were excise duties, both a tax on importation and an inland duty, which greatly increased the price of the tea. So high was the tax that smuggling of tea was a major problem. It was a challenge to avoid the East India Company's monopoly. Few, if any, smugglers had the resources to ship direct from Canton. But one way to make money was to buy the tea in London, export it to the continent of Europe and obtain a rebate of the taxes. Then smuggle the tea back into England or Scotland. Or smuggle from Holland tea obtained by the Dutch. Bo'ness harbour had a history of smuggling, although the Custom House had been established there in 1707 – but this was legal tea.

It was difficult to avoid the consequences of taxes. The fact that the tea could be landed at all at Bo'ness was partly due to an Act of Parliament in 1744[10] which had laid a duty of two pounds Scots, or a sixth part of a penny sterling, upon every Scots pint of ale or beer, brewed, bought or sold in Bo'ness. The money gathered was used by trustees to repair the Bo'ness harbour, which had been prone to silting. The same applied at the destination of the tea, Greenock. The expansion of the port of Greenock was boosted by an Act of 1751 which imposed similar duties on ale and beer within Greenock to raise money for the

8 Thomas J Salmon, *Borrowstouness and District being Historical Sketches of Kinneil, Carriden, and Bo'ness* (1550–1850) (1913), especially pp 325–327.
9 Benjamin W Labaree, *The Boston Tea Party* (1964), p 5.
10 17 Geo II c 21.

repair of the harbour.[11] This was a common method at the time in Scotland of local taxation, partly because it could be added to, and collected at the same time as, excise duties. It did raise questions of interpretation of the statute, of the type loved by lawyers, as to what counted as Bo'ness beer when someone brewed their own or brought in beer from outside.[12] It was the precursor in some senses of a form of local government finance, because later statutes could be extended to use the money for repair of streets or to provide lighting and other matters.[13]

MESSRS ROBERT AND ALEXANDER SINCLAIR

The buyers of the teas from London were merchants in Greenock. Greenock was one of the places to be in Scotland in the middle of the 18th century if you wished to make money. It was the centre of the trade to the northernmost colonies of America. It was easier to get from there to Newfoundland or Nova Scotia or parts of Canada than from London. Greenock was growing rapidly, from a population of 2,000 in 1700 to 17,500 by the end of the century.[14] Along with Port Glasgow, Greenock played a part in the extensive tobacco trade and later the sugar trade with the Caribbean.[15] By 1780, Greenock had the largest number of ships in Scotland on its register, most engaged in foreign trade.[16] Scotts of Greenock were to establish shipbuilding operations in both Greenock and Saint John, New Brunswick.[17]

Amongst the merchants in Greenock in 1770 was a partnership of Robert and Alexander Sinclair. Nothing is known about their origins, but they had a trade in tea in Glasgow and also elsewhere in Scotland. It was to be alleged that they sold to merchants in Falkirk and Lanark. They also had a trade with Messrs Sinclair and Ward in Kingston,

---

11 24 Geo II c 38.
12 NLS: Petition of James Main and others to the Rt Hon Lords of Council and Session, 8 July 1762, APS.3.82.29; Salmon, *Borrowstouness and District (1550–1850)*, pp 237–239.
13 Salmon, *Borrowstouness and District*, pp 227, 245.
14 T M Devine, *The Scottish Nation: A Modern History* (2012), p 156.
15 T M Devine, *To the Ends of the Earth: Scotland's Global Diaspora, 1750–2012* (2011), pp 37–40.
16 Hamilton, *An Economic History of Scotland in the 18th Century*, p 287.
17 J M Bumsted, "The Scottish Diaspora:Emigration to British North America, 1763–1815" in Ned C Landsman, *Nation and Province in the First British Empire: Scotland and the Americas, 1600–1800* (2001), pp 132–133.

Jamaica. Their great excitement in 1770 was not the purchase of some chests of tea, a very ordinary affair in more than one sense, but rather their plans to make their fortune by trade with the North American Colonies and the West Indies. To do this, they had to buy, stock, crew and sail a ship. They were looking for finance. They persuaded two Leith merchants, John Brebner and William Sibbald, to join them in the venture. A contract of co-partnership for the firm Sinclair Brebner & Company was signed on 4 September 1770 with three partners, Sibbald, Brebner and the firm of Robert and Alexander Sinclair.[18] The firm of Robert and Alexander Sinclair was a partner in another firm. A firm or partnership was a separate legal person and this arrangement was possible in Scots law, but not English law.

The brigantine *Katty* was bought complete with six guns and pounders.[19] Brebner went to America for about three years, and, on his account, did very well. But, on his return, he accused the Sinclairs of mismanagement of funds. The Sinclairs became bankrupt, so Sibbald, the remaining solvent partner, had to deal with the consequences of the subsequent, very complicated and lengthy, litigation.[20]

Sinclairs became insolvent and were sequestrated in 1781 or 1782 with debts of about £27,000 owed to 59 creditors who, by the time of the second distribution of dividends, had received 2s 9d for every pound owed.[21] That process was not comfortable for them, not least because the Cashier to the Merchant Banking Company of Glasgow, a bank only operational from 1769,[22] petitioned the court to have their protection from personal diligence removed, ie to have them imprisoned for debt. They were apprehended and had to appear before the Court of Session in Edinburgh, in those days a court of between nine and 15 judges. The court ordered them to be held in the custody of the macer until they found caution (or a guarantee). This was quickly provided by friends and the bond of caution bears the signature of the two Sinclairs – in neat, almost identical,

18 NAS: CS228/B/7/30 Court of Session: Unextracted Processes, 1st arrangement, Adams-Dalrymple office 1664–1865.
19 NAS; CS 96/1414, Brebner Sinclair & Co, merchants Greenock, Journal; CS 96/1413, Brebner Sinclair and Company, merchants Greenock, letter book, 1778–1782.
20 See process in n 19.
21 NAS: Court of Session: Unextracted Processes, 1st arrangement, Currie-Dalrymple office: CS 230/SEQNS/S/14.
22 *Glasgow Journal*, 18 May to 25 May 1769 (the weekly newspaper did not have a single date which is our present custom).

handwriting. Trading as an individual, or as a partnership, had risks in the 18th century which would scare a modern business person.

The case with which we are concerned starts with the attempt by Messrs Sinclairs to sell, in Glasgow, part of the cargo of the *Sir Laurence*: two of the three chests of Bohea tea.[23] We do not know what happened to the other chest but, perhaps, it did make the long journey to Newfoundland. Sinclairs wrote a letter to Archibald Campbell in Glasgow. This listed a variety of teas, namely ordinary Bohea, Congo and Suchong at various prices. Campbell was not to sell under those prices, but he could give two or three months' credit. Sinclairs preferred that the teas were to be delivered in Greenock, which suggests the teas reached there and were stored there, but they did contemplate the possibility of delivery in Glasgow. The reason for the sale was that they had "a greater stock of tea in hand than (they) had occasion for". They also had more expensive green teas and offered to provide samples. Campbell had already received samples of the black teas. Samples were important as there were different grades and qualities of teas. Also, it was difficult to tell one tea from another by looking at it. The unscrupulous might mix some cheap into expensive teas or add some smuggled tea.

THE 18TH CENTURY TEAS

The tea imported into Britain in the 18th century came from, or originated in, China. The tea was imported by the East India Company, who, despite its name, did not at this time import tea originating in India. Indian tea was unknown and a trade in it was not developed until the middle of the 19th century as part of the British Empire's attempts to avoid a huge reliance on imports from China.[24]

Bohea tea was the lowest quality of black teas.[25] There were three grades of Bohea: ordinary, middling and good. It had a reputation of containing small leaves like dust, of smelling like dried hay and, on the addition of water, having a deep mahogany colour which some

23 It was later to be alleged that there was no evidence that the three chests on the *Sir Laurence* were the same three sold in Glasgow, but there never was a hearing of evidence and we have to take the statements in the court pleadings as we find them. The dates of all the events are consistent.
24 The attempt to redress the balance by paying the Chinese in opium is one of the scandals of Empire.
25 London Genuine Tea Company, *The History of the Tea Plant: from the Sowing of the Seed, to its Package for the European Market* (1820).

disliked. It was the ordinary Bohea tea, the lowest quality, which was sold in this case. The next in quality was Congou or Congo. Souchong was like Congo. Pekoe was expensive and often added to other teas to improve flavour. By statute in 1772, in an attempt to control fraud, all packages of these teas had to be marked "BLACK". All other teas were marked with the word "GREEN".[26] It was Bohea tea which, in 1773, was thrown into the harbour during the Boston Tea Party, this being a spark for the American War of Independence.[27] This may have had the curious effect that, in certain American quarters in the 21st century, Bohea tea is expensive and much sought after.

Drinking tea in Scotland was almost unknown prior to 1720. By 1750, it was drunk at every breakfast table in place of ale,[28] a fact noted by Dr Johnson on his tour of the Western Islands in 1773.[29] On a morning visit, Mackintosh of Borlum would be asked if he had had his tea.[30] Ladies might gather in the afternoon at the "four hours" for tea instead of their drink in previous decades of ale or claret.[31] This remarkable change in drinking habits in the course of a generation was not without controversy. Some believed tea was weakening and made a man effeminate. Amongst the doubters was Lord President Forbes and there was a movement to try to ban the "Chinese leaf".[32] Nevertheless the growth in the general use of expensive tea was a barometer of a rising standard of living.[33] This was a good time to import and to sell tea, provided you did not import too much.

THE SALE OF THE TEA BY CAMPBELL TO SWORD

Archibald Campbell in Glasgow acting on behalf of his Greenock principals, Messrs Sinclairs, sold 600 pounds of Bohea tea to John Sword, shopkeeper in Glasgow. He did this by a written bargain, called

26 12 Geo III c 46. There was at one time a controversy as to whether green teas came from a different plant. In fact, it is from the same plant but the leaves are picked at an earlier stage and processed differently.

27 Labaree, *The Boston Tea Party*, pp 4–5.

28 The history can be traced in Henry G Graham, *The Social Life of Scotland in the 18th Century* (1950); Robert Chambers, *Domestic Annals of Scotland* (3rd edn, 1874), vol iii; and the *First Statistical Accounts* which are helpfully summarised in Maisie Steven, *Parish Life in Eighteenth Century Scotland* (1995).

29 *A Journey to the Western Islands of Scotland* (various eds) sv "Coriatachan in Sky."

30 Graham, *The Social Life of Scotland in the 18th Century*, p 11.

31 Graham, *The Social Life of Scotland in the 18th Century*, p 91.

32 Chambers, *Domestic Annals of Scotland*, p 613.

33 Steven, *Parish Life in Eighteenth Century Scotland*, p 38.

missives, on 29 August 1770.[34] The missives stated the price of the tea as 2s 8d Sterling per pound. This was the price in the written instructions to Campbell from the Sinclairs. John Sword wrote:

> Sir, I agree to take from you 600 pounds of Bohea tea, at 2s 8d Sterling per pound, to be paid ready money, and delivered within eight days of this date.

> (Sgd) John Sword. Glasgow, August 29, 1770.

> (Addressed) to Mr Archibald Campbell.

Campbell wrote the same day, presumably on the same piece of paper:

> Sir, I hereby agree to deliver you the above quantity of tea, on the above terms, to be delivered you here within the mentioned time.

> (Sgd) Archibald Campbell, Glasgow. August 29 1770

> (Addressed) To Mr John Sword merchant in Glasgow.

When Campbell told the Sinclairs what he had done, their first reaction was that he had made a mistake in the price. They replied immediately saying that he had marked "2" for "3s 8d per pound." But, it was not Campbell's error. Sinclairs had written the wrong figure in their instructions to Campbell. Campbell then had to try to negotiate matters with Sword. Sword offered by way of compromise to take some more tea at another 2d per pound. Sinclairs rejected this as it would involve them selling the tea at a great loss. The cost to them of the tea had been 3s 7½ d per pound. This was tea which had sold in London for 2s 10d per pound before duties and charges. Selling the tea at 3s 8d per pound made a profit, maybe, but, if the profit to be made by Sinclairs was only ½d per pound, they were making less out of the tea than anyone else. As a commercial venture, it was not a great success. If this were typical of their acumen, it is not surprising that their business became completely insolvent ten years later.

With the Sinclairs refusing to deliver the tea – and it never was delivered or the price paid – Sword raised an action before the magistrates in Glasgow claiming £50 damages. It is possible that the magistrates conducted daily courts to hear civil disputes.[35] The magistrates, faced with a written contract in the form of the missives, allowed Sword proof of his loss. In principle, this would have been

---

34 The details are in the original papers preserved in the Faculty of Advocates Library: Arniston, vol 104, no 7 (1770–1771); Ilay Campbell, vol 21, 6 and 7.

35 *First Statistical Account of 1791–99, Glasgow*, vol 5, p 496.

the extra cost to Sword above 2s 8d of buying tea similar to the tea he had contracted for.

Sinclairs appealed the decision of the magistrates to the Court of Session in Edinburgh by a procedure then known as advocation. A single judge, Lord Barjarg, found in favour of Sword. Although they had consistently lost before the courts, Sinclairs appealed to the whole court of 15 Senators of the College of Justice. Despite the written contract, the court declined to follow the previous judges and refused to enforce the contract. Sinclairs won. Why? At the time, judges did not give written reasons for their decisions. There has to be an inference drawn from the court papers or written pleadings of the parties.

In his favour, Sword had the contract and the argument that bargains would be precarious if parties could later argue that the price was too low. He had not committed fraud and, if the price really was too low, he would have taken all 660lbs on offer, not the 600lbs he bought. He also disputed details of the cost to Sinclairs of the tea. On the face of it, these are strong points. There were, however, factors on the side of Sinclairs which won the day.

Archibald Campbell was "a young man, ignorant of these matters, and who did not know there was any mistake". He was "so unlucky as to apply to John Sword, shopkeeper in Glasgow, an old experienced dealer in this commodity". The result was that Sword realised "where the pennyworth lay" and he acted unconscionably. Much of the pleadings are about the true price of Bohea tea and to the effect that 2s 8d was obviously too low. Sinclairs argued that the correct price, looking at other transactions, was about 3s 8d or 3s 9d per pound. Even Sword, in quoting other deals, was mentioning 3s 5d per pound. Sinclairs were saying that 2s.8d would have been the rate for "some very coarse, smuggled stuff, passing under the name of tea".

It seems obvious that the court believed that Campbell and the Sinclairs had made a mistake known to and taken advantage of by Sword. This case is one of the earliest on this type of error in Scots law and, properly understood, it is the foundation of the current law.[36] An error by one party known to and taken advantage of by the other party can invalidate the contract. The case might also be used to show that there is some essential element of good faith in the law of contract. Understanding of this case by lawyers has been hampered because

---

36 W W McBryde, "A Note on Sword v Sinclair and the Law of Error" 1997 JR 281; *McBryde on Contract* (3rd edn, 2007), paras 15-30 to 15-33. See *Wills v Strategic Procurement* [2013] CSOH 26.

the published report of it in Morison's *Dictionary of Decisions of the Court of Session*[37] is a very abbreviated version of the facts and written pleadings. In particular, the arguments about the imbalance in knowledge between Campbell and Sword and the general price of tea are not mentioned. Yet, these must have been critical to the judges' views about the actions of Sword.

JOHN SWORD

None of what happened would have occurred but for the actions of John Sword. Who was he? The question is not easy to answer with certainty because there were several Swords, all related, in Glasgow at the time. They are noted in the Burgess and Guild Brethren records.[38] The probability is that John Sword was the eldest legitimate son of James Sword, merchant. John was admitted to the guild on 24 July 1769. His younger brother, James Sword, was also admitted the following year. John Sword had a son, James Sword, who was admitted to the guild in 1787, and, in turn, James Sword, junior, son of James, was admitted in 1795.

The year 1769 was a momentous and nervous year for the Sword brothers. John and James Sword were indicted for the rape of Janet Orr, spouse to William Brown, "bookseller" in Glasgow. The *Glasgow Journal* more disparagingly described Brown as a "hawker".[39] There may have been a family connection because a John Sword "grocer" had irregularly married a Ms Brown in Glasgow two years previously.[40] Her first name is not given, but it may have been "Mary".[41]

The Swords were tried at Glasgow High Court before Lord Justice-Clerk Glenlee and Lord Kames, it being normal in those days for two judges on circuit to hear a case. On Wednesday 24 May, after a trial in a small hall at the west end of the Tolbooth lasting ten hours, they

37 Mor 14241.
38 Scottish Record Society, *The Burgesses & Guild Brethren of Glasgow, 1751–1846*, ed James R Anderson (1935).
39 *Glasgow Journal*, Thurs 25 May to Thurs 1 June 1769.
40 OPR Marriages, 644/01 0260 0041 Glasgow; 08/09/1767.
41 In *Sword v Sinclair*, John Sword described himself as supplying groceries as well as other products. A Mrs Mary Brown, wife of John Sword esq of Carfin, merchant in Glasgow, died in 1793 (*Scots Magazine*, vol 55, 1793, p 101) and John Sword remarried the following year: OPR Marriages 644/01 0270 0172 Glasgow; 6 July 1794.

were found not guilty by the jury.[42] The *Scots Magazine* reported that "The woman and her husband were the only evidence of the rape; but there was most satisfying evidence that the story was contrived, and the prosecution instigated by them, with a view of extorting money from the [accused]." This was a lucky escape because by immemorial custom the punishment for rape was death.[43]

Nathaniel Jones's *Directory of Glasgow* in 1787 lists John Sword, spirit dealer and manufacturer, St Andrew's entry, Gallowgate, and James Sword, "hard ware merchant, shop Ingram's land, north side Gallowgate, No 15". In the 18th and 19th centuries, the Sword family prospered and, in 1791, a James Sword bought Annfield House, then in the country just outside Gallowgate on the north side of the Edinburgh Road. He died there in 1832, and later proprietors feued out the grounds prior to the eventual demolition of the house. Even that process ended up with litigation before the First Division of the Court of Session.[44] The traces of all this are in the street and place names of today: Annbank Place, Annbank Street, Annfield Place and Annfield Medical Centre; and going from the Gallowgate to Duke Street, near Bellgrove Station, is Sword Street.

A student of the history of the law could take a walk down the High Street, past the original site of the College of Glasgow University, where, in the 1770s, the Regius Professor of Law, John Millar, was acquiring a European reputation,[45] to the Gallowgate, which is at the heart of this case. The Sword businesses were here. It is reasonable to assume that the contract for the tea was entered into in this area, probably in one of the many public houses, as was the custom. To the right of Glasgow Cross is the Trongate where the Tontine Coffee House was built in 1781 and which featured in a creditors' meeting on the bankruptcy of Messrs Sinclairs. The visible remains of that once-famous place is Tontine Lane.

The tall Tolbooth Tower is what is left of a much larger building which contained the Justiciary Court where the Swords were tried[46]

---

42 *Scots Magazine*, June 1769, p 332; James Gibson, *History of Glasgow* (1777), p 145.

43 David Hume, *Commentaries on the Law of Scotland respecting Crimes*, (4th edn, 1844), I. 306, citing cases of 1746, 1790 and 1817. On the other hand, no one was executed for rape in Glasgow in the years from 1765 to 1820; housebreaking, robbery, theft and murder were the usual capital crimes: NLS: *Broadside Listing All the Public Executions that took place in Glasgow between 1765 and 1820*, LC Fol 73 (015).

44 *Dennistoun v Thomson* (1872) 11 M 121.

45 J D Mackie, *The University of Glasgow 1451–1951* (1954), p 233.

46 Ian S Ross, *Lord Kames and the Scotland of his Day* (1972), p 306; Gibson, *History of Glasgow*, p 145.

and where a year later John Sword would have started his civil case before the Glasgow magistrates. Turning left along Gallowgate, heading on what in the 1770s was the road to Edinburgh, very soon takes you to a railway bridge carrying trains from Bellgrove Station. Tucked away against the bridge on the south side of the Gallowgate is a small lane, now unmarked, and maybe soon to disappear as the area is being redeveloped. This is St Andrew's Lane which is as near as anyone is likely to get to the site of John Sword's shop; only a short distance from the Tolbooth. In the 18th century, there flowed here the open Molendinar Burn[47] the line of which on the ground around St Andrews Church later caused John Sword some problems.[48] The area has changed much,[49] but in the 1770s Gallowgate was on the outskirts of Glasgow.[50]

Walking along the Gallowgate to the east would have been familiar to John Sword, because he would have come to the original Saracen's Head Inn, then run by James and Jean Graham, the terminus for the Edinburgh and Ayr coaches and the hub of part of Glasgow's social life.[51] It was where Boswell and Johnson stayed in 1773 and drank tea with, amongst others, the University's Professors of Moral and Natural Philosophy.[52] The Saracen's Head also, being the best hotel in town at the time, was where the judges stayed. Lord Justice-Clerk Glenlee and Lord Kames would have processed from there on foot along the Gallowgate to the Tolbooth to take the rape case against the Swords. The judges dressed in their robes and were accompanied by the Provost, Baillies, Town Officers, and others, all in their finery, along with a military escort. The band and the state trumpeters played.[53]

The name "Gallowgate" was not accidental because a public hanging was a possible result of their day's labours, as it had been at the previous circuit in September 1769 in circumstances which caused distress to

47 Map, Mitchell Library, Glasgow, GC 941.435 REN.
48 *Extracts from the Records of the Burgh of Glasgow* vol vii (1760–80), ed R Renwick (1912), p 542, 24 December 1778.
49 A sketch by James Brown exists of the Trongate and Glasgow Cross in 1774, with commentary, in John G Smith and John O Mitchell, *The Old Country Houses of the Old Glasgow Gentry* (2nd edn,1878). The same book has a sketch of Annfield House.
50 Charles Ross, map of shire of Lanark south west section (insert), 1773: NLS:EMS s 358.
51 Mitchell Library, Glasgow, GC 941.435.GOR.
52 James Boswell, *The Journal of a Tour to the Hebrides with Samuel Johnson* (various editions); entries for 28 and 29 October 1773.
53 Ross, *Lord Kames and the Scotland of his Day*, p 306; Senex, *Glasgow Past and Present* (1864), vol 2, p 478.

the magistrates.[54] The Scottish judicial orders for mutilation of a body, before or after a slow strangulation, would make a gruesome story. Death was sometimes not enough for the judges. The present pub, on a slightly different site, is not a judges' residence. It is affectionately known to Glaswegians, especially Celtic supporters, as the "Sarry Heid". It is a long walk, as befits the original journey to a country estate, to Sword Street.

54 D Macleod Malloch, *The Book of Glasgow Anecdote* (1912), p 273.

A Brave Scottish Advocate of Liberty: Thomas Muir

Clare Connelly[1]

Known as one of the five "Scottish Martyrs", Thomas Muir was among the celebrated reformers of 1792–1793. The reform movements that had developed all over Scotland, England and Ireland gathered momentum with the events in France at that time. In April 1792, an association had been formed in London called "Friends of the People" for the purpose of procuring reform in parliament. This association sought to restore the purity of the British constitution; to curtail the already overgrown influence of the Crown; to secure the independence of the House of Commons; to render its members "representatives of the people"; to consolidate their interests with that of the nation; to check corruption and prodigality; and to avert the horrors of a revolution.[2]

On 16 October 1792, a public meeting was held within the Star Inn, Glasgow chaired by Colonel Dalrymple of Fordel. Muir was amongst many respectable and affluent Glaswegians in attendance and they formed an association under the title "Friends of the Constitution, and of the People" with the purpose of co-operating with the Friends of the People in London in procuring reform of the House of Commons. Unlike parliamentary representation and participation, which at the time was restricted to the landed classes, citizens of every description were invited to attend. However, membership necessitated a declaration of adherence to the government of Great Britain as established by King, Lords and Commons. Muir's radical tendencies also extended to his open criticism of the legal system which he viewed as being biased in favour of the rich. Muir's threat to the establishment peaked with the French Revolution and the execution of Louis XVI. The British ruling classes

---

1 This chapter is dedicated to my Criminal Devil Master, Sarah Livingstone, Advocate.
2 P Mackenzie, *Life of Thomas Muir, Esq* (1831), p 5.

were concerned that these revolutionary ideas would spread to Britain. Muir's was one of a number of show trials, ending with gruelling punishment, that succeeded merely in delaying rather than stopping much needed political reform.

MUIR'S EARLY LIFE

Thomas Muir was born on 25 August 1765,[3] the only son of wealthy parents. He initially lived in a flat above his father's shop in the High Street of Glasgow. Muir's father's commercial success is evidenced in his purchase in the 1780s of the property, Huntershill House, together with adjoining lands. Muir's parents were both orthodox Presbyterians and their son was brought up within the moral and social ethic of "Auld Licht" Calvinism. His early education began at age five under a local schoolmaster, William Barclay. At the age of 10, he was admitted to the "gowned classes" of the University of Glasgow. He attended junior classes for five sessions before matriculating in 1777 when he embarked upon the study of divinity. He graduated with the degree of Master of Arts in 1782. Influenced by the teachings of John Millar,[4] Professor of Civil Law, he abandoned his studies for the church and commenced studying law. Millar was a republican Whig who supported the American struggle for independence and favoured parliamentary reform at home. He sympathised with the French revolutionaries and supported the agitation against the slave trade. Such views were conspicuous at a time when Scotland was chiefly in the hands of the Tories.

Muir's study of law at Glasgow University was cut short following his support in 1784 of Professor John Anderson. Anderson, Professor of Oriental Languages and Natural Philosophy, brought a complaint of embezzlement against the Principal, William Leechman, and Professors Richardson and Taylor.[5] The University was not willing to

---

3 It is suggested in some writings that he was born on 24 August. See www.huntershill.co.uk for a brief account of his life.

4 John Millar (1735–1801) was admitted to the Faculty of Advocates in 1760 and appointed the Regius Professor of Civil Law from 1761 to 1800. He expanded the curriculum and encouraged conversation and debate. Such was his popularity that the number of students studying law rose from 4 to 30–40 each year. He established the university's reputation as a leading law school.

5 Anderson was ultimately suspended from his office as a member of the Jurisdictio Ordinaria. He went on to found the Andersonian Institute in Glasgow, now known as Strathclyde University.

investigate the allegations so Anderson petitioned the Chancellor, the Marquess of Graham, and Ilay Campbell, the Lord Advocate, for assistance in procuring a Royal Commission of Enquiry into the university's affairs. Glasgow University archives hold letters from Principal William Leechman to Ilay Campbell assuring him that the University feared no enquiry into the conduct of the management[6] and urging him to refuse any help to Anderson who was going to London with "seven or eight different petitions for a Royal Visitation".[7] Principal Leechman also wrote to the Marquess of Graham seeking his co-operation against the evil actions of Professor John Anderson.[8] The university archive also holds letters to Henry Dundas, a former Lord Rector, seeking his co-operation against Anderson.[9] These efforts by Principal Leechman to secure support from these prominent figures reflected the fact that Anderson was enjoying widespread support including from the Glasgow Trades who, by a large majority, voted on 24 February 1785 in support of Anderson's cause. The influence of Principal Leechman is reflected in the fact that this vote was reversed a few days later after an appeal by him.

Meanwhile, students petitioned the Lord Rector, Edmund Burke, to exert his influence in favour of Anderson.[10] It is not known whether his response was indifference or a refusal to interfere, but the frustrated students resolved to elect another to replace him. The professoriate were unhappy at this threatened action and used their powerful influence which they exerted by threats and intimidation to successfully secure Burke's re-election in 1784.[11] The senior students supporting Anderson went on to issue a pamphlet entitled "A Statement of Fact" against Leechman and the faculty. The faculty responded to what they viewed as a gross act of insubordination by banning Muir and twelve others from lectures prior to the result of hearings; however, they only did this after Anderson had departed for London. Muir and his fellow students, acting on the principles instilled by John Millar, requested legal representation at the hearings.

6 Glasgow University Library Archive, GUA27344, 1784.
7 GUL Archive, GUA27346, March 1785.
8 GUL Archive, GUA27348, May 1785.
9 GUL Archive, GUA27350, May 1785.
10 Mackenzie, *Life of Thomas Muir, Esq*, p 2.
11 Following this the majority of professors sought to take the election of the Lord Rector into their own hands and deprive students of their only popular privilege. This was unsuccessful. In 1785, Robert Graham Esq, of Gartmore, a genuine Whig, was elected Lord Rector.

The rejection of this request led Muir to give notice of his voluntary self-expulsion from the University.[12] Muir's actions protected the MA degree he had already been awarded and, with the assistance of Professor John Millar, he secured a place at the University of Edinburgh to study law under the Whig Professor of Law, John Wylde. Both of these men furthered Muir's knowledge of law and also his political interest and commitment to republicanism. Muir completed his studies at Edinburgh and was admitted to the Faculty of Advocates in 1787, aged 22.

AN ADVOCATE AND A RADICAL

Muir's student political inclinations did not subside when he commenced practice at the Bar. He soon developed a reputation as a fluent and eloquent speaker who showed great zeal and anxiety for his clients' interests. He was, somewhat unusually, willing to appear in court on behalf of poor clients who could not afford to pay a fee. He maintained his early habits of piety and devotion in respect of his religious beliefs. As an elder of the Church of Scotland, he became embroiled in a bitter dispute with local landlords in his parish of Cadder. Muir acted on behalf of the elders to challenge the local landlords' and heritors' attempts to dominate the selection committee for a new minister with "Parchment Barons". Muir was subsequently appointed as counsel for the congregation and was finally victorious in the General Assembly when the case of the landlords was thrown out.

Muir quickly secured a reputation as a man of principle who was anti-establishment. The hopes of all Whig members in Scotland and England were revived with the occurrence of the French Revolution in 1789. As reform societies grew in popularity, the Foxite Whigs in Parliament and the Lords inaugurated the London association of the "Friends of the People" in April 1792. Despite the entrenched opposition of Henry Erskine, the Dean of the Faculty of Advocates and leading Scottish Whig, the Scottish association of the Friends of the People was formed in Edinburgh on 26 July 1792. Assisted by the publications the *Edinburgh Gazetteer*, the *Caledonian Chronicle* and James Tyler's *Historical Register*, the new movement rapidly expanded. On 16 October 1792 in Glasgow, the "Friends of the Constitution,

12 Mackenzie, *Life of Thomas Muir, Esq*, p 3.

and of the People" was created[13] and, by the end of that year, the reform clubs and societies in Scotland, in particular those in Glasgow, Edinburgh, Dundee and Perth, put in place a plan of organisation, drawn up by Muir and William Skirving, a Fifeshire farmer. Unlike the London society which was elitist, the Scottish reform clubs were open to people of all social classes. Various public meetings, known as a "Convention of Delegates", from all the different reform societies in Scotland were held in Edinburgh during 1792–93 and were frequently presided over by Thomas Muir or his friend Lord Daer (who became the Earl of Selkirk).

In 1792, Muir began corresponding with Archibald Hamilton Rowan, who was Secretary of the Society of United Irishmen in Dublin.[14] Muir suggested a closer association and unity of action between the two movements. Muir was elected vice-president of the movement at the Edinburgh meeting and initiated a general convention of the societies. At the general convention of the Scottish Societies of the Friends of the People in December 1792, Muir wished to read an address from the United Irishmen of Dublin which appealed to Muir's nationalistic sentiments.

> We greatly rejoice that the spirit of freedom moves over the face of Scotland – that light seems to break from the chaos of her internal government; and that a country so respectable in her attainments in science, in arts and in arms [...] now rises to distinction, not by a calm contented secret wish for a Reform in Parliament, but by openly, actively and urgently willing it, with the unity and energy of an imbodied [sic] nation. We rejoice that you do not consider yourselves as merged, and melted down, into another country, but that, in this great national question, you are still Scotland – the land where Buchanan wrote, and Fletcher spoke, and Wallace fought![15]

The Act of Union had been passed in 1707 and appeals to nationalist sentiment were not to the liking of the unionists among the delegates

13 Mackenzie, *Life of Thomas Muir, Esq*, p 7.
14 The Society of United Irishmen in Dublin was founded in 18th-century Ireland as a liberal organisation that sought parliamentary reform. As one of the founding members, Archibald Hamilton Rowan worked alongside such famous radicals as William Drennan and Theobald Wolfe Tone. He was arrested in 1792 for seditious libel when caught handing out "An address to the Volunteers of Ireland", having been reported by the spy Thomas Collins. From February 1793, Britain and Ireland joined the War of the First Coalition against France, and the United Irish movement was outlawed in 1794.
15 F Clune, *The Scottish Martyrs: their Trials and Transportation to Botany Bay* (1969), p 5.

including Colonel William Dalrymple, Lord Daer and Richard Fowler. They were of the view that the address contained treason against the union with England and, whilst their attempts to silence Muir failed and he did read it out, the address was ultimately rejected by the convention. Muir closed his presentation by declaring to the convention: "We do not, we cannot, consider ourselves as mowed and melted down into another country. Have we not distinct Courts, Judges, Juries, Laws etc?"[16]

From this point, Muir was marked as a dangerous man. A government spy who had been in attendance at the convention reported on the proceedings with particular emphasis on the address. Concern that the Friends of Liberty in Scotland were almost unanimously enemies to the union with England was reported by Lord Daer in correspondence with Charles Grey of the London Friends of the People. As Muir busied himself preparing to defend James Tytler who had been arrested on a charge of sedition,[17] the Lord Advocate, Robert Dundas, began an intensive investigation into Muir's activities and is reported to have told his uncle, the Home Secretary, that he would charge Muir with high treason.

Whilst on his way to Tytler's trial in Edinburgh on 2 January 1793, Muir himself was arrested on a charge of treason and brought under guard to Edinburgh. Muir appeared for judicial examination before John Pringle, sheriff-depute of the County of Edinburgh, on 2 January but refused to answer any questions and was liberated after finding sufficient bail for his appearance on some future occasion. Matters became more difficult for Muir as he was regularly shunned by fellow members of the Scottish Bar, whilst others in more elevated positions treated him with rude insolence.

Muir attempted to use his period at liberty to galvanise support for the Scottish Association and so decided to travel.[18] His first port of

16 Clune, *The Scottish Martyrs*, p 5.
17 Tytler had a number of occupations, including apothecary, surgeon and editor of *Encyclopaedia Britannica* (2nd edn), and is also known as the first British person to ascend in a hot air balloon on 25 August 1784, in Edinburgh. Tytler, also a member of the association, expressed sympathy for the French Revolution of 1789 and called on the British not to pay taxes. In one of his pamphlets, published in 1792, his description of the House of Commons as a "vile junto of aristocrats" usurping the rights of king and people and his suggestion that honesty and upright behaviour rather than money should qualify a man for being an elector resulted in his being charged and ultimately outlawed in absentia for sedition in January 1793.
18 Some of his friends felt that this action allowed his enemies to further malign him in his absence.

call was London on 8 January where he discovered there was great panic among the English Whigs over the proceedings of the trial of the French King, Louis XVI.[19] Such was the concern that leading figures such as Charles Grey and Lord Lauderdale were openly discussing abandoning the campaign for parliamentary reform. Muir travelled to Paris in an attempt to intervene in the outcome of the king's trial which he correctly feared would exasperate the other crowned heads of Europe who would lead their subjects into a war and thus retard the growth of freedom. His arrival on the eve of Louis XVI's execution left no opportunity for such intervention. Muir was welcomed in Paris, where he stayed for six months, making many helpful connections, including Barras, Condorcet and La Fayette.

During his period of absence, many of Muir's friends, who had enjoyed his friendship and confidence, were examined by the authorities. Some condescended to gather information for the authorities and others, who were once regarded as friends, joined the ranks of his known enemies. Thomas Muir was indicted before the High Court of Justiciary for sedition with his trial scheduled to start on 11 (and afterwards altered to 25) February 1793. Muir was informed of this by letter, but he was unable to return to Scotland because of the ongoing war with France. He wrote the following address to the Friends of the People in Scotland:

> Upon the evening of the 8th of this month I received letters from my father and from my agent Mr Campbell, informing me that an indictment was served against me in my absence, and that the trial was fixed for Monday the 11th instant. The distance, and the shortness of the time could not permit me to reach Edinburgh by that day. War is declared between England and France, and the formalities requisite to be gone through, before I could procure my passport, would at least have consumed three days. To shrink from dangers would be unbecoming my own character, and your confidence. I dare challenge the most minute investigation of my public and private conduct. Armed with innocency, I appeal to justice; and I disdain to supplicate favours. I have hastened to give you an account of my intention, and I am happy that a private gentleman, who leaves Paris tomorrow, affords me an opportunity for the communication. Thomas Muir. Paris 13th February, 1793.[20]

19 In July 1789, Louis XVI and his family were imprisoned. He attempted to escape in 1791 but was captured and returned to Paris. In 1792, the newly-elected National Convention declared France a Republic and brought Louis XVI to trial for crimes against the people. On 20 January 1793, the National Convention condemned Louis XVI to death, his execution scheduled for the next day.

20 Mackenzie, *Life of Thomas Muir, Esq*, p 16.

Lord Dundas, the Lord Advocate, sought and obtained Muir's labelling as a fugitive from justice on 25 February 1793 before Lord Braxfield, and a sentence of outlawry was granted. As a result, the Faculty of Advocates convened a meeting on 6 March, at which Muir was neither present nor represented, where he was unanimously expelled and his name struck from the roll of the Faculty of Advocates. Mackenzie suggests that this occurrence did not trouble Muir as he planned to retire to the USA if acquitted at trial.[21] The relevant entry in *The Faculty of Advocates 1800–1986* reads:

> Muir, Thomas (27 November 1787 (date of admission to Faculty), son of James Muir of Huntershill, merchant, Glasgow, born 24 August 1765, died at Paris, 27 September 1798. Convicted of Sedition 1794, sentenced to transportation for 14 years, expelled from Faculty 1793.[22]

When Muir did secure passage home from Paris, it was on board an American ship, *The Hope of Boston*, which took him to Belfast, from where he visited Dublin and the United Irishmen before finally returning to the north and sailing to Portpatrick. On arrival in Scotland, he was recognised by a customs officer and immediately taken into custody. Muir was transported to Edinburgh under heavy guard and remanded in custody in the Tolbooth prison until his trial before Lord Braxfield and a hand-picked jury who were anti-reform.[23]

THE INDICTMENT

The libel contained in the indictment is lengthy, but in essence describes sedition in various forms, including speeches and harangues, addresses to meetings and conventions of persons brought together by no lawful authority; and the wicked and felonious advising and exhorting of persons to purchase and peruse seditious and wicked publications and writings calculated to produce a spirit of disloyalty and disaffection to the king and the established government. The indictment went on to narrate various meetings where Muir had been present and had addressed the audience and listed the publications Muir was alleged to have circulated or caused to be circulated.

---

21 Mackenzie, *Life of Thomas Muir, Esq*, p 16.
22 S P Walker, *The Faculty of Advocates 1800–1986: A Biographical Dictionary of Members Admitted from 1 January 1800 to 31 December 1986* (1987), p 157.
23 Mackenzie, *Life of Thomas Muir, Esq*, p 17.

THE TRIAL

Before examining the content of the evidence led at trial and the verdict, there are three peculiarities in criminal procedure in this era that should be noted. The first is that the jury were nominated by the judges of the Court of Justiciary. The Clerk of Court handed to the presiding judge a list of the names of 45 jurymen, who were all cited to attend on the occasion. His Lordship then proceeded to pick out his chosen 15 jurors. The only basis for objection by the accused was on the limited and special grounds of personal malice, misnomer, infamy, minority, deafness, dumbness, insanity or a relationship to the prosecutor. The second peculiarity is that at the time of Muir's trial an accused was not able to give evidence. The fact that Muir represented himself therefore gave him a unique opportunity to both cross-examine the witnesses led against him and also to state his defence to the court. The final difference in criminal procedure at this time was that there was no Court of Criminal Appeal and, therefore, the decision of a jury and the sentence passed were final and could not be reviewed.

Muir's trial for sedition was opened a few minutes after 10am on Friday 30 August 1793, by Lord Justice-Clerk McQueen, and four Lords Commissioners of Justiciary, Lord Henderland, Lord Swinton, Lord Dunsinnan and Lord Abercromby. The Lord Advocate, Robert Dundas, led the prosecution and Thomas Muir presented his own defence. Mr Muir arrived a few minutes late and, following him being reprimanded, the indictment was read out by the depute clerk of court. In addition to the charges of sedition, extracts from the works of Thomas Paine and others, which Muir was libelled to have supplied to Henry Freeland, were read to the court. This included the following extract:

> The act called the Bill of Rights comes here into view. What is it but a bargain which the parts of the government made with each other to divide powers, profits and privileges? You shall have so much, and I will have the rest; and with respect to the nation, it said for your share you shall have the right of petitioning. This being the case the Bill of Rights is more properly a Bill of wrongs and of insult.[24]

The libel made specific reference to Muir reading the address for the Society of United Irishmen in Dublin (referred to above) at various meetings in 1792.

24 T J Howell, *A Complete Collection of State Trials and Proceedings for High Treason and Other Crimes and Misdemeanours* (1817), p 120.

As was the norm, in advance of the trial, Muir had intimated a list of witnesses and a written note of his defence in the following terms:

> The criminal libel is false and injurious; so far from exciting the people to riot and insurrection, it can easily be proved, by a numerous list of witnesses that, upon every occasion, the panel exhorted them to pursue measures moderate, legal, peaceable, and constitutional. The charge of distributing seditious publications and of advising the people to read them, is equally false and calumnious. The panel admits, that on the great national question, concerning an equal representation of the people in the House of commons, he exerted every effort to procure in that House, a full, fair, and equal representation of the people as he considered it to be a measure (and still does) the most salutary for the interest of his country. But the panel offers to prove, that as he considered the information of the people to be the chief thing requisite to accomplish this great object, he uniformly advised them to read every publication, upon either side, which the important question of parliamentary reform had occasioned.[25]

When Muir was asked if he had anything further to state in support of his defence, he said:

> I admit that I exerted every effort to procure a more equal representation of the people in the House of commons. If that be a crime I plead guilty to the charge. I acknowledge that I considered the issue of parliamentary reform to be essential to the salvation of my country; but I deny that I ever advised the people to attempt to accomplish that great object by any means which the constitution did not sanction. I grant that I advised the people to read different publications upon both sides, which this great national question had excited, and I am not ashamed to assign my motives. I consider the ignorance of the people on the one hand, to be the source from which despotism flows … Knowledge must always precede reformation, and who shall dare to say that the people should be debarred from information, when it concerns them so materially? I am accused of sedition; and yet, I can prove by thousands of witnesses, that I warned the people of the danger of that crime, exhorted them to adopt none but measures which were constitutional and intreated them, to connect liberty with knowledge, and both with morality. This is what I can prove. If these are crimes I am guilty.[26]

Following the selection of the first two jurors at his trial, Muir rose and stated that he did not know the men, but that he nevertheless protested against their sitting on his trial because they belonged to an

25 Howell, *A Complete Collection of State Trials*, p 129.
26 Howell, *A Complete Collection of State Trials*, p 131.

association which had publicly condemned his principles and had
actually offered a reward to discover any person who had circulated
any of the political publications which he was accused of circulating
in the indictment. He asked to be tried fairly by an independent jury.
But his plea fell on deaf ears. Muir objected to all of the jurors without
effect and in due course they were empanelled.

The Crown led evidence from witnesses regarding their attendance
at various meetings that Muir addressed. When the Crown called
William Muir,[27] on his refusal to take the oath, the Lord Advocate
moved that he be committed to prison for his contumacy and
informed him that there was no way by which he could ever be set
free, and, in express words declared, that this imprisonment would
be eternal.[28] He later returned, took the oath and gave evidence that
he did not remember Muir speaking against the government, that
Muir did not advise unconstitutional measures and that he heard
him speak about the government. Throughout the trial, Muir objected
to the Lord Advocate putting questions to witnesses in respect of
crimes with which he had not been charged, which included speaking
disrespectfully of the courts of justice to thereby incite the people
against the administration of law. His repeated appeal that no person
should be tried for a crime without fair notice of the crimes charged
was not upheld by the judges who said that all accusations being
made fell within the broad libel of sedition. The address from the
Society of United Irishmen of Dublin that Muir had given at public
meetings was read to the court.

Muir called the following witnesses in his defence: William Skirving;
John Buchanan; William Johnston; Maurice Thomson; Charles Salter;
Peter Wood; David Dale;[29] John Brock; William Cliddesdale; George
Waddel; John Russel; William Riddle; William Reid; George Bell; Rev
Daniel McArthur; James Mcgibbon; Robert Henry; William Orr;
James Craig; and James Richardson. Mr Muir now declared that he
had finished presenting his defence and, whilst he was able to adduce
more witnesses, he deemed it totally unnecessary.

The Lord Advocate then proceeded to make his closing address to
the jury which included a summary of the evidence that had been

27 It is not evident from the record of proceedings what William Muir's relationship
    was to Thomas, but it is clear that he was neither his father nor his brother.
28 Howell, *A Complete Collection of State Trials*, p 145.
29 When this witness was asked if anyone had told him what to say, he replied
    only to tell the truth. When he was asked who had so advised him, he was
    unable/unwilling to say and he was committed to prison for three weeks on the
    basis that he was guilty of concealing the truth upon oath.

heard, reference to Muir's association with the Rev T Fyshe Palmer, who was indicted to stand trial in Perth in a matter of days, and he concluded with the following statement:

> I hope gentlemen, this case will be viewed by you in such a light as that you will protect your king from the attacks of his enemies, that you will protect his temple of freedom from the attempts of the factious, but particularly against that man at the bar, who has been sowing sedition with so liberal a hand. You may now, however, seize him in his career, and by your verdict do justice to your country and honour to yourselves.

Mr Muir then addressed the jury. He explained why his return from France was delayed and challenged the prosecutor's position that he had attempted to evade justice by landing in Scotland in a clandestine manner. He spoke at length of his campaign to secure parliamentary reform which he said was by constitutional measures. He stated that, if the attempt to procure reform in parliament was criminal, then the accusation would extend far and wide to include ministers of the Crown and the lowest subjects. He went on to say that, if the real cause of his standing accused is for having engaged in the cause of a parliamentary reform, he pleads guilty. He stated that he engaged in that cause to save his country as a more equal representation would dry up the sources, as of corruption, would diminish taxes and stop the effusion of blood. That such were his motives appeared from every part of the evidence against him. He reflected on the prosecution evidence led at the trial and invited the jury to look again at the indictment and compare it to the evidence. On sitting down, the audience gave a unanimous burst of applause.

The Lord Justice-Clerk then charged the jury. He began by stating that Muir's indictment was the longest he had ever seen. He told the jury the question for them was whether, on the evidence as a whole, Muir was guilty of sedition or not. On charging the jury in respect of the writings mentioned in the indictment, he advised that the passages should be taken in context and that, to render a book seditious, it was not necessary for it to all be seditious. He stated that, as Muir had brought witnesses to prove his general good behaviour, and his recommending peaceable measures and petitions to parliament, it was the jury's business to judge how far this should operate in his favour, in opposition to the evidence on the other side. The Lord Justice-Clerk then made a clear declaration in support of the status quo by stating:

> A government in every country should be just like a corporation; and in this country it is made up of the landed interest, which alone has a right

to be represented; as for the rabble who have nothing but personal property, what hold has the nation of them? What security for the payment of their taxes? They may pack up all their property on their backs, and leave the country in the twinkling of an eye, but landed property cannot be removed.[30]

The Lord Justice-Clerk finished his address at 1.30am on Saturday 31 August. The court was adjourned until noon that day and the jury were immediately enclosed. They returned at noon and delivered a verdict of guilty of the crimes libelled. The Lord Justice-Clerk told the jury that the court highly approved of their verdict. The judges then delivered a unanimous opinion that Muir should be sentenced to transportation for 14 years. Passing sentence, the Lord Justice-Clerk told Muir that, if during the 14 year period, he should return to any part of Great Britain without some lawful cause and be convicted, he shall suffer death.

TRANSPORTATION

On 15 November 1793, Muir was taken from the Tolbooth prison in Edinburgh by coach to Newhaven where he was sent on board the *Royal George*, excise yacht, Captain Ogilvie, lying in Leith Roads, for London. His parents visited him for the last time before he commenced this journey. He was accompanied by a fellow reformist, Rev T Fyshe Palmer, and other convicts. On their arrival, they were put on board the Hulks at Woolwich. Representations in Muir's favour in the House of Commons and the House of Lords, by the Right Hon William Adam (on 10 March 1794) and the Earl of Lauderdale, respectively, were unsuccessful by an overwhelming majority.[31] Soon after the votes in Parliament, Muir was shipped off to Botany Bay, Australia.[32]

30 Howell, *A Complete Collection of State Trials*, p 231.
31 In the House of Commons there were 32 votes for the motion of Mr Adam and 171 against, the majority against the motion being 139.
32 After the Transportation Act of 1718 had been passed, the number of people sentenced to transportation increased steadily until it was halted when the American War of Independence began in 1776. In 1787, transportation resumed with a new destination, Australia. The first convicts, around 750, arrived in Botany Bay in Australia on 20 January 1788. This was the beginning of the most extensive system of forced exile ever to be undertaken by the British Government. Between 1787 and 1840, 80,000 convicts were deported to New South Wales and 60,000 to Van Diemen's Land in Tasmania. However, unlike England, the Scottish courts only transported those convicted of the most serious crimes and this and the fact of the population being smaller accounts

Muir was accompanied by 82 fellow convicts on board the *Surprise* transport that took him from England to Botany Bay. His fellow reformers, Palmer, Skirving and Margarot, were among them. A rather unexpected fellow convict was a man of the name of Henderson who had been tried by the Circuit Court of Justiciary, two years previously, for the murder of his wife. Muir had been his counsel and was successful in securing a verdict of culpable homicide, which saved Henderson from the gallows but gained him 14 years' transportation.

Muir enjoyed better treatment in Sydney than he had done in Scotland. He was no longer yoked in chains and set to hard labour – instead his gentlemanly deportment commanded respect. Approximately three months after his arrival, Muir wrote to a friend, Mr Moffatt, a solicitor in London. In his letter, dated 13 December 1794, Muir wrote that he was as pleased with his situation as he could be. He, Palmer and Skirving lived in the utmost harmony whilst Margarot was expelled. He stated that he could not speak too highly of his treatment: he had a neat little house and another property at a farm two miles away across the water. Muir laboured with his hands to cultivate the land he had bought, but he also improved the mental and corporeal conditions of the less fortunate felons who surrounded him.

The publication of his trial in the United States resulted in Muir being viewed as a martyr in the cause of freedom. Washington became interested in him, as did some generous benefactors who formed the bold project of rescuing him from captivity. At their own expense and unknown to Muir, an American ship called the *Otter* was dispatched in 1795. The *Otter* anchored in the Cove at Sydney on 25 January 1796. After a few days, Captain Dawes discovered Muir and, on 11 February 1796, he boarded the *Otter* and the vessel instantly set sail. Margarot communicated Muir's escape in a letter to Thomas Hardy in March 1796, which demonstrates that he was fully aware that the *Otter* had anchored in Sydney under the pretence of needing wood and water. Prior to his departure, Muir wrote to the Governor of Sydney acknowledging his kindness and stating his intention to take up residence in the USA. After four months at sea, the *Otter* was shipwrecked. She struck a chain of sunken rocks off the west coast

---

for the fact that there were only about 8,000 Scottish convicts deported to the southern hemisphere during this time. The punishment was harsh, as exile to a foreign land so far away made returning to the home land very difficult.

of North America. Only Muir and two sailors survived. Muir was separated from the other two after they were all captured by Indians and, when he made his escape, he travelled alone across 4,000 miles by foot until he reached Panama.

Muir's linguistic abilities, which included Spanish, assisted him in describing his plight to the Governor who helped him in securing guides to take him to Vera Cruz, the grand sea-port of Mexico, 1,000 miles away. Muir sought passage on an American ship but, as none was available, he secured passage in the first vessel that sailed for Havannah. Unknown to Muir, the Governor of Vera Cruz had intimated to the Governor of Havannah that he thought a man of Muir's principles was dangerous and that he should be sent to Spain in order that the king might determine what should be done with him. Muir was detained in prison for four weeks in La Principe on the north side of Cuba before sailing to Spain in one of two Spanish frigates, both with a rich cargo.

Close to the harbour of Cadiz, the two Spanish frigates were spotted by a British squadron. On 26 April 1797, the *Emerald* and the *Irresistible*, two frigates of that squadron, gave chase to the Spanish vessels. Within hours, they approached each other within pistol shot. Two hours of fierce and bloody action followed. Towards the close, Muir was struck by a cannon ball and lay prostrate with the dead. The Spanish vanquished, some of the officers of the *Irresistible* boarded the frigate, and amongst the dead found a man with one eye and the bone and lower part of his cheek missing. The sailors, presuming he was dead, lifted him to throw him overboard. Muir uttered a sigh and his bible, bearing his name, fell from his hands and was picked up by an officer who recognised the name of his childhood friend. Aware of Muir's predicament, the officer concealed his identity and instead ordered for him to be taken ashore to Cadiz with the other wounded Spanish sailors.

After two months in hospital, Muir was able to speak a little and by unknown means communication of his situation reached Paris. The French Directory ordered their agent at Cadiz to meet Muir's expenses and to supply him with money. In September 1797, Muir received a communication from the government of France offering him the privileges of a free citizen and inviting him to spend the remainder of his life in France. He arrived in Bordeaux in early December and, when he rose to offer thanks at a public dinner, attended by upwards of 500 on 4 December 1797, he fainted in the arms of the American consul. He reached Paris on 4 February 1798. He recorded his gratitude to the French Directory in a letter of 6

February 1798 for his liberty, his life and for the liberty of his country. He declared his devotion and gratitude and stated that he would remain faithful to his adopted country until his last breath. The wounds Muir had sustained were incurable. Prior to his death on 27 September 1798, aged 33 years, he packaged up the bible his parents had long since gifted to him that had accompanied him through all of his travels, and left instruction that it be returned to them. It was in due course received by them with mixed feelings of satisfaction and grief. They survived their son by approximately two years.

CONCLUSION

As Muir correctly anticipated, his trial survived history. Electoral reform did occur and the men convicted of sedition and transported to Botany Bay soon became known as the Scottish Martyrs – celebrated reformists who paid a high price in the name of democracy. Muir is celebrated across Scotland with monuments and heritage trails. He is also remembered in the form of the Thomas Muir Society in the Faculty of Advocates. Muir is perhaps best summed up as "Brave Scottish Advocate of Liberty", the acclamation that accompanied a toast to him in Bordeaux in December 1797.

Downfall of a Racing Man:
Udny v Udny

David Carey Miller and Anne MacKenzie

Colonel John Udny lived life to the full. Litigation that arose from his private life culminated in a decision of the House of Lords in 1869 that, to this day, remains a definitive authority on the determination of domicile. The domicile of Colonel Udny became an issue shortly before his death in 1861 but its resolution called for consideration of circumstances and events from his entire life to determine whether he retained his Scottish domicile of origin or whether he had acquired an English domicile of choice. This issue was critical to the question of the legitimacy of his son, John Henry Udny. That this son was born out of wedlock was not in dispute but the effect of the subsequent marriage of his parents was the issue which necessitated a decision between the two British legal systems. According to the law of Scotland, the illegitimate child of unmarried parents became legitimate by the parents' subsequent marriage, but in English law this consequence did not follow. In both systems, legitimacy was a prerequisite to the right of succession – in this case, the right to inherit the Udny family estate.

PLACE AND FAMILY

The estate of Udny lies on the flat and windswept North Sea coast some 12 miles north of Aberdeen and south of the town of Ellon. The village of Newburgh was also part of the Udny estate. Although a quiet and relatively prosperous part of the country, in the mid-19th century, it was to become the focus of a dispute about its ownership which was to last for several years.

In *The Thanage of Fermartyn*, published in 1894, the Reverend William Temple notes that "The barony of Udny, in the parish of the same name, has been in the possession of the present family for at least five centuries."[1] Temple traces the family from the first recorded member, the late-14th century Patrick de Uldeny, through the Udnys who were anti-Covenanters, including one who apparently joined the Jacobite Rebellion of 1745. About him, it is said: "John Fullerton [Udny] of Dudwick out in 1745; was especially exempted from the general amnesty, and it is said travelled the country disguised as a packman."[2] As with most Victorian genealogies, this narrative must be treated with some caution, but what emerges is that the Udny family was one of considerable antiquity and some importance in Aberdeenshire where they married into other prominent families including, notably, the Gordons, Earls of Aberdeen.

About the parish of Udny, the Reverend John Leslie writes in the second *Statistical Account of Scotland* of 1834–45:[3]

> Udny derives its name from a family, which, for many centuries, has possessed the barony of Udny, on which the kirk stands. ... The parish is almost circular, except on the north-east, where it juts out to a considerable extent. It is supposed to contain about 16 square miles.

The minister notes that the estate of Udny comprises lands also in the parishes of Foveran and Ellon. He also describes in detail Udny Castle, at that date in a state of disrepair, an attempt to repair it begun in 1801 having failed. The condition of the castle was to feature considerably in the case and the minister has this to say about it:

> The walls are thick enough to admit of bed-closets within them. The two under-stories are vaulted, the upper one of which contains a spacious hall, the whole length and breadth of the castle. It is neatly floored or rather pavemented, with oblong hexagonal granites, very neatly joined. Its height to the top of the arch is about 20 feet ...The castle is said to have been the work of three successive proprietors, who all lived the ordinary period of life ... It is noted that all three were nearly ruined by it. This is not to be wondered at, when we consider that they had only the barony of Udny, not 400 Scots acres in extent.

Vaulting ambition above the limits of its income appears to have been long-standing in the house of Udny. The case of *Udny v Udny*[4] centred

---

1 W Temple, *The Thanage of Fermartyn* (1894), p 425.
2 Temple, *The Thanage of Fermartyn*, p 432.
3 Accessed 20/04/13 through www.edina.ac.uk.
4 (1869) 7 M (HL) 89. The original process including the closed record and some productions and witness statements are in the National Registers of Scotland, at reference CS244/1483. All references to witness statements, productions, pleadings etc are to these documents.

on the early 19th century ornament of that ancient name, the larger than life figure of Colonel John Robert Fullerton Udny. Born on 14 November 1779 in Leghorn (Livorno) in Italy where his father was British Consul, in 1802 he was served as heir to the estate, succeeding his uncle Robert Udny. The estate was entailed by Alexander Udny of Udny upon the colonel's grandfather, James Udny, Advocate in Aberdeen and Burgess of the City, and his heirs male. The parish records of Aberdeen note that on 20 December 1716 James Udny married Jean Walker (according to Temple,[5] the daughter of the Lord Provost of Aberdeen and on her mother's side descended from the family of Irvine of Drum) and that several children were born to the couple and baptised in Aberdeen. The baptism of the colonel's father, John Udny, is recorded as taking place on 21 March 1727. The witnesses being John Irving (sic), the brother of the deceased Alexander Irving of Drum and also the son of a previous Lord Provost of Aberdeen, lend credence to the claim that Consul Udny's mother was connected with these families.

Having no hope of succeeding to the estate at Udny, John Udny went to Italy, initially to Venice, where he operated as a merchant, trading largely in antiquities and works of art. On the departure and the recommendation of the incumbent, he became British Consul at Venice and subsequently gained the office of Consul at Leghorn in Tuscany, then an important British naval base. As a perk of that office, he had the right to supply the British fleet, a not inconsiderable financial benefit. At Pisa on 21 August 1777, the consul married Miss Selina Shore Cleveland of Devonshire. It is perhaps telling that, in his childhood, Colonel Udny profited from no example of marital harmony. When he was only five years old his mother left her husband and returned to England. This was not a return merely to ensure the education of children but signified a clear estrangement between the couple. Consul Udny returned only on leave in 1799 after his property was confiscated by the French and he died while in England in 1800.

Before leaving Italy, Consul Udny sent various works of art home to Britain, largely to his brother, the laird Robert Udny. Some of these paintings, including Titian's *Triumph of Love,* now in the Ashmolean Museum, were on board the ship *Westmorland* when it was captured by the French on 7 January 1799.[6] As this may suggest, Robert Udny, the colonel's uncle was no simple Scottish country laird. His published

5 Temple, *The Thanage of Fermartyn*, p 433.
6 See www.ashmolean-grandtour.org/westmorland-10-Titian.asp, accessed on 27/04/13.

obituaries narrate that he was a successful West India merchant and noted collector and connoisseur of works of art. These were displayed in a gallery, designed by Robert Adam, at Mr Udny's house in Teddington, Middlesex (now in Richmond on Thames). He was twice married and his second wife, who survived him, became under-governess to Princess Charlotte and also allegedly the mistress of the artist who drew her portrait, now in the British Museum. In his notes on this picture, the curator states that Robert Udny's most notable acquisition was the life-size cartoon by Leonardo da Vinci for *The Madonna and Child with St Anne and the infant St John the Baptist*, now in the National Gallery. His taste was noted among his contemporaries and his obituary, which was widely published, reads:

> Mr Udny possessed a very ample fortune, part of which he acquired in commerce as a West India merchant ... Having early in life conceived a passion for the fine arts he distinguished himself by an elegance and correctness of taste, superior to most men of the present age.[7]

It also notes that he spared no expense in amassing his collection and enlisted the help of his brother, Consul Udny, in its acquisition. He himself had twice made a tour of Italy.

According to the website of the Twickenham Museum, it is said that Robert Udny's collection attracted the interest of King George III to the extent that he and Queen Charlotte visited the house in Teddington to view it and were entertained to breakfast. Whatever the truth of that story, all accounts agree that Mr Udny was noted for his hospitality and generosity. Sadly, although Colonel John Udny inherited his uncle's disposition for sparing no expense, the colonel failed to inherit the talent for earning money which his relative clearly had.

In his evidence, taken on commission because of his fragile state of health, Colonel Udny stated that he was schooled first at Richmond and then at Hackney. Later, at the age of approximately 14, he was sent to the University of Edinburgh. In Edinburgh he lodged with the family of a clergyman, Daniel Sandford, who later became Bishop of the Scottish Episcopalian Church. The judgments narrate that his education in Edinburgh was at the insistence of his uncle Robert, who intended that his nephew and likely heir should read for the Scottish Bar. The young man, however, had other ideas.

7 *Lancaster Gazette*, 23 January 1802.

LIFE AWAY FROM HOME

Following his period in Edinburgh, John Udny began his military service, joining the 1st Foot Guards at the age of 17. He saw service abroad in Holland, the Mediterranean and Spain during the Peninsular Wars. It is a matter of record that he took part in the arduous and dispiriting retreat to Corunna in the winter of 1808 and at the subsequent battle, which saw the death of General Sir John Moore.[8] The award of the Corunna Clasp to Lieutenant Colonel Udny is recorded in the medal rolls kept at the National Archives in Kew.[9]

One of his fellow officers was Captain Sir John Warrender, Bt, an East Lothian landowner, who would later give evidence on behalf of Colonel Udny's son. He spoke of the closeness between the brother officers. This came to an end in 1812 when two significant events in the life of Colonel Udny took place: he left the army and married Emilia Fitzhugh, daughter of Thomas Fitzhugh, gentleman of Denbighshire. The couple set up home in a rented house in Grosvenor Street, London. Thomas Wilsone, solicitor in Aberdeen, testified that the colonel's income consisted of the rents of his estate in Aberdeenshire, stated in the *Statistical Account* to be just over £830, but that he also benefitted by around £16,000, a sum which would have roughly the present-day spending power of £890,000, from his wife on his marriage.

The upright Sir John Warrender noted that the friendship between him and Colonel Udny ended when the latter left the army. In a telling but discreet sentence, he said, "He became a racing man and took a different view of life from myself."

The London to which the 32-year-old colonel returned was at the height of its Regency flamboyance and extravagance. George Bryan "Beau" Brummell dictated the form of a gentleman's attire, Walter Scott made all things Scottish fashionable, and a notorious personality with Aberdeenshire connections, Lord Byron, intrigued and scandalised society in equal measure by his poetry and his very public affair with the married Lady Caroline Lamb. Gambling and reckless spending were rife among the upper classes. Taking their example from the future George IV, many gentlemen thought nothing of risking a fortune on the turn of a card or the outcome of a race. Colonel Udny took full advantage of the spirit of the times.

8 See the history of the Grenadier Guards at www.grengds.com, accessed 18/04/13.
9 Series WO 100.

In later years, Colonel Udny confessed to many friends and professional counsellors that he bitterly regretted the extravagance of his youth which, he said, made it impossible for him to build himself a home on the Udny estate and live there among his tenantry. However, there is no evidence of any twinges of conscience in the contemporary accounts of his career as a man of the turf. Indeed, the success he enjoyed in both the sporting and social contexts would suggest that he spared no effort on these activities. In the sporting pages, he figures as the owner of several notable race-horses, including a chestnut filly called Pantoufle, Corinne, a four-year old in 1819, Abjer, a bay colt, Amphion, Sontag, Comte d'Artois, Tarandus and Plumper. The most successful, however, appear to have been Mirandola, a chestnut filly who won a Gold Cup at Newmarket in 1822, and Emilius, a bay colt bred by the Colonel from his own mare Emily, who crowned a very successful season in 1823 by winning the Derby. Surviving paintings of the horse show him to be a handsome bay stallion, who ended his career at stud. Slightly less successful was the chestnut colt Barmecide about whose performance in the Newmarket October Meeting in 1822 the *Sporting Magazine or Magazine of the Transactions of the Turf, the Chase and Every Other Diversion Interesting to the Man of Pleasure, Enterprise and Spirit,* Volume 11, 1823, said:

> Barmecide, a horse of great speed, some time ago, got beat the last race of the day by Augusta, at even weights. One must have improved in speed very much, or the other gone back. It appeared as if Augusta wore her dancing pumps and Barmecide his clouted shoes

A bay filly belonging to Lord Exeter, Augusta's performance was no flash in the pan as the following year she ended the unbeaten run by Emilius.

Along with racing success, the colonel enjoyed entry to the highest levels of London society. His uncle's reputation for taste and hospitality must have contributed to this to some extent, but his own success in sporting matters will also have ensured his acceptance in the world where these pastimes were highly valued.

The *Morning Post* of 23 May 1828 lists Colonel Udny's name along with those of many leading members of society, including the Dukes of Richmond, Grafton and Rutland and the Earls of Jersey and Sefton, whose wives ruled feminine society, among the distinguished persons present at the close of the races at Epsom. On 17 June 1824, the same journal has the following interesting information:

> The Duke of York also entertained a select Party at Frogmore, consisting of The Duke of Rutland, Earl Verulam, Earl Darlington, Lord Cavendish,

Lord Foley, Lord Clarendon, Lord Egremont, Sir John Shelley and Mr Udny.

A son, John Augustus, was born to the colonel and his wife Emilia on 30 July 1817 and baptised on 7 May 1818 in St George's, Hanover Square. The succession to the Udny estate must then have seemed relatively secure; but founding a family was not enough to encourage Colonel Udny to curb his spending. Given the uncertainty of life at that period, one might have expected a spare heir to be born to the family, but no further children came. It seems that the relationship between the colonel and his wife was not good. The wastage of the money she brought into the marriage may have contributed somewhat to the strain between the couple. Perhaps the naming of one of his best horses after her merely added insult to injury.

ESCAPE FROM CREDITORS

Whatever his domestic and financial difficulties, the colonel's social standing showed no sign of suffering. The *Caledonian Mercury* of 18 April 1844 lists him as among the guests at the wedding breakfast in London of Lord Francis Russell and Miss Peyton.

Inevitably this mode of life could not be sustained. His expenses would always exceed his income and, a few months later, the colonel left London to live in Boulogne. In his evidence in court, the colonel frankly stated that he left London because he had many debts and no means to pay them. He stated that all his goods and furniture, including those of his wife and sister, were sold, but somewhat casually noted that he "cannot remember whether or not there was an execution in the house". Whether or not diligence was being done in the household, the colonel, following the example of, among others, Mr Brummell, felt obliged to escape his creditors to continental Europe. Had he not fled, he could have ended up being imprisoned for debt.

Apart from a brief visit in 1845, the unfortunate Mrs Udny did not join her husband abroad and died in 1846. By the time he left London, the colonel had made the acquaintance of Miss Ann Allat, believed to have been born in Yorkshire, the daughter of pianoforte maker David Allat. Ann Allat is referred to throughout the court proceedings as Mrs Allat, but she was not previously married. In the 1841 Census, she can be found in London, an unmarried daughter in her father's house. In her evidence, she claimed not to have known when she first met the colonel that he was married. In due course, they formed a household together in lodgings in Boulogne. Three children were born to the couple, one stillborn child, a daughter born in 1844 who died aged seven, and finally John Henry, ultimately the defender in the case. He was born in Camberwell on 9 May 1853; the colonel had wanted Miss Allat to be confined in England as he was not happy with the standard of care in Boulogne.

The birth of his younger son appears to have triggered in Colonel Udny a plan to improve his own financial situation and ensure the succession to the Udny estate. John Augustus, his elder, legitimate son was aide de camp to the Lord Lieutenant of Ireland, based in Dublin, and showed no sign of marrying. At some point, the colonel resolved to return to Scotland and marry his mistress, Miss Allat, thus, he believed, legitimating his son, John Henry.

Letters lodged as productions for the pursuer show that Colonel Udny took advice on the legal consequences of his remarriage, going as far as to take counsel's opinion. He also shared his plans with John Augustus, but kept them from Miss Allat for fear of disappointing her. John Augustus was supportive of the plan. Various reasons for this support could be posited, but the likeliest is that stated by the Lord Chancellor in the leading judgment in the House of Lords, that by those means he and the colonel believed they could more easily break the entail. In this way, the colonel and John Augustus – who seems to have inherited his father's talent for economic management – could be relieved of the worst of their financial embarrassments.

The advice must have been positive as, in November 1853, bringing their infant son, the couple left Boulogne, came to Scotland and hired a house in Ormiston, West Lothian. On 2 January 1854, John Robert Fullerton Udny and Ann Allat were married by the minister, Mr Thomson. Though questions were raised during the evidence about the legal formalities of the marriage, both Mr Thomson and the Session Clerk attested to the couple's having fulfilled the residence requirements, and no serious objection was taken on this basis.

In his judgment, the Lord Ordinary generously imputed motives for marriage to the colonel which were more noble than venal:

> It is ... impossible to say that it was otherwise than right on Colonel Udny's part to endeavour to repair the wrong done to a female whom he had led astray, and to his issue by her, by an act which he might hope would remove in some respect the stain which had rested upon them.

Others – including their Lordships in the House of Lords – appeared to take a more cynical view.

Following their marriage, Colonel and the new Mrs Udny took up residence in Edinburgh. Various letters between the now elderly colonel and his son were lodged in court which indicated that the colonel felt disgruntled to be obliged to live in Scotland and, with his creditors again threatening, he would be happier to have been able to return to Boulogne.

Despite this, the colonel was to remain resident in Edinburgh until his death there on 29 November 1861. His death certificate narrates that he died from the decay of nature caused by old age, and congestion of the liver and jaundice. In contrast to his time in London, the family lived in modest circumstances. The 1861 census for 1 Bruntsfield Place, Edinburgh shows that they had only two female servants.

During his time in Edinburgh, an event occurred which, while lessening his financial pressures, must have caused the colonel grief. His elder son, John Augustus, died in Dublin in 1859, aged only 40. The colonel had propelled the succession of the Udny estate to John Augustus in 1839; part had been reconveyed by deed of 1851 but, in any event, his son's death meant that the colonel stood reinvested of the whole estate. John Augustus had succeeded in having the entail of a more minor family estate, that of Dudwick, set aside due to an irregularity in its constitution shortly before his death, but the Udny estate remained entailed.

Another aspect of the death of John Augustus was that the payment of some insurance policies on his son's life made the colonel's financial circumstances easier. He could once again afford to set up his carriage. The man who once rubbed shoulders with royalty and owned numerous highly bred racehorses now had to be grateful to own a pair to draw his own conveyance. The death of John Augustus was also the trigger for the case under discussion.

Should the colonel die without a legitimate heir, the property would devolve on George Udny, a barrister in London, the son of Consul Udny's brother Ernest. On the death of John Augustus, he not unreasonably considered that he should become the heir to the estate. Accordingly, before the death of Colonel Udny, he raised an action against John Henry Udny seeking to have him declared a bastard.

LAW, EVIDENCE AND OUTCOME

The case was heard first before the Lord Ordinary on 23 January 1866 and appealed to the Second Division. It was finally decided in the House of Lords in 1869 in favour of John Henry Udny. Doubtless with a view to limiting the exorbitant cost of such a long-running dispute, George Udny argued his own case in the House of Lords, doing so, as Lord Chancellor Hatherley observed, "with very considerable ability",[10] if ultimately unsuccessfully.

The argument put forward by George Udny was to the effect that Colonel Udny, not being a domiciled Scotsman, either at the birth of John Henry or at the time of his marriage to Miss Allat, could not render his bastard son legitimate by marrying the child's mother. The crux of the matter was the difference between the laws of Scotland and England in that regard. Scotland, in common with most civil law jurisdictions, recognised the possibility of legitimation by subsequent marriage, whereas England did not; for an Englishman, once a bastard, always a bastard.

Bankton noted the difference:

> There is properly, by the law of England, no legitimation of children born before marriage, by the subsequent marriage of the parents; as there is by our law, in conformity to the civil and canon law; but by the rules of the church, conform to the canon law, such children are holden as legitimate; and an application was made by the clergy in England to the parliament, for an act to alter the law temporal in that respect; but the answer given them unanimously was, *Nolemus leges Angliae mutare, quae huc usque usitatae sunt et approbate*; The laws of England, hitherto used and approved, must not be altered.[11]

George Udny argued first that Consul Udny had abandoned his Scottish domicile by his residence for many years in Italy and that thus Colonel Udny never acquired a Scottish domicile by birth. This argument stood little chance of success given that, for most of his stay in Italy, John Udny the elder was acting as consul for his native country. In the Second Division, Lord Neaves delivered an extensive exposition of the role of a consul and the history of the post. He set the appointment firmly in its historical context and took pains to stress something easily overlooked at a distance of years, that the consul's first appointment took place only 14 years after the end of the last Jacobite rebellion and that the appointment would have been made only on the assurance of the consul's unequivocal support for the unpopular Hanoverian dynasty. In addition, for much of the latter half of the 18th century and the early part of the 19th, Britain was at war with France. A loyal subject would therefore be needed in such a sensitive part of the world to look after Britain's interests and, in co-

---

10 (1869) 7 M (HL) 89 at 92. See also *Dundee Courier*, 10 April 1869.
11 Bankton, *An Institute of the Laws of Scotland* (1751; W M Gordon (ed) 1993), Book I, Title V, (Observations on the Law of England).

operation with such luminaries as Lord Nelson, to ensure that the fleet was well provisioned.

More telling was George Udny's argument that the colonel had lost his Scottish domicile of origin at the time of the birth of his son, John Henry, and his subsequent marriage to Miss Allat. As is apparent from the preceding narrative, Colonel Udny had lived in Scotland for a short time only, while at Edinburgh University. He spent most of his adult life in London and only quit England when forced to do so by his financial embarrassments. On what possible basis could the colonel be held to have remained or become again a domiciled Scot?

In both houses of the Court of Session, it was held that the colonel never lost the Scottish domicile he acquired through his father. Much evidence was led of the connection he maintained with his estates in Aberdeenshire. In his evidence, he stated that, while living in London, he made frequent, almost yearly, visits to his estates and took a lively interest in the management of the properties through his agents, Mr Crombie and Mr Brebner. On these visits, he stayed at hotels in Aberdeen, the Inn at Udny Green (which still exists as a fine dining restaurant with rooms) or with neighbouring landed proprietors such as Lord Aberdeen or Mr Gordon of Esslemont. Early in life he became a Burgess of the City of Aberdeen and later a Deputy Lieutenant of Aberdeenshire. Certainly, contemporary newspaper accounts record on several occasions the visits of Colonel and sometimes also Mrs Udny to the area. The *Caledonian Mercury* in 1840 notes their arrival at the Royal Hotel in Aberdeen.

During the course of the case various Aberdeenshire residents gave evidence about the interest which Colonel Udny showed in his estates and the number of times he visited. As lamented by Leslie in the *Statistical Account* referred to, the estates were entailed and the longest lease which could be granted was 19 years, which necessitated relatively frequent renegotiations with tenants about leasing terms and compensation for improvements. Colonel Udny was said to have taken an interest in each of these transactions and on some occasions dealt with them personally.

Most loquacious among the witnesses was George Stodart, a 79-year-old farmer at Cultercullen. He related that the colonel had dealt personally with the renewal of his lease and the extent of his farm and added, "When in the country he always went round the most of the farms." This venerable farmer also related that Colonel Udny gave a dinner for the tenants when John Augustus came of age. However, perhaps the most striking image from his testimony is of the colonel's visit at the time of the first election after the Great Reform Act of

1832. He observed that the colonel supported the Honourable Captain Gordon, a brother of the late Lord Aberdeen, and painted a picture of the colonel striding through the Aberdeenshire countryside at the head of the tenants to register his vote: "I saw Colonel Udny on that occasion. The polling place was at Ellon. Colonel Udny met the tenants at a place close to Ellon and we all walked down with him."

Whatever his shortcomings, Colonel Udny was not ungenerous and seems to have inspired considerable loyalty among his tenants. William Duguid the tenant of Ardmore, and James Cruickshank, an elderly tenant on Dudwick, spoke of his helping out tenants in difficulty; the latter said, "He never gave me seed corn but in two bad seasons he gave seed corn for some of the other lands where he thought the tenants needed it. He did so in 1812 and 1816."

While in Aberdeenshire, Colonel Udny did not abandon his social activities. In evidence, James Giles, the artist, described driving out from Haddo House with a group including Colonel Udny to sketch local castles; he recalled that on one occasion the late Lord Justice-Clerk Hope, then Dean of Faculty, was one of the party. These convivial outings followed the Romantic fashion for admiring and sketching ruins, including Tolquhon and Udny Castles and featured discussions about restoring Udny. At one such outing, Lord Aberdeen is quoted as having said, "Well, Udny, have you made up your mind yet to be my neighbour?"

In 1840, the colonel is recorded as having attended the Formartine Agricultural Association Meeting as a guest of its chairman Lord Aberdeen.[12] In the course of a lively social evening, Colonel Udny was toasted by his host and addressed a toast to the "Wives and Daughters of the Tenantry" who were, needless to say, not present. In this male-only environment, it is likely that this toast featured some, one would hope, gentle ribaldry, an impression reinforced by the chairman saying that it could be followed only by a toast to "Breeding in all its Branches". Sadly, it seems that this meeting ended in what could only be described as a "rammy", but not, fortunately, until the gentry had departed homewards.

Much of the evidence focused on why Colonel Udny never had a settled home in Scotland. Even once established in Edinburgh after 1853, he rented various houses and all his many schemes to buy a house or have one built came to naught. It was never disputed that Udny Castle at that period was not suitable for habitation and the possibility of living in any of the other houses on the estate was

12 *Aberdeen Journal*, 2 September 1840.

excluded for various reasons. The best of these appeared to be Ythan Lodge, but this was already occupied by a Doctor Gordon.

During his time in Edinburgh, the colonel was at pains to tell anyone who would listen, and probably several who were not at all keen to do so, that the only reason he had never lived on his estate or had a settled home there was lack of funds – he also freely admitted that his own extravagance was the reason for this. Various witnesses who knew him well at that period testified to this, chief among them Sean Ramsay, Dean of the Diocese of Edinburgh and Minister of St John's where Colonel Udny was a communicant member. This reverend gentleman appeared convinced of the colonel's sincerity and repentance. Under cross-examination he asserted,

> He made me to understand that he regretted not being more among his people on account of the habits of his early life ... Speaking in a religious point of view he wished me to know all his early habits.

There was also evidence of Colonel Udny's ambition to become a member of the New Club. This was founded on in support of the contention that he intended to remain in Scotland. Various witnesses also spoke to Colonel Udny's wish that his son should be brought up and educated in Scotland, indicating a preference for "Scotch education".

The death of John Augustus Udny in 1859, however much it will have grieved him, provided the colonel, then over 80, with the opportunity to reinforce his connection to the Udny estate and to indulge, probably for the last time, his taste for the dramatic. Following the interment of John Augustus in the family vault at Newburgh, the colonel gave a luncheon in a grain loft. Alexander Mitchell, who was by then living at Ythan Lodge, described the funeral as a large one with the tenantry and the local gentry present and went on to describe how the colonel appeared at the luncheon and introduced Mrs Udny and John Henry,

> He said he had lost one son that he dearly loved but there was another that, though young, he hoped might one day fill his shoes and he trusted he would be as well beloved to the tenantry as he had been himself.

The image thus conjured up is of a bewildered small boy of six, doubtless uncomfortable in stiff formal mourning for a brother he could barely have known, clutching his mother's voluminous black skirts while being presented by his elderly father to a host of strangers.

This child, however, was indeed destined to be Laird of Udny. Convinced by all the evidence that Colonel Udny retained his connection with Aberdeenshire, both houses of the Court of Session found that he never lost his Scottish domicile. Perversely, it counted in his favour that he had never had any occupation in London but confined his activities there to wasting rather than earning money.

The Lord Chancellor was less convinced and described that opinion as "a point of great nicety" but one which he was not prepared to depart from. However, he was of the opinion that what mattered was not whether the colonel was domiciled in England up until 1844 but his domicile thereafter and, most specifically, at the time of his marriage to Miss Allat and earlier at John Henry's birth.

The Law Lords agreed that, had the colonel been domiciled in England at the time of his son's birth, he could never acquire a legal connection with his bastard child. As a result, a subsequent change of domicile could not operate to permit him to legitimate the child by his marriage. However, all agreed that, even had he abandoned his Scottish domicile of origin and acquired an English domicile by virtue of establishing a permanent home, his original Scottish domicile would revive when he left England in 1844, never to return. This decision was made on the basis that every man must have a domicile which regulates his position and the effects of his actions at law. It was also accepted that the domicile of origin, though it can be lost by a man's actings and intent, is never truly extinguished but will revive by default when another domicile of choice is lost.

AFTERWARDS

Sadly, Ann Allat did not enjoy a long life and outlived the colonel by only nine years. Her death certificate records that she died in Edinburgh in 1870, aged 49, of disease of the liver and dropsy. Did the tribulations of life drive her to drink?

John Henry was confirmed as Laird of Udny, a position he held until his death at the age of 81 in 1934. It may be noted that, despite his father's preference for a "Scotch education", he followed a period at Glenalmond by attending Eton and graduated from Trinity Hall, Cambridge.[13] His obituary states that, in 1874, he married Amy Camilla Sinclair, daughter of G J Tollemache Sinclair of Ulbster in Caithness. She died in Monte Carlo in 1925. Although the couple had no children, in many ways John Henry succeeded where his father failed. Mrs Udny's obituary in *The Scotsman* notes that, in the year before her death, they celebrated their golden wedding. This suggests that the marriage was probably happy and at least successful and long-lasting.

13 Cambridge University Alumni, 1261–1900.

As well as leading a successful domestic life, John Henry transformed his family home of Udny Castle by renovating and extending it. He is said in his *Scotsman* obituary to have taken a great interest in his estate with its grounds and woodlands and to have been, as his father hoped, "greatly esteemed" by his tenants. On his death, he was succeeded by a cousin, Lord Belhaven and Stenton, whose descendants demolished the Scottish baronial revivalist extension built in 1874–75 for John Henry. The original tower house remains; it is occupied and can be seen just north of Udny Green.[14]

14 I Shepherd, *Aberdeenshire, Donside and Strathbogie: An Illustrated Architectural Guide* (2nd edn, 2006), p 204.

Did She or Didn't She?
The Case of Madeleine Smith

Sheila A M McLean

Under the headline, "The 19th Century Amanda Knox", Judith Flanders, writing in *The Guardian* on 6 October 2011, notes that "Sex sells: death sells". In this brief article, she notes the similarities between the case of "Foxy Knoxy" and Madeleine Smith, both young, upper middle class women, accused of murder and – arguably just as importantly – "accused" of having a sexual appetite. Indeed, in the Madeleine Smith case, the fact that she had seemingly not only instigated sex, but had apparently also enjoyed it and had committed this to paper, was given as a reason why she might have killed her lover, Emile L'Angelier. As Douglas MacGowan notes, sexual activity outside marriage was something that was "unheard of for proper Victorian ladies".[1] Enjoying it, presumably, made it even worse!

THE DRAMATIS PERSONAE

Madeleine Smith

Madeleine Hamilton Smith was born in 1835 in Glasgow, Scotland, the first child of James and Elizabeth Smith. She was born and raised in privileged circumstances. Her father was a wealthy architect and her grandfather was also a famous architect whose designs helped to shape the city of her birth with elegant buildings that remain today. Despite the economic adversity that for a while stopped the family in its tracks, life for the Smiths was generally good. As seems to have been the custom of the day, the family rented property in Glasgow for the winter months, and decamped to the country for the summer months. Madeleine's father designed a large country house –

---

1   D MacGowan, *The Strange Affair of Madeleine Smith: Victorian Scotland's Trial of the Century* (2007), p 41.

Rowaleyn – on the Clyde coast at Row (now known as Rhu) near Helensburgh which became their summer residence. Madeleine appears to have been an attractive, even if not classically beautiful, young woman, who enjoyed the pleasures open to young women in her circle: balls, dinner parties and strolling in Sauchiehall Street, which was a main shopping street in Glasgow, with her sister or friends, sometimes even unaccompanied. In their fascinating account of Madeleine's story, Gordon and Nair note that, although there is a lingering assumption that young women of her era lived closeted and limited lives, in fact Madeleine seems to have been relatively free to move unchaperoned around the major shopping streets of Glasgow, and led an extremely active social life.[2]

Pierre Emile L'Angelier

Known as Emile, as his name suggests, he was of French extraction (something that, as we will see, played a not unimportant role in the forensic rhetoric at Madeleine's trial) on both his mother's and father's sides. His father and uncle left France to escape the social and political unrest there and settled in the Channel Island of Jersey. Emile was born on 30 April 1823. At the age of sixteen, Emile was apprenticed as a nurseryman. Three years into his apprenticeship, his father died and a wealthy client, Sir Francis Mackenzie of Gairloch, found him a position with an Edinburgh seed merchant. Although it seems he left Edinburgh for a while, 1851 sees him back in the city. In 1852, he moved to Dundee following a "disappointment" in love. Seemingly, he had believed himself to have won the affections of a wealthy young woman, described merely as coming from Fife. Even at Madeleine's trial, the court declined to name this young woman, who was said to have "titled connections", leaving it unclear on what basis Emile held his expectations. One thing that does seem clear, however, is that, irrespective of the degree of intimacy of this relationship, her family would never have tolerated a marriage between the impecunious Emile and their high-born daughter. In September 1852, Emile relocated to Glasgow, setting in train the events leading to the tragedy of his death and the accusations against Madeleine.

---

2 E Gordon and G Nair, *Murder and Morality in Victorian Britain: The Story of Madeleine Smith* (2009), particularly ch 3.

THE BEGINNING OF THE END

Virtually all accounts of Emile describe him as vain; confident in his personal charms and his ability to attract women – not just any women, of course, but rather those who might be expected to bring considerable wealth as a dowry. However unrealistic, it does seem that Emile did not accept that the mores of the day would almost certainly preclude his marriage to a wealthy woman. Whatever his personal attractiveness, his social, and particularly economic, status effectively ensured that families, such as the Smiths, would not see him as an acceptable suitor. This, however, does not seem to have deterred him in his apparent search for a rich wife. As we have seen, Madeleine was relatively free to promenade the fashionable shopping streets of Glasgow, and Emile was determined to engineer an introduction to the vivacious, attractive young lady. As MacGowan notes, "[t]he strict rules of Victorian society forbade a man from simply walking up and speaking with a lady – he needed to be introduced by a mutual acquaintance."[3] While it is not known specifically where Emile first caught sight of Madeleine, since she was a member of a prominent family, it is likely that he was aware of her identity. The search for the right person to effect the introduction was finally successful, in the shape of one Robert Baird. In February or March 1855, in Sauchiehall Street, Emile and Robert saw Madeleine and her sister, Bessie, enter a draper's shop. It appears that Emile was able to persuade the reluctant Robert to invite Madeleine to come out of the shop and be introduced to him. Thereafter, it seems they pursued a friendly relationship, taking walks together and meeting elsewhere in the city.

The nature of this early relationship is not clear, but it seems that Madeleine was sufficiently impressed with her suitor to begin a correspondence with him which ran to hundreds of letters over a period of years. Commentators have noted that from the outset Madeleine seems to have been very much influenced by Emile, to the extent that in her first letter to him from Rowaleyn shortly after their first meeting, she declares, "I am trying to break myself of all my very bad habits – it is you I have to thank for this, which I do sincerely from my heart."[4] In fact, despite Madeleine's apparent, albeit

---

3 MacGowan, *The Strange Affair of Madeleine Smith*, p 10.

4 All quotations from Madeleine's letters are taken from MacGowan, *The Strange Affair of Madeleine Smith*; Gordon and Nair, *Murder and Morality in Victorian Britain*; and J P Campbell, *A Scottish Murder: Rewriting the Madeleine Smith Story* (2007).

relative, independence, deference to Emile's opinions as to her character and behavioural flaws is a recurrent and pervasive theme in her letters to him; and his letters to her show him not to be reticent in trying to shape her behaviour to his satisfaction.

It seems clear that Madeleine's father became aware of the correspondence between the two reasonably quickly and expressly instructed Madeleine to bring it to an end. Despite her relative youth, and the expectation that young women would unhesitatingly obey their fathers, after an early – and not very convincing – attempt to break off the relationship, Madeleine flew in the face of convention and continued to write copiously to Emile. More than that, she also, in clear defiance of her father's wishes, began to engineer opportunities for clandestine meetings with him. Deluded about his chances as he seems to have been, Emile pressed her for an introduction to her father, presumably in the belief that a personal approach would change Smith's mind about him. This Madeleine initially resisted, perhaps more realistically recognising that nothing but trouble would be likely to follow. In later correspondence, however, she does seem to countenance such a meeting, although how serious she was about this is a matter of conjecture. Certainly, she must have been all too aware that her father would never sanction a continuing relationship with Emile, far less a marriage. Indeed, despite the increasingly amorous tone of Madeleine's letters, it is tempting to speculate that part of Emile's attraction resulted from the very fact that the liaison was both clandestine and socially unacceptable, rather than from any realistic expectation of a satisfactory outcome. Rebellious teenagers, it seems, are not a 20th- or 21st-century phenomenon!

A second breaking-off of the relationship by Madeleine was apparently greeted with silence from Emile. Perhaps this was a clever tactic on his part. If so, it was successful, with Madeleine begging him within a week to write to her. Emile's reply shows yet again his sense of offended *amour propre*, claiming that Madeleine had behaved badly towards him and expressing mystification (surely somewhat disingenuously) as to the reason for Mr Smith being averse to his relationship with his daughter. In her letters, Madeleine had taken to signing herself as "Mimi" or occasionally adopting his surname. This Emile took as a solemn promise and certainly Madeleine made no secret of her desire to marry him, protesting that she could be happy on his pitiful wages (although in at least one letter it appears that she was somewhat surprised to discover just how pitiful they were) and living in simple accommodation with him. Indeed, a wedding date was agreed between them, although it was continuously moved forward as the practical difficulties – including the need to post banns in public – seemed insurmountable. Even at this early stage, Emile shows his willingness to threaten Madeleine, however obliquely. In his response to her plea that he write to her again, having first cast aspersions on her character for seeking to break off their relationship, he says, "[t]hink what your father would say if I sent him your letters for a perusal. Do you think he could sanction your breaking your promises. ... I flatter myself he can only accuse me of want of fortune."

Despite these ups and downs, the couple continued to write regularly and to contrive opportunities to meet. In this, they were greatly assisted by two people: the Smiths' maid, Christina Haggart, and Emile's friend, Miss Mary Perry, a spinster who had come to know him through her church. Given that Madeleine's mother had also become aware of the correspondence and had added her objections to those of her husband, a strategy was devised whereby Emile's letters to Madeleine were addressed not to her but to Christina. When the family moved to No 7 Blythswood Square, and also at their previous lodgings in India Street and at Rowaleyn, Christina was on occasion instructed by Madeleine to leave outside doors unlocked so that Emile could visit, although it is not clear how often he was entertained within the house. As often as not, it seems, their meetings were conducted with him stationed outside her bedroom window, which in Blythswood Square was conveniently in a sub-basement. Given that Madeleine's younger sister, Janet, shared this bedroom, arranging these meetings might have been hazardous and certainly speaks to the sense of adventure that may well have had something to do with Madeleine's involvement in this grand deceit. Madeleine also corresponded occasionally with Miss Perry, with whom Emile was in frequent contact.

Despite the difficulties of meeting, MacGowan reports that it was in 1856 – and in a flagrant breach of Victorian morality – that Madeleine and Emile first made love. [5] The response of each to this momentous event is instructive, and highlights that Emile's almost Machiavellian control of Madeleine extended also into their intimate lives. While Madeleine seems to revel in the intimacy they shared, L'Angelier declares himself distraught, but, in an interesting twist, manages to blame everything on Madeleine and her family. Why, he asks, did Madeleine capitulate when she had promised that there would be no such intimacy until after they were married? In fact, he concludes that her parents are "to blame for it all". While it seems

5 MacGowan, *The Strange Affair of Madeleine Smith*, p 32.

that the sexual act was consensual, there is a resonance in his attitude even in modern life when all too often women are blamed and sometimes shamed for "giving in" to (or even seducing) men, particularly when the outcome is an unwanted pregnancy.

In retrospect, it is difficult to be sure of exactly why Madeleine allowed – in fact, actually encouraged – the relationship for as long as she did. Equally puzzling is why she was prepared to flout not only the clearly expressed wishes of her parents but also the social conventions under which she lived. On the one hand, it could be said that she showed courage in her refusal to submit to the will of others or to the narrow values of the Victorian age. On the other, her behaviour was both reckless and potentially enormously hurtful to her family, and perhaps in particular to her sisters who might be "tarred with the same brush" were her indiscretions to become public. In fact, neither of her surviving sisters ever married. Whether this is in consequence of personal choice or a side-effect of the scandal that surrounded Madeleine is not known for sure, but certainly their marriage prospects might reasonably be assumed to have been negatively affected by the notoriety surrounding their sister. Can Madeleine's self-centred pursuit of this relationship be characterised as a bold rejection of "Victorian values" or merely as the behaviour of a deluded, pleasure-seeking egotist?

On reading the extensive literature available, the answer to this question is unclear. Madeleine's letters are certainly passionate, although the level of that passion seems to decrease as the relationship goes on. She is also, as we have seen, apparently very much influenced by Emile's evaluation of her character, although she is also on occasion both deceitful and provocative. Emile's jealous evaluation of her "flirtatious behaviour" is greeted with protestations of innocence, yet does not seem to have inclined her to modify her behaviour. Her busy social life, indeed, seems unaffected by her expressed commitment to Emile and is sometimes used in a way that seems deliberately designed to provoke a jealous and condemnatory response from him. He, on the other hand, continues with what can be seen as vaguely threatening exhortations about her behaviour and reminders of the extent to which she has committed herself to him both by her words and her deeds. What stands out for this author is that, despite the fact that it must have been blindingly obvious to both that their relationship was doomed, they remained seemingly so much in thrall to it that discretion and realism are pretty much entirely absent from their interaction. Certainly from Madeleine's perspective, she is phenomenally indiscreet in what she writes, while

Emile seems to have been meticulous in storing her every word. Did he already foresee that her letters could be used against her?

THE END OF THE BEGINNING

While presumably Madeleine's parents and family believed the relationship to have been abandoned, and indeed Christina had been rebuked for her part in it, a new character was to appear on the scene. A young man named William Minnoch became the tenant of an apartment above that of the Smiths in Blythswood Square. Although considerably older than Madeleine (in his mid-thirties), he was a respectable and well-off young man who became a regular visitor to the Smiths and was well liked by her father. His name then begins to creep into Madeleine's correspondence with Emile fairly regularly, whether or not in an attempt to make him jealous. In one letter, Madeleine even refers to a rumour that she and Minnoch are what would nowadays be called "an item" and entreats Emile to ignore any such stories. Whether or not such a rumour existed in fact is not clear, but reference to it would certainly be unsettling for Emile who believed that Madeleine had so far compromised herself with him that there was no turning back – and, in having kept pretty much all of her letters, he had the evidence to prove it!

While being courted by Minnoch, with the support of her parents, it must have been obvious to Madeleine that trouble was brewing, yet she continued her correspondence with Emile, albeit that her letters were sometimes a bit less effusive than they had been previously. Sure enough, on 28 January 1857, Minnoch proposed to Madeleine and was accepted. Apparently, her next letter to Emile was not well received by him and his response – which included returning the letter to her – gave her precisely the opening that she needed to escape from the relationship.

She protested his treatment in returning her letter, saying "I felt truly astonished to have my last letter returned to me. But it will be the last you shall have the opportunity of returning." Seizing the opportunity with both hands, she proceeded to tell Emile that she no longer loved him and demanded the return of her letters and a likeness she had previously given him. His failure initially to respond was greeted by a further demand for return of her letters, and what must have been increasing panic for Madeleine. True to form, Emile then threatened to send her letters to her father. Doubtless, he would profess some "honourable" motive for doing this, but he must have been aware of the consequences for Madeleine should he do so. Certainly, he cannot have seriously believed that doing this would endear him to her father!

For Madeleine, this was surely a complete disaster. Should her father have access to her letters, and the evidence not just of her failure to follow his instructions but also of her shameful behaviour according to the values of the time, he might well have entirely disowned her. In addition, her social standing would have been profoundly threatened and her marriage to Billy Minnoch would not have gone ahead. Despite, or perhaps because of, her terror, Madeleine continued to deny that she was involved with anyone else and never acknowledged her engagement. At around midnight on 11 February 1857, Emile was at No 7 Blythswood Square and met Madeleine in Christina Haggart's room. At this time, he also began to write a diary and recorded three occasions when he became unwell after meeting Madeleine. At her trial, Madeleine's defence made reference to the oddity of his having started to write this diary "out of the blue", but at a crucial time in the events of this period. He also confided to his friend, Mary Perry, that he had become unwell after having been given a cup of hot chocolate by Madeleine and insinuated that she may be trying to poison him.

His first episode of serious ill-health occurred on 19 February after a claimed visit to Madeleine. Of course, had she been attempting to poison him, she would have to have been in possession of the means to do so. On three occasions, in fact, Madeleine had purchased arsenic, ostensibly as an aid to her complexion (although this was not the story she gave to the pharmacist). Unfortunately for Emile – if indeed he was trying to set Madeleine up – her first purchase, made quite openly and after she signed the required poisons register and had the purchase charged to her father's account, did not take place until 21 February. On 6 March, in the company of a friend, Madeleine bought a further ounce of arsenic. That same day, she and her family travelled to Bridge of Allan in Stirlingshire and did not return to Glasgow until 17 March. Apparently, Emile also had thoughts of visiting Bridge of Allan, but Madeleine discouraged him from doing so. On 18 March, Madeleine bought a third portion of arsenic, again using her own name and making no attempt to disguise her identity.

Emile finally left for Bridge of Allan on 19 March. He was apparently expecting a letter from Madeleine and asked that, should one arrive, it should be forwarded to him. A confusion as to dates seems to have arisen and Emile hurried back to Glasgow believing that Madeleine had arranged to meet him on Sunday, 22 March, when in fact she had not anticipated the delay in her letter reaching him, and had merely proposed a meeting "tomorrow night". As she had a habit of not always dating her letters, the confusion is understandable. To his landlady's surprise, Emile reappeared at his lodgings on 22 March, ate a small meal and then asked for a pass key as he was going out and expected to be late. He was seen in Sauchiehall Street, which is close to Blythswood Square, at around 9 pm, and thereafter called on a friend who was unfortunately not at home. From then until the wee small hours of Monday, 23 March, his whereabouts are unknown. What is known is that, when he returned to his lodgings, he was extremely ill and his landlady sought out his doctor, who recommended treatment but did not at that stage attend. Emile rejected the doctor's recommendations and became increasingly unwell. At 7 am, his landlady again sought out the doctor who returned with her. He applied a mustard poultice and left. A few hours later he returned and pronounced Emile dead.

A post-mortem examination was undertaken and a very significant amount of arsenic was found in his body. Madeleine's letters and Emile's diary were subsequently found and retained eventually by the fiscal (prosecutor). As for Madeleine, she was made aware of Emile's death following a visit to her mother by Mary Perry, who informed Mrs Smith that the relationship had endured to the present time, much to the fury of Madeleine's parents who had believed it to have ended some time before this. It is a matter of speculation what went on in the Smith household following these revelations, but on the following Thursday Madeleine left the house at Blythswood Square unannounced. She was tracked down by her brother and Mr Minnoch aboard a steamship bound for Helensburgh (presumably on her way to Rowaleyn) and returned to Blythswood Square with them that same night.

Emile was buried on that same day. At that time, it seems that there was no direct suspicion of foul play. However, analysis of his stomach contents detected a considerable amount of arsenic and an order to exhume his body was made on 30 March. On 31 March, Madeleine was arrested. In a statement, she accepted that she had known L'Angelier for around two years, but also declared that she had not seen him for around three weeks prior to his death. She completely denied ever having given him poison. She was charged with two counts of attempted murder on 19 or 20 February, 22 February and murder on 22 March. After Madeleine had spent around three months in prison, her trial began on 30 June.

THE TRIAL

Unsurprisingly, the facts and allegations in this case excited the public imagination. The court was packed every day of the trial and the media, not just in Scotland but throughout the UK, were fixated on every aspect of the trial. Its fascination lay not only in the fact that a murder had taken place, but also in the scandalous behaviour of a wealthy young woman, whose family were pillars of the community. Every detail of the evidence was picked over with glee, and strong opinions were formed as to her guilt or innocence. In addition to the dramatic facts of the case, two of Scotland's most senior law officers were lined up against each other: the Dean of the Faculty of Advocates, John Inglis, for Madeleine's defence and the Lord Advocate (Scotland's senior law officer), James Moncrieff, for the prosecution. The scene was set for a forensic tussle of epic proportions.

There is insufficient space here to discuss all of the nuances of the trial, but some aspects of it are of particular interest. The first – and again there are echoes of Amanda Knox here – was the intense interest in the behaviour of the accused. Madeleine's demeanour was of particular interest. She remained calm throughout the trial, a fact that was widely reported in the media, sometimes as a sign of her courage and at other times as a sign of her callousness. Only on one occasion was she reportedly less than calm, even cheerful. Since Scots law at the time precluded Madeleine from speaking in her own defence, arguably more might have been inferred (on either side) from her demeanour than was merited.

As for Emile, he was painted as a vain hypochondriac, who had threatened suicide on more than one occasion and was known to use laudanum (on one account to excess). Even the prosecution could not disguise their distaste for the man, a distaste occasionally expressed in terms that can only be described as xenophobic. For example, the Lord Advocate did not attempt to refute the suggestions that L'Angelier was volatile, preferring rather to argue that this volatility made suicide less likely, as "[i]t is more characteristic of our neighbours on the other side of the Channel". Gordon and Nair record that he "described him [Emile] as 'a kind of gasconading, boasting man, such as a Jersey man might be.'"[6] Inglis, too, was not indifferent to the "foreignness" of Emile (despite the fact that he was, of course, a British subject). While not referring to it directly, his description of Emile as

---

6   Gordon and Nair, *Murder and Morality in Victorian Britain*, p 136.

a "Frenchman" and an outsider clearly implied similar sentiments to those of the Lord Advocate.

Inglis laid the blame for Madeleine's disgrace firmly at Emile's feet, despite the fact that Madeleine seems to have encouraged sexual activity and indeed often spoke in her letters – before the passion died – of wanting to repeat the experience. For Inglis, "her fall from grace could only be attributed to her having been corrupted by L'Angelier ... The fact that L'Angelier was of French extraction, although a British subject, compounded his sins and was evidence of the inferior moral standards of foreigners."[7] In fact, the summation of both the prosecution and the defence showed a great deal of sympathy for Madeleine's plight and precious little concern for Emile. So much so that the Lord Justice-Clerk "delivered a mild rebuke to both counsels for allowing their personal opinions to intrude into their addresses to the jury".[8]

And what of the facts? It was not in dispute that Madeleine had purchased arsenic on three occasions. This she had done without any attempt at subterfuge, beyond not owning up to precisely why she wanted it. This may simply have been embarrassment about the use of any product to enhance her beauty as the use of cosmetics, for example, was still not seen as entirely the "done thing" for respectable ladies. However bizarre it may seem that arsenic would be used as a beauty treatment, evidence was led that this was not an unheard-of practice. The real importance of these purchases, of course, was that it placed the means for murder firmly in Madeleine's hands.

Two important matters flow from this. The first relates to the somewhat unsatisfactory forensic evidence. While arsenic was undoubtedly present in Emile's stomach, it was apparently in the form of a white powder, whereas, by law, the arsenic that Madeleine had purchased was stained with other substances. The expert witnesses made no mention of any such colouration – one of them indicating that he had not looked for it because no one had asked him to! Might it not have been obvious even to an untrained eye? On this same point, the dose of arsenic was so far in excess of what would have been needed to kill someone that it was questioned how anyone could have drunk so much without noticing it, as it was doubtful that all of the arsenic would have been dissolved even in a hot liquid.

Second, and of greatest importance, it had to be shown that Madeleine had the opportunity to poison Emile. On this, there was

7 Gordon and Nair, *Murder and Morality in Victorian Britain*, p 139.
8 Gordon and Nair, *Murder and Morality in Victorian Britain*, p 139.

no evidence that she had purchased arsenic on any occasion other than the three to which she freely admitted. As Emile first became ill several days before her first purchase of arsenic, she could not be tied to this charge and, unsurprisingly, on this count she was found not guilty. As for the second two charges, the problem for the prosecution was to show that Madeleine and Emile had in fact met on the dates when he became unwell. As to the alleged attempted murder on 22 February, no evidence substantiated any meeting between the two. Indeed, Emile's landlady testified that he had not asked for a pass key on that date, which was usually necessary when he met Madeleine as their meetings were generally held after the family had gone to sleep.

Finally, the murder charge itself must be considered. It has already been said that Madeleine was not expecting Emile that night; due to the confusion of dates engendered by his late receipt of her letter, she had expected him on the Saturday. In addition, Christina Haggart testified that, on the night of 22 March, she had no reason to believe that Madeleine had arranged any meeting with Emile (bearing in mind that she was often complicit in such meetings). Madeleine's sister, Janet, testified that she and Madeleine had gone to bed at the same time and that she heard nothing in the night to suggest Emile's presence. Did a meeting, in fact, occur despite this evidence? Unfortunately for Madeleine, from the time he called on his absent friend (around 9.20 pm) until around 2.30 the following morning when he woke his landlady and was clearly extremely ill, no account of Emile's movements could be found.

THE VERDICT

With an admonition from the presiding judge that only evidence and not sentiment should guide their decision, the jury withdrew to consider their verdict at 1.10 pm on 9 July. Less than 30 minutes later, the jury returned with their verdict. As instructed by the judge, Madeleine was found not guilty on the first charge. As for the two remaining charges, these were found not proven. Not proven is a verdict peculiar to Scots law. Some cynically say that it means "we know you did it, but we can't actually prove it". Certainly, while doubtless relieved that she did not face execution, Madeleine was not fully satisfied with the outcome. Interestingly, the debate about the not proven verdict subsists to this day, with recent proposals having been made that it should be abolished. On 10 December 2012, it was reported that the Scottish Government would consult further on whether or not it should remain as an option.[9] This followed a review by Lord Justice-Clerk Carloway of various aspects of Scots criminal law which recommended, amongst other things, that the not proven verdict should be abolished.[10]

Whatever the merits or demerits of the not proven verdict, it undoubtedly leaves questions unanswered. Does it mean that the jury believed Madeleine to be guilty, but could not quite find a final piece of evidence to satisfy them beyond a reasonable doubt? Does it mean that they felt her to be legally guilty, but that Emile was morally guilty? Or was it simply a reflection of the difficulty in choosing between alternative explanations? MacGowan, for example, argues that there were only five explanations for Emile's death. To summarise, he describes them as follows.[11]

First, that Emile accidentally poisoned himself. This is unsatisfactory for a number of reasons, not least that he was known to dislike taking medicine, and, second, that there was no evidence of his having purchased arsenic. Second, that Emile committed suicide, perhaps even intending to frame Madeleine. This, MacGowan says, is not entirely plausible since, if Emile wanted to destroy Madeleine, he already had the ability to do so merely by producing the letters. One caveat for MacGowan here is that Emile's sudden decision to write a diary in the last months of his life might have been designed to provide evidence that Madeleine did indeed have the opportunity to kill him.

Third, someone other than Madeleine killed him, deliberately or accidentally implicating her in his death. A major problem with this theory is that it would have required that person both to know of Emile and Madeleine's relationship and to know that Madeleine had purchased arsenic. Fourth, that Emile was killed by someone who did not know about his relationship with Madeleine. This, MacGowan argues, would stretch coincidence and credibility too far.

Finally, of course, is the possibility Madeleine did indeed murder Emile. This, he believes, is unlikely. She would know that his visits to her could be proved, raising circumstantial evidence against her. She made no secret of her purchases of arsenic and did not retrieve the letters which would be her downfall and which, presumably, would have been her motive to kill him.

9 See http://www.bbc.co.uk/news/uk-scotland-scotland-politics-20782115 (accessed on 14/05/2013).

10 The Carloway: Report and Recommendation (2011), available at http://www.scotland.gov.uk/About/Review/CarlowayReview (accessed on 14/05/2013).

11 MacGowan, *The Strange Affair of Madeleine Smith*, pp 132–34.

In other words, there really does not seem to be an explanation that is fully satisfactory. As Gordon and Nair say "[i]t is difficult to envisage a scenario that encompasses all the facts and makes some kind of cohesive sense."[12] While Madeleine may have been naïve and even deceitful, what would she have gained from killing Emile while he still had possession of the incriminating letters? In fact, his death probably guaranteed that they would become public, whereas she may have hoped that continued pressure on him might have resulted in his "doing the decent thing" and relinquishing them to her. On the other hand, there was no other person identified who would have wished Emile dead. He may not have been popular in some circles, but nothing emerged that would suggest he was loathed to the extent that murder would have ensued; and, indeed, some witnesses spoke warmly of him. Perhaps suicide, then, is the most plausible explanation, but again this begs the question of how Emile managed to obtain arsenic. If he did so, it was certainly not in his own name. Equally, having been disappointed in love before, and not killing himself, would this particular rejection have been so much more devastating that it would lead him to kill himself? Bear in mind that Emile seems not to have lacked confidence in his ability to attract women – why should another not fall for his charms in the future, allowing him to satisfy his desire for a rich wife?

EPILOGUE

Following what might be seen as a narrow escape from the hangman's noose, Madeleine clearly could not stay in Glasgow. Perhaps fuelled by the not proven verdict, the case continued to be a subject of discussion and debate in the public and the media. Her ravaged family too moved away from Glasgow, although her father continued to work in the city for some time afterwards.

As for Madeleine, a long – and apparently happy – life was to follow. Not long after the trial, she and her brother Jack moved to London where she met and married George Wardle and had two children. Making no secret of her past from the Wardle family (although it seems that her own children were not privy to her past), Madeleine and George moved in artistic circles and Madeleine became actively involved in the Socialist movement. She and George parted and he moved to Italy. In 1893, Madeleine moved to the United States where

---

12 Gordon and Nair, *Murder and Morality in Victorian Britain*, p 191.

her son, Tom, already lived. On arrival in New York, she apparently gave her age as 36 although she was in fact 58. Somehow (and obviously without the surgical assistance of today's world) she managed to maintain the fiction of her age! Apparently, perhaps because of a new relationship with a William Sheehy, who was more than 20 years her junior, Madeleine continued to shave years off her age, claiming in 1910 to be 45 years old. She and Sheehy lived together, but whether or not Lena (as she was now known) and William married after George's death in 1910 is not agreed upon by all commentators. What is known is that she died on 12 April 1928 and was buried as Lena Sheehy.

Unconventional Madeleine certainly was – guilty of murder; who knows? Whether this apparent disregard for convention allows her to be classified as an early feminist or merely a conniving egotist is likely to be the subject of debate until interest in her case dies, if it ever does. During her lifetime, her story became the subject of academic commentary, at least one movie and several plays. Rumour even has it that she turned down an invitation to star as herself in a movie!

In conclusion, it is interesting to speculate what would have been the outcome of her trial had the not proven verdict not been available. She would certainly have been found not guilty on the first charge but, as to the other two, the picture is less clear. Had only the stark choice between guilty and not guilty been available, would the circumstantial evidence that seemed to implicate her have resulted in a conviction? Such speculation is probably unhelpful. I do, however, suspect that the jury in this case was almost certainly extremely relieved that the option of not proven was available to them. Whether it will remain available is yet to be seen.

Jane's Story:
A Tragedy in Three Acts
Woods and Pirie v Cumming Gordon[1]

Kenneth McK Norrie

PROLOGUE

It is a truth universally acknowledged, that a young woman of genteel birth but indifferent fortune must be in want of a husband; and if she cannot or will not have a husband she must perforce become a governess. However uncertain of giving happiness, an independent income acquired through personal endeavour acts both as a preservative from want and as a foundation for self-respect. Suppression of Sapphic desires, to take another case, may reduce internal contentment but will tend to the increase of the esteem shown by others; their indulgence, if known, would invariably be regarded by right-thinking members of society as being entirely inconsistent with the only sure guarantee of happiness, respectability. No city in Europe, perhaps, takes its reputation for respectability more seriously than Edinburgh, and in few cities can scandal be more destructive. William Roughead, writing in 1929, could say of Scotland's capital city: "above and beyond [all] tributes to her physical perfection does she plume herself on her respectability. She sits upon her hills as Caesar's wife, above suspicion, and contemplates with complacency the shortcomings of her sister cities."[2] All the more true was this of Edinburgh in the Regency period.

1 Neither the judgments nor the transcript of proceedings in this case appears in any law report, but they are held in the Advocates Library (*Session Papers* Moncrieff Collection, vol xxi (1811–21)) and were extensively researched by Professor Lillian Faderman for her (somewhat misleadingly titled) book *Scotch Verdict* (1983), from which much of the information for this chapter is taken. The case is also fully discussed by William Roughead in his article "Closed Doors: Or, the Great Drumsheugh Case" 1929 JR 91, and in his book *Bad Companions* (1931). The *Edinburgh Evening News* carried, on 25 February 2009, a feature on the case, as did the *Signet Magazine* (Issue 4, January 2013 and Issue 5, August 2013).

2 Roughead, "Closed Doors: Or, the Great Drumsheugh Case", p 91.

SETTING THE SCENE

Miss Jane Pirie was the daughter of a writer of religious books and her maternal grandfather had been a minister of the Church of Scotland. Both she and her elder sister, left little in the testament of respectable but indigent parents other than a fierce Presbyterianism, had no choices in life other than to apply themselves to the education of the daughters of families of position. The younger sister was doubly blessed for, being endowed with a sharp mind and a quick temper, she also enjoyed the advantage of an especial friend upon whom she could call for emotional support and personal fulfilment, Miss Marianne Woods, an orphan who had spent her formative years with her uncle, an actor in the theatre, and his wife Mrs Ann Woods. The uncle, on retiring from the ardours of stagecraft, turned to the teaching of elocution and Marianne, English-born like her uncle and therefore genteelly-accented, assisted him; he, however, died within a year of that retiral, leaving his widow and his niece in circumstances straitened enough to elicit sympathy but no practical assistance from anyone other than Miss Pirie.

The pleasure grounds of Drumsheugh were at the time in question (the first years of the 19th century) being developed as a residential neighbourhood, less grand than its near-neighbour the New Town of Edinburgh, where the inhabitants of Charlotte Square and Heriot Row might well have *heard* of Drumsheugh Gardens but could no more be on visiting terms with its residents than invite them to the New Town to drink tea in their withdrawing rooms. Yet in a house newly completed at that address Miss Jane Pirie sank her small savings, that she might establish a school and become, with Miss Woods, mistress of children and, more importantly, of her own destiny. The house being available in the spring of 1809,[3] the two young ladies signed a lease, took possession on Whitsunday of that year and looked forward to a not wholly disagreeable existence together. Miss Pirie, however, was contractually obliged to fulfil her role as governess with a private family[4] for a further six months and so Miss Woods, accompanied by her aunt Mrs Ann Woods, moved into the house in

---

3 The year in which the Battle of Corunna in the Peninsular War was fought; Gladstone and Darwin were born; Thomas Paine died.

4 The Campbells, coincidentally the same family name as that of the family with whom Jane Fairfax in *Emma* (1816) resided. Jane Fairfax, like Jane Pirie, was always destined to be a governess and (another coincidence) her only living connections were the much-reduced Mrs Bates and Miss Bates whose penurious circumstances exactly paralleled those of Mrs Woods and Miss Woods.

Drumsheugh Gardens before Miss Pirie, in order that it might be made ready for the opening of an educational establishment for girls of superior background, Miss Pirie to join them at Martinmas, the term of her current employ. Two pupils, including a Bishop's daughter (for Miss Woods was as Episcopalian as Miss Pirie was Presbyterian), were enrolled before November. In the meantime, it pleased Mrs Woods to make herself useful by such contributions as choosing furniture and arranging credit with local merchants; Miss Woods spent her time (if without noticeable success) seeking additional pupils.

Shortly after the November reunion of the two close friends, the newly established school came to the attention of a lady whose potential patronage was a consummation devoutly to be wished. Lady Helen Cumming Gordon, in whose daughter's household Miss Pirie's elder sister (who now fades from our attention) was governess, was looking for a school in which to educate her granddaughter, the child of a son who, on being sent to India at the age of 18, had done as so many well-born young men at that time did, and both fathered a child by a serving native girl and shortly thereafter died of one of the many diseases indigenous to our Indian possessions. This grandchild, "unfortunately wanting in the advantages of legitimacy and a European complexion",[5] was christened Jane Cumming. With a determination as unexpected as it was uncommon for the age, Lady Cumming Gordon insisted that the child be educated as a lady and treated as a full member of her own family. What indignities the child suffered at the hands both of her family, who valued her only as a reminder of the father she had never known, and of others, who felt no need to see further for their estimation of her worth than her dark complexion and long straight hair, can with no great difficulty be imagined and surely with compassion. Her skin tone proved to be a cause of some difficulties at her original school in India where other children of the ruling (and paler) class were educated, and so at the age of 8 or 9 she was brought to Scotland to complete her education and to take her place in society. What that place was, could not but be in doubt.

After some years of quiet country schooling which imparted little of worth into the agile mind of Miss Cumming, Lady Cumming Gordon who, when in town, maintained an establishment at 22 Charlotte Square, Edinburgh (and a country estate at Gordonstoun, near Elgin, which over 100 years later was to establish its own

5 Per Lord Meadowbank in his judgment, as reported in Faderman, *Scotch Verdict*, at p 258 and Roughead, "Closed Doors: Or, the Great Drumsheugh Case" at p 96.

educational reputation) determined that this new school at Drumsheugh would be ideal for her very particular needs. Miss Jane Cumming, by now 15 years of age, became a boarder at the Drumsheugh school just before Christmas 1809 – notwithstanding that it took day pupils and her grandmother's residence in Charlotte Square was barely half a mile distant. During the summer holidays following, when the school mistresses retired to no less respectable a resort than Portobello, Lady Cumming Gordon found it convenient to pay Miss Pirie and Miss Woods to look after her granddaughter there while she herself retired into Morayshire and her estate at Gordonstoun. The girl's own feelings are nowhere recorded, other than that she developed a fondness for Miss Woods which found no reflection in her feelings for Miss Pirie. For these two ladies, however, Lady Cumming Gordon's patronage proved as powerful as they had hoped for; on the recommendation of Lady Cumming Gordon to her friends and acquaintances, their school at Drumsheugh enrolled a further dozen pupils.

The house in which the school operated had been built as a residential property, with two large, and two smaller, bedrooms. The boarders slept in the large bedrooms, each sharing a double-bed, and Miss Pirie slept in one of these bedrooms (sharing a bed with the dark-skinned scholar, Miss Jane Cumming) while Miss Woods slept (with another scholar as bedfellow) in the other large bedroom. Mrs Ann Woods, as was appropriate to her matronly dignity, slept alone, in one of the smaller bedrooms at the back of the house.

ACT ONE: A SCHOOL IN DRUMSHEUGH

Domestic felicity from this happy arrangement was denied the two school mistresses, and best friends, who were marked out from the start by misfortune. The relict aunt, Mrs Ann Woods, proved to be the source of many small, and as many substantial, discontents. She had on one occasion taken it upon herself to reword an advertisement for the school that Miss Pirie had drafted, shifting emphasis from Miss Pirie's description of the instruction in the arts of geography, geometry, literature, history, philosophy and religion that the scholars would receive, towards the polishing of young ladies for the comforts of a genteel life that the school would provide. Mrs Woods was no Mr Gradgrind who saw the school as a place for the imparting of facts: rather she conceived it as a place for the acquisition of respectable accomplishments, as described in the best known of Miss Austen's works: "A woman must have a thorough knowledge of music, singing, drawing, dancing and the modern languages to deserve the word ['accomplished']; and besides all this she must possess a certain something in her air and manner of walking, the tone of her voice, her address and expressions, or the word will be but half-deserved."[6] The unauthorised alteration of the advertisement caused substantial friction between Miss Pirie – who saw the school (had she been favoured with the gift of foresight) as the spiritual ancestor of Marcia Blaine's School for Girls – and Mrs Woods; nor was this by any sensible measure the worst dispute.

Shortly after joining the school that had been established with her own small capital, Miss Pirie attended a map shop at which an account for the school had been opened with the intention of purchasing a globe for the better instruction of her pupils in the mysteries of geography. She was told by the shop keeper, however, that he would not give credit on her signature but that she should speak to "her mistress, Mrs Woods". It was not very wonderful that Miss Pirie's warm temper suffered this indignity not in silence and the unhappy matron who had caused it was left in no doubt as to the former's very substantial displeasure. This and countless other episodes of disputatious intercourse between Miss Pirie and her friend's aunt set the character of the first nine months of the school's existence. By the autumn of 1810,[7] continuation of the present circumstances had become intolerable to Miss Pirie. Angry people are not always wise and Miss Pirie informed Miss Woods that her aunt could no longer continue her residence at Drumsheugh. Miss Woods agreed, but with a reluctance that speaks as much for her family feeling as her loyalty to her friend, and she took no steps to put the agreement into effect; the arguments between the two friends became more bitter as time went on and Miss Pirie's hatred for the aunt overwhelmed her love for the niece. The two women's arguments, recriminations and tears were witnessed by the servants, the scholars, and neighbours. Their reconciliations tended to a more private nature, but were witnessed by the dark eyes of Miss Jane Cumming.

The lenient hand of time, which might have assuaged these hurts, was afforded no opportunity to do so, for a blow infinitely more ruinous than domestic disputation befell the school on 14 November 1810. On that date Lady Cumming Gordon, in so many respects the

6 *Pride and Prejudice* (1813), per Miss Bingley.
7 In this year Napoleon divorced Josephine de Beauharnais and married Princess Marie Louise of Austria; Lord Byron swam the Hellespont.

foundation of its fortune, suddenly removed her granddaughter and wrote to the families to whom she had recommended the school informing them that she had done so: within two days, all the pupils had been removed by their concerned parents and guardians. For Jane Cumming, the Indian scholar, had told her grandmother a remarkable story. The two school mistresses, said she, "had conceived for one another an inordinate affection, which they did not scruple to display in the very presence of their pupils".[8] Indeed, Miss Cumming went on, Miss Woods was habituated to come into the bed that Miss Pirie shared with Miss Cumming and, believing Miss Cumming to be asleep, would lie atop Miss Pirie and make the bed shake and disturb Miss Cumming's sleep. This occurred also, and often, during the holidays when the other boarders were away from the school and there was no call for any sharing of beds by ladies of respectable habits. Upon receiving communication from Lady Cumming Gordon, the other parents removed their daughters from the Drumsheugh school to its utter ruin, and it was the passing of this information to these parents that Miss Pirie and Miss Woods founded upon in their suit against Lady Cumming Gordon for defamation.

ACT TWO: THE COURT OF SESSION IN EDINBURGH

Early in 1811,[9] the case called before the Second Division of the Inner House of the Court of Session which at that time acted as a Court of First Instance and not, as today, exclusively an appeal chamber. The proof commenced on 15 March 1811 under the chairmanship of Lord Justice-Clerk Hope, scion of a great legal family whose distant descendant was, precisely two hundred years later, Deputy President of the United Kingdom Supreme Court. Thus it was that an action by two ladies against a third, where the witnesses were exclusively female, and which would turn on female behaviour in an exclusively female environment was subjected to the judgment of a bench that would remain exclusively male for another 185 years.[10]

8 Roughead, "Closed Doors: Or, the Great Drumsheugh Case", p 106.
9 In this year the Prince of Wales became Prince Regent, and Miss Austen in her first published novel, *Sense and Sensibility*, introduced the world to a very near namesake of Miss Marianne Woods, that heroine of sensibility, Miss Marianne Dashwood.
10 Lady Cosgrove became, in 1996, the first judge of the Court of Session to lack the advantage of a Y chromosome.

An early witness was Charlotte Whiffen, who had held that least desirable of all domestic positions, the maid of all work, at the Drumsheugh school. Miss Jane Cumming had told her grandmother that she had discussed the mistresses' behaviour with Charlotte (notwithstanding that it was expressly forbidden for the pupils at the school to converse with the maid, for fear of corruption by a member of a class whose low morals were notour) and that Charlotte had responded that "it was a pity they could not get a man" and that she herself, through a keyhole, had seen Miss Pirie and Miss Woods together on a couch in an intimate embrace indulging in practices that were as infamous as they were unspeakable. The defender intended Charlotte to speak to these events, and provide the corroboration that was at that time needed in all Scottish court cases, whether civil or criminal. In the witness box, however, and to the obvious disconcertment of the defender's counsel, Charlotte denied everything Miss Cumming had said about her and the corroboration of the latter's tale to her grandmother fell away. If Miss Cumming was being truthful in respect of her conversation with the maid Charlotte then that maid was not, either in what she said to Miss Cumming or in what she said on oath to the court. A judicial inspection of the house and the room where the couch was situated convinced the judges that Charlotte could not have seen that article of furnishing, or anyone on it, from the keyhole and they would have sent Charlotte immediately to the prison for perjury, but for the fact, as frustrating for the judges as it was inconvenient for the defender, that the layout of the house indicated that she had lied to Miss Cumming and not, on oath, to them.

The primary witness for the defence of Lady Cumming Gordon always was going to be her own granddaughter. At this time, however, the rules of evidence rendered incompetent to testify partial witnesses, that is those who had an interest in the outcome of the proceedings or a connection with the parties – though in exceptional circumstances such witnesses could be tolerated under reservation of their credibility. The pursuers objected to Miss Cumming's competency as a witness, as being too close to and completely dependent upon the defender, but the court rejected that objection on the basis, which reveals the full majesty of the law's introspection, that Miss Cumming was not, after all or at least in the eyes of the law, any granddaughter of the defender but merely the natural child of the defender's legitimate son. The granddaughter was therefore allowed to give her evidence, without which the defender's case was naught. In response to the questions put to her by her grandmother's counsel, Miss Cumming told her story with confidence, if with a sufficiency of tears to remind their lordships of her youth and innocence. She was talkative to an extreme, remembering event after event in which her two schoolmistresses had joined each other in her bed, describing the lifting of their nightshifts, the positioning of their legs relative to her own as she lay awake in the bed she shared with Miss Pirie, and noises which, when pressed, she described as being like "putting one's finger into the neck of a wet bottle". (She subsequently accepted that she never did put her own finger in a wet bottle nor had ever heard anyone doing so.) She repeated conversations she overheard between the schoolmistresses, which included the phrases "you are in the wrong place" and "you are hurting me" and "will you promise not to take me in your arms nor come again into my bed until the holidays?" and other such comments as suggestible as they were ambiguous.

In response to questioning from counsel for the pursuers,[11] Miss Cumming could not but allow that she much preferred Miss Woods to Miss Pirie and would often bespeak the former's arm when out walking and sit next to her at work and had asked to share her bed when Miss Pirie was absent; she allowed as well that Miss Woods showed no favouritism towards her in response to these needful approaches but, on the contrary, had made her the frequent recipient of punishments for misdemeanours at a school where discipline was much harder than she had been accustomed to. A disinterested reader of the evidence might well consider it in plain sight that Miss Cumming, a friendless young girl in a foreign land, an obvious outsider who was utterly dependent on the continued approval of a grandmother grieving for her own son's death, had reached out for affection from whatever source it might be obtained, but had suffered the punishment of an attachment without enjoying any of its advantages. If her reaction to rejection was revengeful, sympathy for her plight was not to be maintained.[12]

---

11 John Clerk, later (and briefly) Lord Eldin, defender of Deacon Brodie's co-accused: see "Pronounced for Doom: Deacon William Brodie", p 1 supra.

12 No sympathy whatsoever is shown by Roughead, who places all the blame for the subsequent events on the "precocious wickedness" of Miss Cumming ("Closed Doors: Or, the Great Drumsheugh Case", p 107). It was not, he surmised, that she had no heart but "that she had, and one to match her complexion" (pp 100–101). His entertainingly written account of the case doubtless reflects the prejudices of the time, but to modern eyes it is unutterably spoilt by his inability to hide his distaste for the black-hearted "half-caste", "Asiatic", "daughter of the Philistines" who "imported into the Water of Leith the bane which she had gathered on the banks of the Ganges".

The judges saw and heard a witness of much darker skin than they were used to hearing from, and yet felt confident in drawing conclusions as to her character from that very skin tone.[13] Lord Meadowbank[14] records as "an historical fact and matter of notoriety" that "the language of the Hindoo female domestics" (amongst whom, it may be recalled, Miss Cumming had spent her early years, her own mother being one such) "turns chiefly on the commerce of the sexes. The instructions of Hindoo nurses to their female infants are also frequently on the same subject and are calculated to excite anticipation of its nature, even before the venereal instincts have begun to exist in a girlchild." Miss Cumming, the judges felt competent to surmise, was more knowing of the intricacies of sexual intimacy than a wholly European young lady of her age and position in society could be expected to be. The question became whether thus informed she was in the position to recognise improper and indecent behaviour from the schoolmistresses' interactions with each other which would be inexplicable or even invisible to a more properly brought-up girl, or whether as "a child of India" she was the possessor of such knowledge as allowed her to fabricate a tale otherwise inconceivable from the imagination of a European-complexioned young lady of her years.

There was one further witness of note. Lady Cunynghame, wife of Sir William Cunynghame, was the mother of one of the boarding pupils at the Drumsheugh school but, alone of the parents, she had refused to remove her daughter from the school on the word of one even so worthy as Lady Cumming Gordon without an investigation into the matter. But on learning that all other parents had so responded, and being furnished with further and better particulars by that lady herself, Lady Cunynghame eventually did as the others without her hesitation had done. She spoke nevertheless of her high regard for Miss Woods, of her complete absence of complaint against the school until she was obliged to remove her daughter, and of the difficulty she now had in finding a school willing to take her daughter whom society perceived as indelibly contaminated by having previously attended at the establishment in Drumsheugh Gardens. The evidence of Lady Cunynghame spoke nothing to the truth or falsehood of the allegations, but spoke eloquently of the fact that its

---

13 This aspect of the case is discussed by Geraldine Friedman in "A School for Scandal: Sexuality, Race and National Vice and Virtue" (2005) 27 *Nineteenth Century Contexts* 53–76.

14 Faderman, *Scotch Verdict*, p 153.

publication abroad lay entirely at the hands of the defender, Lady Cumming Gordon.

In June 1811, the judges delivered their verdict. Each judge who spoke felt obliged to record his disgust at the allegations, and his unshakeable disbelief that, in such a morally respectable society as Scotland (as opposed to other, eastern, realms), female sexuality could find any expression without male involvement. On the matter before them, Lord Justice-Clerk Hope, Lord Boyle and (the first) Lord Meadowbank held the allegations that the defender had made to be not established and so found for the pursuers. Lord Boyle alone considered the defence that in a later age would be called qualified privilege: that the defender was duty bound to speak out as she did, irrespective of the truth or falsehood of the allegation. He acquitted her of acting with malicious purpose but could not acquit her of liability for the enormity of the damage she had caused.[15] Lord Meadowbank, perceptively, saw disturbing analogies with allegations of witchcraft in a previous age, "where the very allegation was evidence of its own truth". These judges were, however, in the minority. Lord Robertson (a near neighbour of the defender's Charlotte Square home), Lord Glenlee (father to the defender's son-in-law) and Lord Newton (a high Tory of the old school and staunch defender of both the aristocracy and its vassal cousin the baronetcy), could find no reason to disbelieve Miss Cumming and therefore found for the defender (though Lord Newton did regret that the charge was not a criminal charge, allowing the defence of "not proven"[16] to be available to the court). The casting vote fell to the final (and always the least) member of the Second Division, Lord Polkemmet who, it may be noted with curiosity, had not attended any of the proof but who claimed to have read the transcripts. He found, without giving any reason for so finding, that Lady Cumming Gordon was not guilty of defaming Miss Marianne Woods and Miss Jane Pirie, and so the defender was assoilzied.

Nine months later, in a procedure no longer apt to a court whose functions are now clearly divided between first instance and appeal, the Second Division reviewed its own decision, though with some differences in personnel since Lord Justice-Clerk Hope had in the meantime become Lord President and moved to the First Division, Lord Newton had died and Lord Polkemmet had retired. They were

15 Today, the effect of qualified privilege is that the pursuer must establish that the defender acted with malice: absence of malice is otherwise irrelevant to liability in defamation.
16 The "Scotch Verdict" adverted to by Lillian Faderman.

replaced by Lords Woodhouselee, Craigie and Gillies. Lord
Woodhouselee, finding for the pursuers, pointed out the various
malign motives that the dark-skinned witness who had been brought
up in an Eastern climate might have had to construe her
schoolmistresses' behaviour in the way she did. Lord Craigie, finding
for the defender, held that Lady Cumming Gordon had been duty-
bound, given the nature of the allegations, to inform other parents –
and in any case the allegations had been proven to the satisfaction of
reasonable judges. Lord Gillies held that all the allegations, of night-
visits, shaking beds and the like, were as explicable by innocent as by
guilty explanations and so found for the pursuers. In the end, a four-
three defeat in the Court of Session for Miss Woods and Miss Pirie
became, in 1812,[17] a four-three victory against Lady Cumming
Gordon.

ACT THREE: THE HOUSE OF LORDS IN LONDON

Appeal from the Court of Session in Edinburgh has been possible
since just after the Union to the House of Lords in London,[18] and in
this case was taken by the losing defender, who could afford to do so.
That court proceeded at a pace that was as magisterial as it was painful.
It took that ultimate court more than seven years to reach its decision
but finally, in 1819,[19] the House of Lords affirmed the Court of Session's
decision that Lady Cumming Gordon should pay damages to Miss
Woods and Miss Pirie. They did so with a delicacy that is one of the
first refinements of a polished society but which had proved
impossible in the lower court, and their reported decision[20] said no
more than that damages were due by Lady Cumming Gordon "for
having spread sundry reports of a nature tending to the ruin of [the
pursuers'] establishment". The story was not yet ended, for neither
the Court of Session nor the House of Lords had considered it
necessary to set the amount that was due on a finding of liability
which became, therefore, a matter of further negotiation marked,
unsurprisingly, by ill-temper on all sides (including the judges). The
pursuers claimed £10,000 for loss of profits and a solatium for their
hurt feelings, which even today are the two main heads in any

17 The year of Borodino, and Napoleon's retreat from Moscow.
18 *Greenshields v Magistrates of Edinburgh* (1711) Robertson 12.
19 In this year Sir Stamford Raffles landed in Singapore, and a Princess, christened
   Alexandrina Victoria, was born to the Duke and Duchess of Kent.
20 *London News*, 18 July 1819.

successful action for defamation.[21] Lady Cumming Gordon initially refused to pay a farthing and the pursuers, by now of course living in penury (though not, it may be recorded with some sadness, together) dropped their claim for solatium and suggested that the remaining claim for economic loss be submitted to the Jury Court for determination. That court had been established, along the English model, in 1816[22] and was therefore not in existence when the original proof was heard, and so it remains a matter of speculation whether a jury of Edinburgh burgesses (as masculine as any bench of judges and perhaps more so) would have been more or less likely to find in favour of the pursuers. But liability had already been established and any reference to the Jury Court could be solely to determine the amount of damages due on that liability. There is, however, no record of that court ever hearing the case, nor of any further judicial involvement, and a private settlement was finally reached[23] in 1821, the year before George IV, who as Prince Regent had given his name to the era, visited Edinburgh and confirmed once and for all that city's (though perhaps not all its citizens') irreproachable respectability.

EPILOGUE

The case above discussed finds no permanent record in the formal law reports: whether from a delicacy that recoiled from the scandal of the subject-matter or from the fact that the decision was made in that crepuscular period of Scots law between the publication of the final volumes of Mr Morison's famous *Dictionary* in 1807 and the first of Mr Shaw's annual reports in 1821 I leave to be settled by whomsoever of my readers cares to speculate. Nor is the case noticed by the writers on the Scottish law of defamation, and it is not referred to in the few subsequent actions based on allegations of homosexuality (a word that would have gained no recognition in 1811). Defamation is, of course, a concept that bends and sways with the winds of public opinion, and the court's response to defamatory allegations is peculiarly

---

21 See K Norrie, "The Scots Law of Defamation: Is There a Need for Reform?" in N Whitty and R Zimmermann (eds), *Rights of Personality in Scots Law: A Comparative Perspective* (2009).
22 Jury Trials (Scotland) Act 1815.
23 Professor Frances Singh reports in the *Signet Magazine* (Issue 5, August 2013) a private letter to Dame Helen Cumming's son, dated 5 March 1821, in which it is revealed that a sum of £4,000 was paid to the pursuers.

apt to reveal to the historian changing fashions in social attitude. The judges of the Second Division in 1811 felt no need to explain *why* an allegation of sexual activity between persons of the same sex was so destructive, for the matter was too obvious at the time to everyone (whether of superior or inferior birth) for any explanation to be wanting. As it had been for 1800 years previously so it would remain for almost another 200. Homosexuality was axiomatically a state that both deserved and received the utmost contempt of respectable people and allegations thereof remained, long after Miss Pirie and Miss Woods were resting in their graves,[24] self-evidently actionable. Just over 100 years after their great cause, social attitudes to same-sex relationships and activity remained entirely unchanged from the Regency period, as is revealed in the case of *AB v XY*,[25] where two office clerks sued the office manager who, on discovering them together in the office toilet, immediately dismissed them and declared to their fellow workers that the two were "not men, they are beasts".[26] (It is intriguing to note that in *Woods and Pirie* the maid of all works Charlotte was reported by Miss Jane Cumming to have told her that her mistresses were "worse than beasts".) A dozen years later, when the Drumsheugh case is first discussed in the legal literature,[27] the author takes pains to dissociate himself from the allegations. "Had the accusation been well-founded", declared he robustly,[28] "nothing would have induced me

---

24 To which they departed, respectively, in 1833 and 1870. Jane Cumming, we are informed by Professor Singh (n 23 above) was married in 1818 to a schoolmaster, William Tulloch, who then, through the exercise of her grandmother's patronage, became minister of a parish in Morayshire. In gratitude (perhaps) Tulloch adhered to the Church of Scotland at the 1843 Disruption (caused in large part by the long-running dispute over the issue of patronage) but his wife, his patron's granddaughter, left with the Free Church. The marriage had not been a happy one, due to the minister's sexual infidelities which caused scandal but no court case. Jane died in 1844 and her husband one year later. They were survived by three children.

25 1917 SC 15.

26 The claim for defamation was dismissed on the ground that the manager enjoyed the benefit of qualified privilege. Lord Dundas expressed regret that the clerks had raised the action and thereby given further publicity to the scandal, from which they could never hope to escape. Illustrating the continuing validity of Lord Meadowbank's witchcraft analogy, where the allegation alone is as damaging as the fact, Lord McAlpine's settlement of a defamation claim against "Twitterers" has more recently shown that allegations of paedophilia exemplify the same phenomenon in the modern age: see *McAlpine v Bercow* [2013] EWHC 981 (QB).

27 Roughead, "Closed Doors: Or, the Great Drumsheugh Case".

28 Roughead, "Closed Doors: Or, the Great Drumsheugh Case", p 107.

to deal with it." He could write, wittily enough, about alleged lesbians, but his respectability would not allow him to treat of actual lesbians.

Thereafter it was not until 1997 that a defamation action involving an allegation of homosexuality again graced the Scottish law reports, by which time homosexual behaviour between males had been lawful for 17 years,[29] and social attitudes were, at last, shaking off the dead hand of organised superstition. In *Prophit v BBC,*[30] an allegation made during a popular radio comedy quiz show that the pursuer was a "lesbian nun" whose handling of charitable funds had been dishonest, was held to be clearly defamatory, though that conclusion was founded more on the allegation of dishonesty and the fact that, as a nun, sexual chastity was much to be expected, than on the allegation of lesbianism itself. *Quilty v Windsor,*[31] the next case to raise the issue, was decided in the year in which the House of Lords held that a same-sex couple could constitute a "family",[32] and in which the European Court of Human Rights finally accepted that sexual orientation discrimination was prohibited by the non-discrimination requirements of article 14 of the European Convention on Human Rights.[33] In *Quilty,* Lord Kingarth questioned whether, on its own, an allegation of homosexuality remained, in the modern world, one that could found an action for defamation as lowering the subject in the estimation of right-thinking members of society.[34] Most recently, in *Cowan v Bennett,*[35] decided but two months before the Scottish Government published its plans to allow couples of the same sex access to that ultimate badge of respectability, marriage, Sheriff McGowan specifically held, in rejecting an action for defamation on the basis of an allegation of homosexuality, that such an imputation is not today defamatory, because it does not lower the subject in the estimation of right-thinking members of society, save in very exceptional circumstances (perhaps involving nuns and the like[36]).

29 Criminal Justice (Scotland) Act 1980, s 81.
30 1997 SLT 745.
31 1999 SLT 346.
32 *Fitzpatrick v Sterling Housing Association* [1999] 4 All ER 707.
33 *Da Silva Mouta v Portugal* (2001) 31 EHRR 47.
34 This being, since *Sim v Stretch* [1936] 2 All ER 1237, the accepted test for determining whether a statement is defamatory or not.
35 2012 GWD 37-738.
36 See *Kuchi and Rothe v Austria* Appl Nos 5115/06 and 6490/07, 24 January 2013, ECtHR.

Today, respectability and homosexuality might be found residing without conflict in the heart of the same person, and any aspiration to the former need no longer be frustrated by public acknowledgement of the latter. No teacher in 21st-century Scotland loses her or his job or livelihood or the esteem of others – at least those whose esteem is worth having – on being revealed as lesbian or gay. Who, today, lose their jobs are those who cannot reconcile themselves to the long-overdue shift in social attitudes towards homosexuality and so refuse to provide their employers' services to gay men and lesbians.[37] This is as it should be. One awaits eagerly the first claim for defamation brought by an individual who is lowered in the eyes of right-thinking members of society by being accused (wrongly) not of homosexuality but of homophobia. Only then may the spirits of the tragic schoolmistresses from Drumsheugh rest in peace.

37 *McClintock v Department of Constitutional Affairs* [2008] IRLR 29; *Ladele v Islington Borough Council* [2010] 1 WLR 955; *McFarlane v Relate (Avon) Ltd* [2010] IRLR 872. In *Eweida v United Kingdom* (2013) 57 EHRR 8 Ms Ladele and Mr McFarlane lost their claims that their right to religious freedom under article 8 of the European Convention on Human Rights had been infringed by their dismissals.

The Collapse of the
City of Glasgow Bank

Robert S Shiels

On 2 October 1878, a large crowd gathered outside the offices of the City of Glasgow Bank in Virginia Street, Glasgow. The bank had closed its doors for business the previous day. Many members of the public were there to see if it would open again so that they might get their money from the bank. The whole of Scottish society and the business world were shocked at the suddenness of the event and its implications. The sums of money that were lost to account holders were enormous and business confidence generally was shaken.[1]

The collapse of the City of Glasgow Bank in 1878 was a significant event in the history of banking in Scotland.[2] It was not, however, unprecedented as the Ayr Bank had collapsed in 1772, and that was followed by the Western Bank of Scotland in 1857.[3] The latter bank collapsed as the result of a combination of trade recession and bad management. The 1857 failure led to litigation, although, in terms of volume and demand on the courts, it was all overshadowed by events in 1878.

Mismanagement finished the City of Glasgow Bank and when it closed the immediate impact of the event was traumatic, although pressure was eased by the other Scottish banks' prompt decision to honour all the City of Glasgow Bank notes and to offer banking facilities to its customers. Widespread concern created a groundswell in favour of reform and company law changed the following year to limit the liability of shareholders.[4]

---

1 E A Cameron, *Impaled Upon a Thistle: Scotland since 1880* (2010) puts the collapse in its wider historical context.
2 S G Checkland, *Scottish Banking: A History, 1695–1973* (1975) provides a general history of the banking industry in Scotland.
3 See Checkland, *Scottish Banking*, pp 466–469 for a description of the collapse of the Western Bank.
4 C Mackie, "From Privilege to Right – Themes in the Emergence of Limited Liability" 2011 JR 293.

THE CITY OF GLASGOW BANK

The City of Glasgow Bank started business as a banking company in 1839 with a head office in Glasgow and many branch offices throughout Scotland. At its peak, the total of branch offices was 133. The bank continued as a going concern until it ceased trading in 1857, about the same time as the Western Bank of Scotland failed. The City of Glasgow Bank, however, resumed business in 1858. It was registered under the Joint Stock Companies Act 1862 and continued trading until 2 October 1878. There were contemporary doubts that the City of Glasgow Bank was ever really solvent after the problems of 1857.

There were, in all, 1,249 partners connected with the business and the paid-up capital amounted to £1 million. At the beginning of 1878, the reserve fund was stated to be £450,000, the dividends and surplus profits in hand stood at £148,501, the deposits at £8,382,712 and the "circulation, acceptances, etc" at £2,114,229. Taken at the quotations made in the course of December, the price per £100 of stock for the three years prior to the collapse was £228 in 1875, £228 in 1876 and £243 in 1877, huge sums by the standards of the time.

On 3 October 1878, the directors of the City of Glasgow Bank placed the books of the bank in the hands of Alexander McGrigor of McGrigor, Donald & Co, solicitors, and William Anderson, a chartered accountant of Kerr, Anderson, Muir and Main, accountants, with instructions to investigate and prepare a report of the state of the affairs of the bank for the shareholders' meeting later.[5] By 5 October 1878, after an admittedly cursory study of the books, the directors were advised that it was impossible for the bank to continue in business and that it would be advisable for the bank to wind up its affairs. The complicated nature of the matter meant that a full report was not available until 18 October 1878.

The preliminary view was that the bank had lost £6.2 million, that is to say, the whole of the paid-up capital reserve fund, with £5 million (the sum of £6.2 million alone would be about £467 million in current values). The report referred to falsified accounts, securities entered at fictitious levels, bad debts taken as good assets and gold which ought to have been held on statutory authority against note issue being deliberately squandered to the extent of over £300,000. That was the evidence in support of the history of incompetence within the bank.

---

5 The report was published as an appendix to an account of the criminal trial (along with the earlier bail hearing): C T Couper, *Report of the Trial of the Directors and Manager of The City of Glasgow Bank* (1879), pp 467–473.

CRIMINAL BUSINESS

The prosecuting authorities acted very fast in the case of the directors and the manager.[6] Once the report of the investigators was made known, the first steps were taken towards the prosecution of those who had taken part in the frauds which that report had revealed. That meant, in practice, that arrest warrants were obtained and, by 29 October 1878, all the directors and the manager had been arrested and detained.

There was a question of bail for the directors and manager of the bank: the public was outraged by the collapse and there must have been a real risk that some of the accused would disappear or hide. Seven applied for bail, of whom only the secretary to the company was allowed bail, with the consent of the Lord Advocate, with two sureties for the sum of £5,000. The applications of the others were refused on the ground that the offences for which they had been committed for trial were so serious. Appeals to the High Court of Justiciary in Edinburgh against the decision to refuse bail were soon heard. In the bail appeals, it was held that the petitioners had failed to satisfy the court that the facts, as alleged in the petition that went before the sheriff at the committal stage, were insufficient to sustain a serious charge of theft or fraud.[7]

When the criminal trial commenced on 20 January 1879, there were seven men named as accused in the indictment and who were in the dock.[8] John Stewart, Lewis Potter, Robert Salmond, William Taylor, Henry Inglis, John Innes Wright and Robert Summers Stronach were the accused. Charles Samuel Leresche, the company secretary, had been named in the indictment but was not prosecuted; he gave valuable evidence for the prosecution.

The indictment for the trial remains exceptional in its complexity.[9] However, after preliminary discussion about the correctness of the indictment, the trial took place on an unamended indictment. The trial was in the High Court of Justiciary in Edinburgh before the Lord

6 This part of the chapter is based on my more detailed article: "The Criminal Trial of the Directors of the City of Glasgow Bank" 2013 JR 27.

7 For the bail hearing, see Couper, *Report of the Trial*, pp 1–25.

8 For evidence at the 12-day trial, see Couper, *Report of the Trial*, pp 87–462. A further but less detailed account appears in W Wallace, *The Trial of the City of Glasgow Bank Directors* (1905).

9 The indictment is reproduced in Couper, *Report of the Trial*, pp 26–44. It seems likely that this case showed up the need to reform Scots law in regard to drafting indictments.

Justice-Clerk (Lord Moncreiff of Tulliebole) and Lords Mure and Craighall and a jury. The Lord Advocate and the Solicitor-General (the senior law officers) both appeared for the Crown, with the assistance of others as well. The seven accused each had two members of the bar appearing for them.

The indictment contained in essence the common law charges of (1) falsehood, fraud and wilful imposition; (2) falsification of balance sheets by directors or officials of a joint stock banking company for the purpose of concealing and misrepresenting the true state of the affairs of the company with intent to defraud and uttering the same with intent to defraud whereby members of the company and of the public were defrauded; (3) using and uttering by directors of false balance sheets knowing them to be false with intent to defraud and whereby shareholders and members of the public were imposed upon and defrauded; (4) theft; and (5) breach of trust and embezzlement.

The evidence in support of these charges was that the formal accounting books for the bank had been altered: liabilities were simply reduced, cash in hand overstated, and so too were government stock and other securities. The true market values of assets were less than that stated in the books. The bank purchased its own stock in order to maintain its market price and give a yield similar to that of other Scottish banks. The false balance sheets enabled the City of Glasgow Bank to declare profits and dividends that were comparable with those of competitors.[10] They also suggested that the bank was doing a volume of business commensurate with the size of its liabilities and with adequate liquid reserves.

The evidence overall indicated a deliberate falsification of accounts. False returns concealed the true, bankrupt, state of the business. The initial problem may not have arisen out of fraudulent conduct; it was a bank that had been notable among Scottish banks for endeavours to establish branches all over Scotland, throwing away millions of the money of its depositors to support hopelessly-rotten firms in the East India trade, investing in doubtful or altogether speculative securities and generally behaving recklessly. The criminality arose, on the evidence, out of the need to hide the erroneous business decisions. Little was heard from the accused about the matter as they were not allowed in law to be witnesses on their own behalf and their

10 Couper, *Report of the Trial*, reproduces the actual accounts in the appendix to his book and these, with the alterations and corrections, make for a stark indication of how it all went wrong.

declarations (statements made to a sheriff on first being brought before a court) added little.

The Lord Justice-Clerk in essence reminded the jury prior to their decisions that all the charges in the indictment alleged dishonesty against the directors and the manager in their respective capacities. That being so, there were three questions that arose on each of the charges to be kept in mind: first, whether these balance sheets were false; secondly, whether the accused, each of them or any of them, had knowledge that they were false; and thirdly, whether what they did with the balance sheets, namely, the circulation and publication of the report with each balance sheet, was done with the intention of deceiving the shareholders and the public. The jury was out for about two hours.

The verdicts were returned on Friday, 31 January 1879: two of the accused were found guilty of the first three charges on the indictment: that is to say, fraud, falsification of balance sheets whereby members of the company and of the public were defrauded; and using and uttering false balance sheets knowing them to be false with intent to defraud and whereby shareholders and members of the public were defrauded. The five remaining accused were found guilty of publishing and uttering the accounts. All the accused were found not guilty of the remaining charges.

Sentencing was deferred to the following day, Saturday, 1 February 1879. The first two accused had been found guilty of the three charges of falsifying and fabricating the balance sheets of the bank; each was sentenced to imprisonment for 18 months. The other five accused had been found not guilty of fabricating or falsifying the balance sheets, but of uttering and publishing them, knowing them to be false. Given that they had been in prison awaiting trial for about four months, they were each further imprisoned for eight months.

These sentences were said by many at the time to be ridiculously light. Given that the accused were probably ruined financially and socially, and they were comparatively old, there was reason behind the sentences imposed, but that is not how the public saw it. With criminal convictions, the actions of the directors and the manager were tainted as beyond mere inefficiency or naiveté. Neither could the markets be blamed. The accused were stuck with the disposal; as there was then no competent means of reviewing the judgments or sentences, that was an end to the whole matter in the criminal courts.[11]

11 The public interest continued to the extent of *The Times* reporting on 2 October 1879 and 2 August 1880 the release of the directors and the manager from jail

In the criminal case, there were three areas that illustrate the internal dynamics. First, on bail, the Crown had approached this matter as a wholly fraudulent activity for personal gain. At the conclusion of the Crown case, the Lord Advocate intimated to the court, as he was entitled to do, that he confined the charges to the first three charges on the indictment. These were lesser charges of dishonesty. It seems probable that, while there was evidence of some dishonesty, much of the evidence was equally consistent with utter incompetence. The Lord Advocate appears to have taken the view that conviction was certain on the lesser charges but not very likely on the major charges.

Secondly, the indictment itself was the subject of criticism: experienced counsel said to the jury that he had rarely seen a document more calculated to strike terror into an accused than the indictment then before the jury. This is very much an historical phenomenon given that the intense style of drafting indictments at that period was reformed not much later, possibly as a result of the anachronistic practices in the bank prosecution becoming patently unsuitable for a new age. Some of the allegations in the highly detailed charges were ambiguous in the sense that they alleged matters that were not necessarily criminal: four directors were charged that, during their tenure of office, contrary to their duty, they allowed overdrafts on current accounts or cash credit accounts to be made without security or upon wholly inadequate security. The latter point was objected to as being too indefinite. What remains notable is that the indictment was allowed to go to the jury in a pristine state, unamended or without deletions. The court wanted the jury to hear all the evidence.

Finally, there was the trial. The accounts of the City of Glasgow Bank for the three years before the collapse were a mess. That proposition does not appear to have been challenged by any of the accused: they individually sought, through their lawyers, to minimise their understanding of what was going on around them in the bank. The essential point at trial was the approach taken by the Crown: the initial presentation of the collapse as having been due to criminal activity driven by personal gain was replaced in effect by a narrative of a lesser form of criminal activity due to personal and professional inefficiency. The Lord Advocate was entitled to do what was done,

at the end of their sentences: five directors were released from Ayr Prison on 1 October 1879 (after eight months' imprisonment) and a director and the manager were released from Perth Prison on 30 July 1880 (after 18 months).

but, with the withdrawal of the most serious charges on the indictment, the remaining charges proved easily or at least were likely to be far more acceptable to the jury. At least, meaningful criminal convictions were obtained on what was proved.

CIVIL LITIGATION

There was very extensive litigation immediately following the collapse in 1878.[12] That ought to be seen against the background of the Western Bank litigation that included the crucial decision of *Lumsden v Buchanan*,[13] in which it was held in the House of Lords that trustees entering into a trading partnership such as existed at the Western Bank were personally liable in the obligation incumbent on the parties. That applied both towards creditors and also amongst themselves unless their liability was limited expressly by special stipulation, and in the circumstances of that case; and generally, it would seem that there was in fact nothing to limit responsibility.

The extent of the business from the City of Glasgow Bank collapse was such that thirteen appeals were later taken from the Court of Session to the House of Lords. None of the City of Glasgow Bank cases was reversed on appeal to London. The first reported case, about a month after liquidation, followed a request by some creditors of the City of Glasgow Bank to appoint an accountant in London as an additional liquidator, and that was refused. The remaining cases that were reported seem to fall into three main categories. First, attempts were made to rectify the register which was the list of contributors to whom calls for payment might be made to clear the liabilities of the bank. The creditors of the bank were entitled to rely on the statutory register of members. Many of the cases were about the facts by which those liable tried to have their names removed from the register.

Secondly, problems arose from the legal relationship between husband and wife, the *jus mariti*. This was a right by which a husband acquired to himself absolutely the personal property of his wife, but it meant that he was liable for any call to contribute to the losses of the bank. Many cases sought to separate the husband from the wife for the purposes of assessing liability for payment.

12 This part of the chapter is based on my more detailed article "Civil Litigation and the Collapse of the City of Glasgow Bank" 2012 JR 155.
13 (1865) 3 M (HL) 89.

Thirdly, the preservation of assets by trusts was also tested, in regard to the liability *personally* of trustees.[14] The liquidators made up a list of contributors as at 7 November 1878 and, on 13 November 1878, they made a first call of £500 on each share of £100. A group of trustees soon presented petitions to the Court of Session under the then company law: *Muir v City of Glasgow Bank Liquidators.*[15]

The legal problems that beset the trustees across Scotland were grounded in the intricacies of the law of joint stock companies. The law, as settled in the House of Lords 12 years earlier in *Lumsden v Buchanan*, was against them in their claims in regard to the City of Glasgow Bank. The liquidators opposed the petitions and, on the authorities as they then were, the First Division of the Court of Session refused the petitions.

The essence of the decision in *Muir v City of Glasgow Bank Liquidators* was that persons who accepted a transfer of stock of a joint stock banking company "as trust-disponees" of other persons and were then so entered in the register of members of the company thereby became, as individuals, partners of the company and, in liquidation, they were subject to calls as "contributories in their own right".

The appeal by the trustees to the House of Lords failed and the Lord Chancellor (Cairns) expressed sentiments of sympathy as to the adverse effects of the decision, although he did go further and say that the sympathy was "peculiarly due to those, who without any possibility of benefit to themselves, and probably without any trust-estate behind sufficient to indemnify them, have become subject to loss or ruin by entering, for the advantage of others, into a partnership attended with risks of which they probably were forgetful or which they did not fully realise".

It seems likely that the concluding observations of Lord Penzance, who noted the "national calamity", were nearest what might be thought of as the reality of practice:

> [It] is a matter for deep concern, not unmingled with surprise, that the legal effects attaching to these contracts of trustees, having been thus asserted as exposed in a notable case as long ago as 1865, people should have been found still willing to enter into them. But in all probability the profound conviction with respect to the great banks in Scotland

14 See Kenneth G C Reid, "Embalmed in Rettie: The City of Glasgow Bank and the Liability of Trustees" in A Burrows, D Johnston, and R Zimmermann (eds), *Judge and Jurist: Essays in Memory of Lord Rodger of Earlsferry* (2013).

15 (1879) 6 R (HL) 21.

that such a thing as loss or liability was not to be practically apprehended at all may have led to widespread indifference as to the legal consequences of this improbable event, should ever come to pass.

Remaining cases concerning trustees were directed at liability in law in varying circumstances.

The four liquidators themselves produced one of the most interesting actions because questions had arisen amongst the liquidators as to the remuneration to be paid to them: *City of Glasgow Bank, Petitioners.*[16] They were ordered by the court to lodge statements specifying the time occupied and the work done by each in the liquidation. The court looked at the whole circumstances of the case, fixed the total amount of the remuneration at a commission of three-eighths per cent on the first three dividends and of half a per cent on the last two (the intromissions leading to these being smaller and the trouble greater), and distributed the amount by awarding three-fifths of the gross sum to the two who had taken a leading part and the remainder to the other two who had taken a subordinate part in the liquidation. In practical terms, two liquidators received £10,500 each and the other two £7,200; these sums were equal to about £800,000 and £550,000 at current values.

In their search for the recovery of funds, the liquidators looked at the actions of William Mackinnon, who had been a director of the bank from 1858 to 1870. They sought from the Court of Session an order ordaining him to repay £311,667. That sum was alleged to have been paid improperly as dividends to shareholders while he had been a director. This very substantial action was lost because, after a proof, it was held that (1) the liquidators had no title or legitimate interest to make the claim; (2) the claim was barred by a lapse of time, combined with certain events after Mackinnon left the company and the conduct of the liquidators in disposing of the railway securities in issue; and (3) there was an entire failure to establish that Mackinnon was party to any proceedings which could properly or fairly be described as paying dividends out of capital.

There were inevitably bankruptcy hearings in Glasgow Sheriff Court for those associated with the bank. The problems associated with the winding-up concluded formally with the City of Glasgow Bank (Liquidation) Act 1882 which was given Royal Assent on 24 July 1882. The long title of the Act included reference to two calls on the partners of the Bank, the first of £500 and the second of £2,250,

---

16 (1880) 7 R 1196.

each in respect of every £100 of stock held by such partners respectively. The main purpose of the 1882 Act, however, was to establish The Assets Company Limited as a company to take over the assets of the City of Glasgow Bank. The memorandum of association for the new company was contained within the 1882 Act, in the first schedule, and the transfer of the assets to the new company was in accordance with an agreement between the bank and the new company in the second schedule.

Not long after the 1882 Act came into force, the liquidators were in dispute with the new company. The liquidators argued that The Assets Company Limited had no absolute right to the documents that were then a matter of question between the parties, that being a matter for the court and The Assets Company disputed that. The company did not intend to review the work of the liquidators, but it was entitled to have compromises (agreements to settle for lesser amounts) set aside on the ground of fraud. The court held that all documents disclosing the particulars of compromises and discharges made by the liquidators were to be given up unreservedly. Thus, the 1882 Act signalled the end of the civil litigation.

The central legal point of the collapse, however, was the unlimited nature of the liability of shareholders who, doubtless much to their horror, discovered that they were *partners* in the business: the principle of unlimited liability was one that had been strongly insisted upon by Scottish joint stock bankers. The reason for that approach was that all the resources of all the shareholders had stood behind the banks' obligations and that, to limit liability, was to reduce public confidence in a bank which would harm the business. The standard view has been that the failure of the City of Glasgow Bank revealed inherent weaknesses with unlimited liability, but that has been questioned in modern time and thus the central role of that collapse in the demise of unlimited liability doubted.

Joint stock companies had had a long history.[17] But whatever the traditional views of the law, two points arose: first, in the context of these democratic but toxic commercial organisations, the most critical point was that trustees who entered into a partnership might limit their liability in a question with the other partners to the trust estate, but they could not do so in regard to third parties. They were personally liable to them to the full extent of the partnership

17 See Checkland, *Scottish Banking*, ch 11 for the history of the joint stock company when in the ascendant.

obligations except in so far as they had made special arrangements with individual creditors.

Secondly, the collapse of the City of Glasgow Bank in 1878 led to the Companies Act 1879 which introduced by section 5 the principle of "reserve liability" by which banks could acquire subscriptions for additional reserve capital which would not be called on, except in the case of illiquidity or failure. Moreover, the 1879 Act by section 6 required a compulsory and independent audit and a uniform balance sheet. This was then a novel approach for most banks, as it had been strongly felt that outside investigations or accountability were incompatible with the privacy necessary in dealing with the financial affairs of customers. To emphasise responsibility, the 1879 Act by section 8 required auditors and directors, or at least three of the directors, to sign balance sheets submitted to annual general meetings.

WHY DID THE BANK COLLAPSE?

Many of the staff of the City of Glasgow Bank had been through the crisis of 1857 but seemed not to have learnt anything from it. The Western Bank had collapsed because it had pursued business without much in the way of reserves. A substantial interest had been developing in the American market that was highly unstable. The recipients of loans and discounts from the bank were in a large degree the shareholders of the bank. That dangerous policy was compounded by a strong concentration of loans to a small group of firms. The law at the time did not require financial information about the nature of a bank's lending and assets policy to be made available generally, so that the public were unable to judge the soundness of the bank. Short-term financial pressure elsewhere led to the perilous state of the Western Bank becoming known and it ceased trading.[18]

The City of Glasgow Bank had pursued a very active branch policy with 133 offices by the mid-1870s, with associated expenditure. The bank became heavily dependent on the London money market but it had minimal resources in saleable securities. The bank developed financial interests in India and America, to which was added large-scale speculation in New Zealand. The books of the bank showed credit for interest due from American railroads which had not actually

18 See Checkland, *Scottish Banking*, pp 466–469.

been paid and seemed unlikely to be paid. Further, the financial interest in New Zealand was through a single company which, being unsupported by any other bank, became the sole liability of the City of Glasgow Bank.

The City of Glasgow Bank also made a fundamental error in allowing a small number of large businesses to increase their borrowings to notable sums until the sums lent were concentrated in a few firms. This had a double disadvantage: the City of Glasgow Bank could not end these financial relationships without ruining the firms who owed them money; and, to add to the pressure, these firms began to require further borrowing to survive adverse financial conditions.

All this led to a progressive deterioration of the lending position of the City of Glasgow Bank and to that must be added the mismanagement. The more important businessmen had departed by the mid-1870s. This left those whom one historian has described as "mediocrities, men of straw", heavily indebted to their own bank. It would seem that the directors had failed to understand the true financial position of the bank for which they had responsibility. The manager did, however, and for some years the accounts had been falsified to hide the true position.

That position had been the result of cumulative incompetence hidden by deliberate inaccuracies in the accounts. Latterly, the integrity of the bank began to be questioned publicly. The share price began to slip and the management of the bank tried to stabilise matters by buying its own shares. It also became obvious to the market that many of the bills of exchange were fictitious as new ones were used to settle debts due under existing liabilities. Notwithstanding assistance from other banks, the City of Glasgow Bank had lost all confidence and it ceased trading on 1 October 1878. There had been a boom in the value of the bank in the early 1870s but, by 1878, the bank had become an empty shell. Against liabilities of £12.4 million, there were assets of only £7.2 million. Advances stood at 132.7% of deposits. The shareholders, in addition to losing their paid-up capital of £1 million, had to find another £4.4 million.

The failure of the City of Glasgow Bank was a traumatic experience for the reputation of the Scottish banking business.[19] The Caledonian Banking Company had owned shares in the City of Glasgow Bank and, when the call was made for a contribution, there was a panic

---

19 It had an effect on British banking: see M Collins, "The banking crisis of 1878" (1989) 42 *The Economic History Review* 504–527.

amongst the proprietors of the Caledonian and they put their shares on the market. Confidence fell away rapidly, but a guarantee fund was raised and that allowed the Caledonian to resume business after some months. The result of the collapse was traumatic for the individuals and the families who suffered severe financial loss and many were ruined. This aspect of the history has been neglected: the location and loss was probably spread over much of the wealthier class of mid-Victorian Scotland.[20]

The collapse of the Bank affected profoundly the attitudes of the Scottish banking profession: no-one who lived through the crisis ever seems to have forgotten what happened. Subsequent generations of various professions seem not to have been overly anxious to discuss the collapse and many years passed before any historian wrote of the event. Further, the events of 1878 raise doubts about the nature and extent of the legal advice given when so many people exposed their personal assets and their accumulated family fortunes to unnecessary risk. It remains a mystery how some lawyers maintained such an extraordinarily lax attitude. The mood of public life was depressed by the enormous financial loss sustained by the collapse of the City of Glasgow Bank. In the context of the United Kingdom, however, no English banks were seriously shaken by this collapse and there was no public inquiry.

---

20 For further discussion, see G G Acheson and J D Turner, "The death blow to unlimited liability in Victorian Britain: The City of Glasgow failure" (2008) 45 *Explorations in Economic History* 235–253.

Keeping Bon Accord Square Beautiful: Tailors of Aberdeen v Coutts

Douglas J Cusine

This case, which was about conditions applying to the ownership of land, is in a small category of cases which have twice gone to the House of Lords – in the *Tailors of Aberdeen* case, once in 1839 and then in 1842.[1] Taking a case to the House of Lords was expensive, as would be an appeal to the Supreme Court, as it now is. There was an appeal in civil, ie non-criminal cases, to the House of Lords from 1707, following the Union of the Parliaments, until 1 October 2009 when that was replaced by an appeal to the Supreme Court, which replaced the House of Lords as an appeal court for Scottish civil cases.[2] Before going into the details of the *Tailors of Aberdeen* case, some background information about landownership in Scotland will hopefully assist.

LANDOWNERSHIP IN SCOTLAND

Until 2004, virtually all of the land in Scotland was held under the feudal system of landownership.[3] This system came to Scotland in 1124 when David I became King of Scotland. Prior to that, he had been in England and he was impressed by two things, both of which he brought to Scotland with him. One was the office of sheriff (which still exists) and the other was the feudal system. Such a system was

---

1 (1837) 2 Sh & McL 609; (1842) 1 Rob 296. A more detailed account of the history can be found in The Stair Society, *Miscellany V*, vol 52. The Stair Society publishes volumes on Scottish legal history.
2 Since the passing of the Human Rights Act 1998, the Supreme Court deals also with human rights issues arising in Scottish civil and criminal cases.
3 A more detailed account can be found in a number of publications, eg *Stair Memorial Encyclopaedia*, vol 18 (Property); W M Gordon and Scott Wortley, *Scottish Land Law* (3rd edn, 2009), ch 2.

common in Europe and came to England with William the Conqueror in 1066. It was eventually abolished for Scotland by an Act of the Scottish Parliament, the Abolition of Feudal Tenure etc (Scotland) Act 2000, but with effect from 28 November 2004, and with it, the requirement to pay feuduty. (It had been abolished in England and Wales in 1295.) The essence of the feudal system was that, unless land had been disposed of, it belonged to the Crown/sovereign. The Crown was referred to as "the ultimate superior". When the Crown disposed of land, the Crown became the "superior" and the person who acquired it was the "vassal", also known as the "feuar". The property acquired would be described in legal terms as "the feu".

Although most of the land in Scotland was subject to feudal tenure, there were a number of other types of landholding where there was no superior/vassal relationship. One of these was land owned by the Crown which had never been feued. Another example was burgage tenure which existed only in royal burghs, of which there were 70 in 1707. They were created from 1124 onwards. Examples are Aberdeen, Glasgow, Edinburgh, Dundee and Stirling. They were abolished in 1975 after the re-organisation of local government. Not all land in a royal burgh was held on burgage tenure, but, where the tenure was burgage, the owner of the property held it directly from the Crown. Burgage tenure was a feature of the *Tailors of Aberdeen* case. Yet another example of non-feudal landholding was udal law which applied only to land in Orkney and, more significantly, Shetland.[4] These islands had originally been pledged to Scotland for an unpaid part of the dowry of Margaret, the daughter of the King of Denmark, in relation to her marriage to James III and were forfeited in 1472 because the dowry was not paid. (In 1962, there was litigation between the University of Aberdeen and the Crown over the ownership of the St Ninian's Isle treasure, which consisted of nearly 30 pieces of silver, or silver plate, which had been discovered in 1958 when the University was excavating a site on the island on which a mediaeval chapel had stood. The Crown claimed that, as treasure, they owned it, whereas the University and the landowner claimed that the issue was governed by udal law, in which event it would have belonged to the owner of the site. The court held that udal law did not apply to treasure and so the Crown succeeded.[5])

---

4 For further details, see *Stair Memorial Encyclopaedia*, vol 18.

5 *Lord Advocate v University of Aberdeen* 1963 SC 533, 1963 SLT 361. See D L Carey Miller, "St Ninian's Isle Treasure" in J P Grant and E E Sutherland (eds), *Scots Law Tales* (2010), ch 7.

The final example of non-feudal landownership relates to the King's
Kindly Tenants of the Four Towns of Lochmaben. The towns were
Hightae, Smallholm, Heck and Greenhill, the king was Robert the
Bruce and they were survivors of the more widespread Kindlie Tenants
or Rentallers, who existed throughout Scotland, except in the
highlands. They held their land on a lease, but, provided the rent was
paid, their right was perpetual. In that respect, the Kindly Tenancies
were similar to feudal tenure. All of these unusual forms of
landholding were converted to absolute ownership under the 2000
Act.[6]

As has been said, under the feudal system, all of the land in Scotland
was owned by the sovereign. He would give land to nobles in return,
initially, for services, in the form of men to fight wars, usually against
the English. Each noble, in turn, might give smaller bits of land to
others, also in exchange for services, and so this arrangement formed
a type of pyramid with the sovereign at the top and each layer under
that owing service of some kind to the person next above. Below the
sovereign, each person could be a superior and a vassal at the same
time, until the ultimate vassal, or owner, was reached. As a superior,
the person could enforce land conditions and insist on the provision
of men by the vassal to fight a war, and latterly to collect feuduty
from him. As a vassal, that same person was bound by the land
conditions and had to provide the men, or, later, to pay feuduty to the
next person, "the superior", who was on the next level further up the
pyramid, or rung on the "feudal ladder", as it was sometimes called.

In time, military service was replaced by a monetary payment called
feuduty, and many bodies and organisations, such as insurance
companies and the National Trust for Scotland, derived considerable
income from feuduties. When land was given off, in addition to the
obligation to pay feuduty, the purchaser would have other conditions
imposed, and in more recent times, it was not uncommon to find
conditions such as prohibiting extensions to or subdivisions of
properties, requiring that they be used for the occupation of only one
family and prohibiting their use for any trade, occupation, or
profession. In some titles to tenement properties, one could also come
across conditions such as not burning brick, or making cudbear (a
kind of glue) and not allowing piano lessons. The conditions were
designed to ensure that the nature of the neighbourhood was
preserved and/or that owners of property, especially flats, were free

---

6 These unusual forms of tenure are also dealt with in *Stair Memorial Encyclopaedia*,
   vol 18.

from practices which might have an adverse effect on the quality of life of all of the owners. It was, of course, possible to have these conditions relaxed, but that required the consent of the superior, the next person up the feudal ladder or pyramid. Because of difficulties experienced by some proprietors, eg a stubborn superior, or even one who could not be traced, in 1970[7] a system was introduced whereby the Lands Tribunal for Scotland could vary or discharge these conditions, but there was no certainty that an application to the tribunal would be successful. Most cases were, particularly when the local planning authority had granted permission for something which also required the consent of the superior. Such conditions obviously still exist, even after the demise of the feudal system in 2004 – more of which later.

In Scotland, from the early part of the 19th century onwards, there was a lot of building of houses, following upon the agricultural and, of more significance, the industrial revolution. Developments of note are the New Town in Edinburgh and the west end of cities like Glasgow and, later, Aberdeen. The owners of the houses which were built had conditions imposed by the superiors, the object being to preserve buildings of quality. The fact that they remain can be attributed in large measure to the insistence by these superiors on compliance with the feuing conditions; town and country planning legislation did not exist in Scotland until 1947. Some local authorities had Deans of Guild who developed a jurisdiction over the construction of new buildings and additions and repairs to existing ones, but the conditions imposed by the superiors still played a very important part in preserving the original plans for these developments.

When it came to enforcement of land conditions, the relationship between the superior and the vassal was a contract. Put simply, in exchange for the price, the purchaser would get the property, but under certain conditions, such as those mentioned above. However, as a general rule, a contract is binding only on the parties to it, and so, if the intention was to preserve the nature of a property and the neighbourhood, it would be of no assistance if the conditions imposed did not bind all subsequent proprietors, as well as the original one. These subsequent proprietors are referred to in legal terms as "successors in title", or "singular successors". Conditions would be personal if they were binding only on the original parties. If they were to bind subsequent owners as well, they would have to be "real";

7 Conveyancing and Feudal Reform (Scotland) Act 1970, s 1.

in other words they were binding, in a sense, on the land. (In England and Wales and in various other places in the world, eg in the United States of America, land is called "real property".)

The issue in the *Tailors of Aberdeen* case was how to ensure that conditions imposed bound not only the first owner, but, of more importance, all subsequent owners. The Tailors have a lot of the original papers which were discovered by the late William Bruce, who was the Deacon Convenor of the Seven Incorporated Trades, ie the senior person. He kindly drew them to my attention.

THE TAILORS OF ABERDEEN

The Tailors were founded in 1511, and are one of the Seven Incorporated Trades of Aberdeen who can trace their origins back to charters dated 1179 from William the Lion.[8] The other trades in Aberdeen are Shoemakers, Weavers, Bakers, Fleshers, Hammermen, and Wrights and Coopers. The Trades had their original premises near Trinity Quay (which still exists) in the former Monastery of Red Friars of the Holy Trinity. The premises were purchased by Dr William Guild, who was the Principal of Kings College, then a separate university from Marischal College with which it amalgamated in 1860. He was also a minister in Aberdeen and Guild Street is named after him. That purchase was in 1631 and Dr Guild gifted the former monastery property to the Seven Incorporated Trades in 1633. In 1805, they moved to premises in what is now the Trinity Centre in Union Street but, as parking was a problem latterly, they moved again in 1967, further west to the junction of Holburn Street and Great Western Road, where "Trinity Hall" now stands. Other cities, such as Glasgow, have equivalent incorporations, sometimes with more trades. In Glasgow, Trades Hall is in Glassford Street, in the Merchant City.

The Tailors of Aberdeen owned the lands of Craibstone, formerly owned by John Craib and there is still a Craib Stone (possibly a boundary stone) in Bon Accord Square. Some of the other trades owned property in Aberdeen – for example, the Hammermen owned land which is now occupied by Golden Square, Silver Street and Ruby Place. In 1823, the Tailors decided to feu out the lands of Craibstone. The intention was to form a square which is now Bon Accord Square

8 Ebenezer Bain, *Merchant and Craft Guilds: A History of the Aberdeen Incorporated Trades* (1887); Philip G Taylor, *The Seven Incorporated Trades of Aberdeen; Millennium Brochure* (2000).

and part of the land for that square was bought by George Nicol. (The motto of Aberdeen is "Bon Accord".) This plot was on the north side of the square and forms part of what is now West Craibston Street. Nicol became the owner of number 29 in 1824. The conditions imposed were as follows: (a) within five years, the purchaser would build a house of stone and lime, the front walls of which were to be in granite. (Aberdeen is known in Scotland as "the granite city", as well as "the oil capital of Europe". The largest granite building in the world is the monastery at El Escorial, near Madrid, and the second largest is Marischal College in Aberdeen); (b) the Tailors would put a metal railing around Bon Accord Square; (c) the feuars (ie the owners) would maintain the railing, and would pay two-thirds of the cost of its erection; (d) within six months, the feuars would enter into contracts obliging themselves to pay the feuduties and comply with the other conditions of the sale; (e) within three years, the purchasers would form pavements outside their properties. It was discovered in 1825 that the property was held of burgage tenure, mentioned earlier, and so the documentation was changed in 1825 to reflect this. Burgage tenure and feudal tenure were assimilated in 1874. For present purposes, the differences do not matter.

In order to afford to build his house, Nicol borrowed £550, then £150 and then £440 from Adam Coutts, who was one of the two clerks (lawyers) to the Seven Trades. In the interval, the Tailors had built a sewer to carry water away from the square, and the owners of the various properties were under an obligation to contribute to the cost. Nicol acquired other ground in the square which he built on, but he did not build on the original plot. Nicol was made bankrupt in 1826, but, when his trustees in bankruptcy failed to sell the properties, they were given over to, amongst others, Coutts, who had lent him money and who had a mortgage over Nicol's properties in return. The properties were sold to Coutts for £86 and he agreed to pay off the other mortgage holders.

THE LITIGATION

The issue which went to the House of Lords was which conditions in the sale documentation were personal and hence affected only the original parties and which were "real" which meant that they applied to the land and thus affected every subsequent proprietor as well as the original one, and what were the requirements for a condition to be considered "real". On the first occasion when the case went to the House of Lords, they sent it back to the Court of Session for an opinion of the whole court, ie 15 judges, or at least of the eight most senior ones. This was not uncommon because there might not be a Scottish judge in the House of Lords and/or because the issue was one which was peculiar to Scots law. Between 1712 and 1843, 56 cases were remitted from the House of Lords to the Court of Session. It was not until 1876 that an Act of Parliament provided that there should be two Scottish judges in the House of Lords. After that, the practice of referral ceased.

Coutts had been consulted earlier about the legal issues arising from the original sale documentation which has been mentioned above. He had let out some of the properties which he had bought, but, as water had accumulated outside one of them, in order to get rid of it, he instructed a mason to connect the property to the main sewer, something which was done in the middle of the night. The real reason for the court action was that the Tailors were of the opinion that Coutts had acted against their interests because he had failed to make it clear in the title deeds which conditions "ran with the lands", ie were real conditions and not merely personal ones affecting only the original contracting parties. They were also annoyed that he had connected his property to their sewer under the cover of darkness.

The action was raised by the Tailors in the Court of Session on 25 February 1829. That court is the highest court in Scotland, and sits only in Edinburgh. It is a court of first instance and also a court of appeal. The Tailors wanted the court (at first instance) to find that (a) the conditions in the sale documents, the Articles of Roup, were binding on Coutts; (b) he had advised the Tailors that they were effective and so he was bound by them; and (c) he should enter into a contract agreeing to comply with the conditions of sale. They also wanted payment of his proportion of the cost of the railings around the square, and the cost of the sewer, and they wanted the court to say that he was obliged to lay a pavement outside his property.

Arguments (submissions) for the Tailors

The obligations originally imposed on Nicol bound all proprietors. The obligation to pay for a share of the railings was related to the right to walk in the square which Coutts had, and so he was bound to contribute. Coutts was aware of the conditions imposed on Nicol and so he would be acting in bad faith if he accepted a deed which did not give full effect to them. The conditions imposed ran with the lands.

Arguments (submissions) for Coutts

The obligations were personal to Nicol and were not binding on anyone else. In order to run with the lands, the conditions needed to have attached to them what was called an "irritancy clause", ie a forfeiture clause, which would state that, if the conditions were not complied with, the Tailors could get the land back. There was a distinction, he said, between conditions which were stated to run with the lands and were protected by an irritancy clause, and others.

There was a legal debate and evidence was given on whether Coutts had deliberately omitted the clause about real burdens in the subsequent deeds, whether he had sold the property in good faith to his brother and whether the connection to the sewer had been constructed at night.

At first instance

On 16 November 1832, the first instance judge, called in Scotland the Lord Ordinary, Lord Corehouse, who sits in what is called the Outer House,[9] gave his decision, which was that some of the obligations imposed on Coutts were personal and these were: (a) the requirement to give an undertaking to perform the conditions in the sale document; (b) the obligation to contribute to the cost of the railing and wall in the square; and (c) the obligation to lay the pavement, and to put up a railing at the east end of Nicol's property. In his view, Coutts had not deliberately omitted any clauses in the deeds, but Coutts had constructed the link to the sewer "under cloud of night". Because the Tailors had been unsuccessful, he awarded expenses (costs) against them.

The first appeal

The case went to the Inner House of the Court of Session, which decided that the conditions had been set out in the ruling clause of the deed in favour of Nicol and that had been recorded in the Register

9 Further information about courts in Scotland can be found on the website of the Scottish Court Service: www.scotcourts.gov.uk.

of Sasines, ie the land register. However, because the first instance judge had proceeded on the wrong basis – he thought that these conditions did *not* appear in the land register – the appeal court sent the case back to him to allow him to reconsider. That was done on 27 February 1833. Lord Corehouse gave his new decision on 19 November 1833. He decided that Coutts did not need to give a personal undertaking to pay the feuduties, nor to perform the other land obligations. He did not need to contribute to the cost of putting up the wall and railings, but he was required to lay the pavement and to erect a railing at the east end of his property. He was also liable for a part of the cost of putting in the sewer as he had benefited from it. That decision was also appealed and the Inner House heard the second appeal, giving their decision on 20 December 1834. Counsel for the Tailors did not get a chance to say anything and counsel for Coutts was stopped during his presentation, as the judges indicated that they had made up their minds. Counsel for the Tailors said that he had not been present at a "more unsatisfactory" decision hearing: "The case positively decided without its merits being touched." The Tailors lost. Their counsel advised them to appeal to the House of Lords.

Offer to settle

There was a meeting on 9 February 1835 between representatives of the Tailors and Coutts, and the latter made an offer to settle the case. The conditions were that he would be reimbursed for the expense of defending himself, and if so reimbursed, he would not take action against any member of the Tailors. He wanted the individuals who had decided to take court action to make that payment (he had spent nearly £1,000) and had lost the income from his clerkship of the Tailors, from which he had been removed. The Tailors, in turn, wanted Coutts to pay for the cost of the sewer, the expenses of the court action and to bear his other expenses himself. The parties, not surprisingly, did not reach an agreement to settle the case.

First appeal to the House of Lords, 23 May 1837

Both the Tailors and Coutts appealed. The case was originally to be heard on 7 April 1837, but for a variety of reasons, it was not dealt with until 13 April, and the decision was given on 15 June – and that was to send the case back to the Court of Session. The House of Lords wanted an answer to four questions which were to be addressed by at least nine judges, who were four in each of the two divisions of the appeal court (Inner House) and the first instance judge. The questions were: (a) which of the obligations imposed in the documentation bound the owner, no matter who that might be; (b) if any of the conditions fell into that category, was it necessary for the deed to have a forfeiture clause; (c) were any of the conditions of such a nature that they would not bind every owner unless they were described as "real burdens"; and (d) was there a difference between a forfeiture clause which affected only the owner at the time and one which had the effect of bringing the whole feu to an end with the result that the land reverted to the superior. While sending the case back, the House of Lords did say that, as far as Coutts was concerned, "misconduct of any kind is out of the question".

Back to the Court of Session

Eleven judges dealt with the case. These were the chairs of the two divisions of the appeal court, four judges of the appeal court and five others. (The First Division is presided over by the Lord President and the Second is presided over by the Lord Justice-Clerk). That was all of the judges of the court, bar two. In 2013, the Court of Session consists of 34 judges.[10]

The legal position was set out by four of the consulted judges, with whom the rest agreed. Using the words of Lord Corehouse, they said:

> To constitute a real burden or condition, either in feudal or burgage rights, which is effectual against singular successors, words must be used in the conveyance which clearly express or plainly imply that the subject itself is to be affected, and not the grantee and his heirs alone, and those words must be inserted in the sasine which follows on the conveyance, and of consequence appear on the record. In the next place, the burden or condition must not be contrary to law, or inconsistent with the nature of this species of property; it must not be useless or vexatious; it must not be contrary to public policy, for example, by tending to impede the commerce of land, or create a monopoly. The superior or party in whose favour it is conceived must have an interest to enforce it. Lastly, if it consists in the payment of a sum of money, the amount of the sum must be distinctly specified. If these requisites concur, it is not essential that any *voces signatae* or technical form of words

10 Each of the Divisions has five judges, and the Outer House has 24. The same judges comprise the High Court of Justiciary which deals with crime, both at first instance and on appeal.

should be employed. There is no need for a declaration that the
obligation is real, that it is a *debitum fundi,* that it shall be inserted in all
the future infeftments, or that it shall attach to singular successors.

What they said requires little explanation, except the following. The
reference to "sasine" means that the condition must have appeared
in the Register of Sasines which was set up in 1617 and still exists.
Sasine refers to a ceremony which originally took place on the land
itself and ownership was transferred once the details of what had
taken place at the ceremony were recorded in the Register of Sasines.
There were local "particular registers" and the general one, kept in
Edinburgh, originally at "Register House". These were registers of
deeds. In 1979,[11] the Land Register was set up. This is a register of
titles. The difference is that, if a deed appears in the Register of Sasines,
this is not guaranteed to give a good title to the property, whereas a
deed which is on the Land Register comes with a state guarantee that
the title is a good one; and the Keeper is required, in general terms, to
compensate an owner who can prove that the Keeper has made a
mistake and that he or she has suffered a loss as a result. Both of these
registers are kept by the Keeper of the Registers of Scotland in
Meadowbank House in Edinburgh and these registers are open to
the public. A *debitum fundi* is a debt affecting the land, eg feuduty.
The need for the person seeking to enforce a condition to have both a
title (ie there is something on the Register of Sasines or the Land
Register to that effect) and also an interest, is now enshrined in statute.

Returning to the *Tailors* case, despite the unanimity of the judges
in the Court of Session, there was a second appeal to the House of
Lords. The reports of the case do not say who appealed, but it would
be safe to assume that, as with the first appeal, both parties took issue
with the decision in the Court of Session.

The second appeal, 3 August 1840

On this occasion, the House of Lords affirmed the decision of the
Court of Session. Coutts was not obliged to grant a personal obligation
for payment of the ground rent, the equivalent of feuduty, nor was
he liable for any part of the cost of putting up the railing in Bon Accord
Square. However, he was obliged to lay a pavement in front of his
house and to put up a railing at the east end of his house, and he had
to contribute towards the cost of connecting to the sewer. The cost of

11 Land Registration (Scotland) Act 1979.

the second appeal was £343 69s, which today is about £30,000. It would be reasonable to assume that the cost of the first appeal would be about the same.

THE SIGNIFICANCE OF
THE TAILORS OF ABERDEEN CASE

The case therefore settled the issue of the criteria which have to be met before a condition relating to land will be binding on all successive owners, but a major change took place in 2000 when feudal tenure was abolished. The Abolition of Feudal Tenure etc (Scotland) Act 2000 followed on a report by the Scottish Law Commission which was set up in 1965 to consider law reform in Scotland. The first section of the Act states quite succinctly: "The feudal system of land tenure, that is to say, the entire system whereby land is held by a vassal on perpetual tenure from a superior, is abolished on the appointed day", ie 28 November 2004. That Act was followed in 2003 by the Title Conditions (Scotland) Act which came into force also on 28 November 2004. The latter set out the law on title conditions in general, but in relation to tenement buildings, there is the Tenements (Scotland) Act 2004, recognising that, to some extent, tenements are a special case, in that the proprietors will own not only their individual properties, but may own other parts in common with the other proprietors, eg the roof and the external walls. The maintenance obligations should mirror the property regime. For example, if an owner has an eighth share of the property in the roof, it would be sensible to have him or her obliged to pay an eighth share of the cost of maintenance of the roof.

The requirements for creating real conditions as set out in the *Tailors of Aberdeen* case remain, but one additional requirement which was introduced in the legislation is that the person seeking to enforce a condition must be able to show that there will be "material detriment" to the value or enjoyment of the property if a condition imposed on an adjoining proprietor is not complied with. The precise ambit of the phrase "material detriment" cannot be defined, as each case will turn on its own facts, but an example would be two cottages in the country which are close to each other. If the owner of one seeks to convert it into a recycling unit, it might not be difficult to satisfy the statutory test. If, however, what is proposed is an extension, that might not, especially if the local authority grants planning permission, because one factor which a local authority must take into account is the effect of a proposed development on the amenity of the area.

There is no doubt that the *Tailors of Aberdeen* case was, and still is, of great importance in that it set out the requirements for the creation and, hence, enforcement of conditions governing the ownership of land where the intention is that these conditions will be binding on all owners and not just the first one. There have been, as one would expect, a large number of cases on the enforcement of particular conditions, both in the courts and in the Lands Tribunal. However, in all of them, the *Tailors* case has been accepted as setting out the framework against which other cases are decided. Although Bon Accord Square was originally occupied by private dwelling-houses, many are now offices, but the essential character of the square still remains, a tribute to the Incorporation of the Tailors of Aberdeen, a body which also still exists.

A Noise All Over Europe:
Douglas v Duke of Hamilton

Lesley-Anne Barnes Macfarlane

The Great Douglas Cause – *Douglas v Duke of Hamilton*[1] – was one of the most highly contested and publicised lawsuits of its era. It offered the 18th-century masses an addictive spectacle of the sort that would, even today, create tabloid sensation: a beautiful heiress and a secret marriage; allegations of kidnapped babies; madness; intimate details of the reproductive and sexual habits of the wealthy; scandalous family breakdown followed by tragic death. The litigation lasted almost a decade, during which time it captivated the whole of Europe.

THE GREAT DOUGLAS CAUSE: BEGINNINGS

The story of the Great Douglas Cause opens with beauty, charm and intelligence – all personified in the remarkable, and resourceful, character of Lady Jane Douglas. Lady Jane, known to her many friends as "Jean", was the daughter of the Marquis of Douglas and the younger sister of Archibald, Duke of Douglas. She was born in 1698 and, following her father's death in 1700, was raised by her mother in Scotland at Douglas Castle. The Douglases were the "A-listers" of their day. They were descended from Henry VII and were one of the wealthiest families in the country. They were also a family about whom everything "seemed destined to be wild and strange".[2]

Archibald, Duke of Douglas, Lady Jean's brother, was widely believed to be insane and lived a secluded life after he killed another young man in a fit of rage. Lady Jean was different. Her beauty and amiability delighted the fashionable world. She had many admirers and as a teenager received proposals of marriage with regularity. It

---

1 Reported as *Archibald Douglas v Duke of Hamilton* (1769) 2 Pat 143.
2 P H Fitzgerald, *Lady Jean: The Romance of the Great Douglas Cause* (1904), p 90.

must have seemed in her youth as if the destiny of this great heiress was mapped out: matrimony, wealth and enviable social status.

However, Lady Jean's life took a series of unexpected, and unusual turns. In 1720, when she was 22 years old, she accepted a proposal of marriage from the Earl of Dalkeith. The engagement was abruptly broken off and a subsequent duel was fought between her former fiancé and her brother Archibald, the duke. The ensuing scandal was such that Lady Jean, jilted and publicly humiliated, disguised herself and fled to France. Her mother later discovered her there and begged her to return to Scotland. Jean was persuaded to come home, but though her life of parties and flirtations and proposals resumed, a quarter of a century passed before she would again countenance marriage.

For more than two decades, Lady Jean ignored all friendly advice that she should marry. It seems her birth, beauty and likeability enabled her to live an extraordinarily free life for a single woman in the 1700s. She travelled widely and had various outlandish adventures. On one occasion, she reportedly aided the escape from Scotland of a well-known Jacobite by disguising him as her servant.[3] Like her brother the duke, Jean began to earn a reputation for being peculiar. Yet, unlike his gregarious sister, the duke never enjoyed popularity: where Lady Jean's escapades were indulged by polite society, the duke's solitude and irascible temper only fuelled the rumours of his madness.

Relations between the Douglas siblings were not always cordial. Although they were apparently fond of each other, they disagreed on many matters from politics (he was a staunch loyalist while she was a diehard Jacobite) to matrimony. The Duke of Douglas, being disinclined himself to take a spouse, was determined that his younger sister would produce the family heirs, and Jean's unwillingness to marry was a constant source of exasperation to him. The spinster was undoubtedly the weaker sibling in family discussions since the duke controlled the family fortune and dictated the terms of Lady Jean's allowance.

Argument raged as the years passed and, inevitably, relations soured. Eventually, in 1744, following a particularly heated row, the duke withdrew his sister's allowance and virtually disinherited her. As Lady Jean approached 50 years of age, cut off by her brother,

---

3 Chevalier de Johnstone, *Memoirs of the Rebellion: in 1745 and 1746* (1820), p xliv–xlv. Some commentators have suggested that the Chevalier in fact accompanied Lady Jean and Colonel Stewart (see main text below) on their way to the Continent in 1746.

increasingly steeped in debt and unmarried, her future prospects appeared bleak. However, the most extraordinary events of "erratic"[4] Jean's life were soon to follow.

A MARRIAGE IS (EVENTUALLY) ANNOUNCED

By 1745, the capricious duke had, it appears, experienced a change of heart and reinstated his sister's allowance. Lady Jean, who was by now 47 years old, began to reacquaint herself with Colonel John Stewart, one of her many former admirers. But, while Jean was still lauded as a lady of "graceful manners and of high accomplishments",[5] Stewart's character was rather less well regarded. He was said to be barely literate and deeply in debt. On learning of his sister's partiality for Colonel Stewart, the duke echoed the sentiments of many when he observed that Stewart was "one of the worst of men – a Papist, a Jacobite, a gamester" and a worn-out old rake.[6] Certainly, at 57 years old, Colonel Stewart, a soldier and a younger son, had no inheritance and few connections to recommend him.

That Lady Jean Douglas, an heiress from "a house and family the most ancient and noble in Europe",[7] would consider entering into wedlock with Colonel Stewart must have seemed surprising indeed. Yet, as the Duke of Douglas was enraged to discover many months after the event, Jean and Colonel Stewart were quietly married in Edinburgh in August 1746.[8] Her motivations invite speculation: consuming love or revenge upon the duke? It is possible that independent Jean had had her fill of masculine whims. She had suffered the shock of a broken engagement in her youth and had for decades negotiated the moods of a volatile brother who held the family purse strings. Older and wiser, perhaps Lady Jean intended to plead for a generous marriage settlement from her brother and simply wanted a spouse who would do as she wished.

---

4 Fitzgerald, *Lady Jean*, p 10.
5 *Archibald Douglas v Duke of Hamilton*, p 144.
6 Fitzgerald, Lady Jean, p 10. See also F Douglas, *Observations on the Douglas Cause: In General; But Chiefly with a View to the Characters of the Parties Principally Concerned on the Part of the Defendant. In a Letter to a Noble Lord, from a Gentleman in Scotland* (1768), p 10.
7 *Archibald Douglas v Duke of Hamilton*, p 144.
8 Most commentators believed the marriage had taken place during the month of August 1746, although a number of different dates have been suggested.

Immediately after the marriage, the couple left Scotland for France along with Lady Jean's companion, Mrs Hewit. There is some debate as to whether the spouses presented outwardly as a married couple before they reached France. Even after they had been living for over a year on the Continent, Lady Jean was observed to be coy as to whether Colonel Stewart was actually her husband. The marriage, at which no relatives or friends had attended, was not widely communicated at home or abroad. It was many months (and in some cases years) before news of the union reached polite society.

THE ARRIVAL OF ARCHIE AND SHOLTO

Lady Jean and Colonel Stewart remained in France for the first three years of their married life, moving between Paris and the cities of Rheims and Aix-la-Chapelle. There was little communication between Jean and her brother Archibald, Duke of Douglas. However, in the early months of 1748, there followed another unexpected turn in Lady Jean's life. On 28 April 1748, Lord Crawford, a friend of the Douglas family visiting France, wrote to the duke about the expectation that he and other "well wishers" would soon see "the family of Douglas multiply".[9] In other words, incredible though the news must surely have sounded to her estranged sibling, Lady Jean Douglas was, at the age of 50, said to be pregnant.

It is telling that the duke did not answer Lord Crawford's letter. However, the months moved on and, as her companion, Mrs Hewit, later attested, fate had struck a double blow, for Lady Jean "was, in Paris, delivered on the 10th July 1748 ... of *two* male children".[10] So, the redoubtable Jean had not only given birth, but had produced both an heir and a spare. She wrote to tell her brother so some weeks after the boys were born:

> Though not a little discouraged by your favouring me with no answer to that under cover of Lord Crawford's acquainting your grace with my change of state (...) I think it my incumbent duty to acquaint you further... with the happy consequences of it (...) last month I was blessed with two boys ...[11]

9 *Archibald Douglas v Duke of Hamilton*, p 148.
10 *Archibald Douglas v Duke of Hamilton*, p 150.
11 J Stewart, *Letters of the Right Honourable Lady Jane Douglas; with Several Other Important Pieces of Private Correspondence. Illustrated with Notes* (1767), pp 9–10.

Lady Jean proposed in her letter to her brother that the elder child take the duke's name, Archibald. The duke was said to be in "high passion and displeasure" at receiving the news, convinced that his sister was attempting to impose on the family fictitious heirs, or "pretenders".[12] He made no response to Jean's letter and withdrew entirely her already modest allowance.[13] But Lady Jean was not so easily daunted: she and Colonel Stewart named the children Archibald ("Archie") and Sholto.

Sholto, a poorly child, was sent into the French countryside with a nurse while Lady Jean, Colonel Stewart and Archie returned in late 1748 to Rheims for Archie's baptism. This was a lavish event attended by distinguished guests. In 1749, after Sholto had returned to Lady Jean, she began to plan the family's return to Britain. No money was forthcoming from the duke and, by this stage, Lady Jean and Colonel Stewart were deeply in debt to friends and acquaintances. In late 1749, they borrowed the money for their homeward journey to London from Lady Jean's great friend, Lord Morton.

But the homecoming was not to be the triumph Jean had hoped for. Her brother, the duke, continued to ignore correspondence from his sister, notwithstanding entreaties made to him by various wealthy and influential figures on her behalf. Lady Jean's allowance was not reinstated and poverty once more threatened. The attitude of fashionable society towards Archie and Sholto was mixed: although the story of the boys' births had met with some suspicion, and even incredulity, most did not believe Lady Jean capable of falsifying the birth of children. Thus, throughout the 1750s, people in London and Scotland remained broadly supportive of the boys' legitimacy – or at least kept their doubts to themselves.

LADY JEAN SEEKS ADVICE ON SCOTS LAW

The indomitable Jean soon began to realise that the future of her sons now depended on her proving the legitimacy of their birth. Between 1750 and 1753, various stratagems were employed. Statements from some of the servants engaged at Rheims around the time of the boys'

12 Fitzgerald, *Lady Jean*, pp 43, 59.
13 Some texts, most notably Sir W Fraser's, *The Red Book of Grandtully* (1868), record that it was some months later (mid-1749) when the duke finally withdrew Lady Jean's allowance of £300 per annum.

births were obtained. In 1750, Lady Jean arranged Sholto's baptism in a ceremony in London. At that event, she and Colonel Stewart publicly acknowledged both of the children as their own. The young boys were regularly introduced as young Douglases to significant figures in society. The outcome of those meetings was unclear: the likeness of the boys to their parents was affirmed by some and denied by others. Her brother, the duke, remained unmoved.

Late in 1750, however, unpaid creditors eventually brought fiscal matters to a head. Colonel Stewart was imprisoned in the King's Bench Prison for debt and Lady Jean, destitute but resourceful still, wrote a letter directly to the King, begging that he exercise his royal bounty in respect of her and her children. The letter was so beautifully written that it apparently moved one of the King's advisers, William Murray (later Lord Mansfield), to tears. Lady Jean's resourcefulness once again brought success and she was granted a rare pension of £300 a year.[14] None of that sum was used to secure her husband's release from prison. Instead, Jean travelled from London with the children to her native Scotland, where she redoubled her efforts to be reconciled with the duke and to secure the position of the boys as rightful Douglas heirs.

While in Edinburgh, Lady Jean sought legal advice from her friend, Lord Prestongrange, a former Lord Justice-Clerk of Scotland. In around 1751, he advised her to continue to let it be widely known that the children were her own. This would, he believed, allow the legal doctrine of habit and repute to operate which would be likely, in turn, to satisfy a Scottish court in the event of any future dispute over the children's legitimacy.

As time wore on, the duke's resolve to cast off his sister and her apparent offspring deepened. Lady Jean grew more desperate. On one notable occasion, in late 1752, she took Archie and Sholto with her to Douglas Castle but was refused entry. A pitiful scene reportedly took place where, as Lady Jean and the children sobbed outside the castle gate, a servant she had known since her own childhood was sent down to the gate by her brother to turn them away. Then, in 1753, when the boys were only five years old, tragedy struck. Sholto, who had never been a strong child, died after a short illness. Lady Jean, who was growing frailer herself, was inconsolable. She too died in obscure lodgings in Edinburgh later the same year, never having

14 A F Steuart (ed), *The Douglas Cause: Notable Scottish Trials* (1909), p 34. The then Prime Minister, Mr Pelham, also pled Lady Jean's cause before the King.

reconciled with her brother and resolutely proclaiming the two boys her lawful offspring to the end.[15]

THE TWO ARCHIES

With his mother and brother dead and his father in a debtor's prison, young Archie must have appeared a forlorn little figure. In the end, the child's vulnerability served him well, for the plight of the little orphan roused compassion in many, particularly those who had admired his beautiful mother. Colonel Stewart was soon freed from debtor's prison. Stewart settled on the Isle of Man where he obtained a small allowance, eventually succeeding to the estate of his brother Sir George Stewart of Grandtully. Although he was to become a participant in the later litigation, the colonel's withdrawal from Archie's early life was probably helpful to the child's cause. While Lady Jean, a popular personality of her day, had won public sympathy, Colonel Stewart was suspected by many to be an adventurer.

Shortly after Lady Jean's death in 1753, Lady Shaw, a wealthy invalid, took the five-year-old Archie under her wing and began paying for his education. On the death of Lady Shaw in 1757, the Duke and Duchess of Queensberry, who had been family friends, assumed responsibility for his upbringing. Archie was educated as a person of wealth and nobility at Rugby and later Westminster School. As he grew from childhood into teenage years, the boy enjoyed a life of considerable privilege. Like his mother, he socialised with influential writers, politicians and aristocrats and was amiable and well liked. Regardless of the attitude of his uncle Archibald, Duke of Douglas, the young Archie behaved, and was treated by polite society (even the doubters), as if he were the genuine article.

From the outset, there had seemed little prospect that the Duke of Douglas would recognise young Archie. After his sister's death, the duke had consented (with great reluctance) to pay for a decent burial. The payment was said to be conditional upon Archie's absence from

---

15 That Lady Jean openly maintained the legitimacy of Archie and Sholto until her death has been recorded often throughout the centuries. In 2008, however, the writer and historian Karl Sabbagh uncovered various papers including an undated, scribbled note while researching the Douglas Cause. He believes that the note was penned by Lady Jean on her deathbed and that its tenor implies she was racked with guilt about something. See M Linklater, "Lady Jane's plea for forgiveness may unlock 260-year-old mystery of a 'lady who lied'" *The Times*, 1 September 2008.

the simple ceremony or at the graveside. However, in the decade that
followed, the Duke of Douglas on occasion appeared to soften in
attitude towards his young namesake. The duke sent out letters
enquiring about his late sister's "pregnancy" and the circumstances
of Archie's birth. In one instance, the duke even consented to see
Archie – but later changed his mind and cancelled the meeting. Then,
in 1758, an event that surprised the whole of Scotland took place: the
Duke of Douglas married (in family style) late, at the ripe old age of
64. His wife, Margaret Douglas of Mains, at 43 years old, was said to
be almost as hot-blooded and obstinate as the duke himself. When
asked why she had married such a man, Margaret Douglas reportedly
responded that "when she was pleased she could be as mad as he".[16]

The union of two such passionate characters was not a peaceful
one. While the duke was tormented by longstanding doubts about
young Archie's birth, Margaret, the new Duchess of Douglas, was an
adamant believer in Archie's legitimacy. At home, she used her position
to argue Archie's cause. This enraged her husband so much that on
one occasion he threatened to cut her throat with a pruning knife. In
1759, the couple separated and when, during their separation, Douglas
Castle unexpectedly burnt down, the duke let it be known that he
thought the fire was the work of the duchess. Although the couple
reconciled some months later, their reunion was subject to a legal
agreement attested by both spouses forbidding the duchess ever again
to mention the names of Lady Jean or the young Archie.

In the years preceding the duke's death, his turmoil concerning
the settlement of the Douglas estate is evident. Influenced to some
degree by failing health, his wife's beliefs and wider social opinion,
the duke changed his mind often. Many conflicting deeds were
prepared and executed. Eventually, on 11 July 1761, the year of his
death, the duke prepared a final deed to supersede all previous deeds
and settlements. This provided that the Dukedom of Douglas should
fall to his "own nearest heirs and assignees whatsoever", including
"heirs whatsoever of his father". Since the duke had no children of
his own, this meant, as the House of Lords later observed, that
"everything in the way of succession depended on proof that [Archie]
was the son of Lady Jean Douglas".[17]

16 Fitzgerald, *Lady Jean*, p 85.
17 *Archibald Douglas v Duke of Hamilton*, p 145.

THE LITIGATION COMMENCES –
AND GATHERS MOMENTUM

The death of the Duke of Douglas in 1761 signalled the start of the Great Douglas Cause. The cause, or court action, that was destined to become the most sensational and bitterly fought of its time, began humbly, with a simple "action for Service" before a jury in Edinburgh. The action, raised on behalf of the 13-year-old Archie, was designed to confirm his right to be "served" as heir to the Douglas estate. Evidence was produced, including statements from those who knew Lady Jean when she was said to be pregnant and correspondence from 1748 concerning Archie's birth. The action for Service was a relatively short and inexpensive process: its outcome was a finding in Archie's favour.[18]

Notwithstanding the previous efforts of Lady Jean and Archie's supporters, questions about his pedigree continued to plague his life. Society had never been entirely persuaded that Archie, the only surviving "heir presumptive" of the Douglas family, was not a pretender. Such doubts provided scope for dispute – and, of course, opportunity. Around the time the action for Service was raised, those who had a claim in the line of the Douglas estate rallied.

A further action was soon raised in the Court of Session, Scotland's highest court, for two purposes: first, to set aside the finding in Archie's favour in the previous action for Service and, secondly, for a determination that he was not the lawful child of Lady Jean Douglas. The first-named pursuer, Archie's opponent, was the Duke of Hamilton, who stood next in line to inherit. Public interest, both at home and abroad, in the emerging scandal involving the aristocracy now rapidly began to ignite.

COURT OF SESSION PROCEEDINGS CREATE
"A NOISE ALL OVER EUROPE"

The action in the Court of Session, which was known as *Duke of Hamilton v Archibald Douglas of Douglas,* began early in 1762 and concluded in 1767.[19] Although Archie and the Duke of Hamilton were

18 *A Summary of the Speeches and Arguments and Determinations of The Right Honourable Lords of Council and Session in Scotland (…) Duke of Hamilton and Others v Archibald Douglas of Douglas* (1767), printed and sold by Francis Robertson, Bookseller (Edinburgh), p 17.

19 See *A Summary of the Speeches and Arguments.*

the named parties in the cause, neither stood alone. Each had friends and money; each was possessed of a team of wealthy and influential supporters determined to win, and neither team spared effort or expense. The finest legal minds in Scotland were sought out and employed. The Scottish lawyer and writer James Boswell produced a treatise on the case, observing:

> The Douglas Cause has now made a noise all over Europe; and indeed no cause ever came before a court of justice so interesting in its nature [concerning] whether a young gentleman ... the only remaining representative of the illustrious house of Douglas, is, after ... possession of his estate, to be deprived of it, and to be reduced to a situation worse than death.[20]

Such was Boswell's conviction that Archie was the rightful Douglas heir that he published a thinly-veiled allegorical tale called *Dorando* about the suppositious child of a great lady cast off by her family. As Boswell was himself much engaged in the case, he was strongly criticised for writing the story. He was not the only professional accused of behaving improperly. As emotions ran high during the Great Douglas Cause, Andrew Stuart, an agent employed by the Duke of Hamilton, fought a duel with pistols against one of Archie's lawyers who had called Stuart a liar. Shots were fired; both missed, and honour was satisfied.

Matters were further complicated in late 1762 when the Duke of Hamilton's agents began concurrent proceedings in the French courts (the *Tournelle Criminelle* in Paris). In the course of the French litigation, public notices were issued calling for witnesses to the circumstances surrounding Archie's birth in Paris. Allegations were made that the French witnesses who gave evidence were intimidated and thereafter rewarded for giving testimony – later described by British courts as "blackest perjury".[21] Although the French proceedings were finally ordered to be withdrawn by the House of Lords in 1764, for a period of two years pronouncements (simultaneous, and at times contradictory) had been made by the Scottish and French courts in the case.

One of the most remarkable features of the litigation was the extent to which the general public and fashionable figures of the day were

---

20 J Boswell, *The Essence of the Douglas Cause: To which is subjoined, some observations on a pamphlet lately published, intitled, Considerations on the Douglas cause* (1740–1795), p 1.

21 *Archibald Douglas v Duke of Hamilton*, p 169.

invested in the outcome. Everyone, it seems, supported one side or the other. Commentators' views were published in pamphlets (the tabloids of their time) that were circulated in Edinburgh and London and translated for wider distribution in Paris and throughout the Continent. Influential writers and social commentators regularly advocated, with tremendous zeal, either the Douglas or the Hamilton cause. Public bets were commonly placed in Scotland and elsewhere on the outcome of the case at various stages of its progress.

TWO SIDES TO EVERY STORY: STOLEN BABIES AND INTRIGUE?

The leaking of salacious details given by witnesses in the course of the Scottish and French actions about the most intimate particulars of Lady Jean's life was a constant source of public interest and discussion. There was no shortage of explicit information, for the records of evidence given in the lengthy Court of Session action amounted to thousands of pages, "exceeding in bulk anything of the kind ever before prepared".[22]

Between 1762 and 1767, Colonel John Stewart (who died in 1764), Mrs Hewit (Lady Jean's companion) and a large number of French and British witnesses gave evidence about Lady Jean's "pregnancy" and the early years of Archie's life. Archie was, of course, by now a teenager. In the course of the litigation, it soon became apparent that, notwithstanding difficulties naturally occasioned by the passage of time, the circumstances surrounding his French birth were very mysterious indeed. Whether intentional or not, the behaviour of Lady Jean and Colonel Stewart at the time of Archie and Sholto's births generated more than a whiff of intrigue. Volumes of strange and conflicting evidence enabled the opponents in the Great Douglas Cause to construct two entirely different stories about Archie's parentage.

The Douglas lawyers, keen to advance young Archie's cause, stressed that he had already proved before a Scots jury his entitlement to be "served" as rightful heir to the Douglas estate. They produced evidence (considered shockingly intimate at the time) of Lady Jean's menstrual cycle and bouts of morning sickness. The lawyers also sought to rely on eye-witness accounts of her enlarged breasts and swollen stomach

22 Fitzgerald, *Lady Jean*, p 106.

at various stages of her pregnancy. Other witnesses provided information about her clothes being let out by a seamstress and spoke of her remarkably youthful appearance. Many of the witnesses thought that Lady Jean was between 30 and 40 years of age, some 15 to 20 years younger than she actually was. Much was also made of Lady Jean's conduct in the months and years following the children's births: the children were acknowledged and baptised as her own; both were accepted (through years of habit and repute) by Lady Jean and Colonel Stewart as their lawful children; Archie and Sholto had been widely introduced as their sons "everywhere, by the world as well as in private circles". This final piece of evidence was "proved by all witnesses" who had come across the family.[23]

However, Archie's opponents also produced much evidence in support of their cause. In seeking to persuade the court that he was not the rightful Douglas heir, the Duke of Hamilton's lawyers principally relied on testimony given by French witnesses discovered by their agent, Andrew Stuart. Madame Mignon, a glassblower's wife from Paris, swore that she had, in 1748, "sold her own child to foreigners" and another witness spoke of a child by name of Sanry, the son of a "rope-dancer", who had been taken from his parents later the same year.[24] This evidence of buying, or indeed stealing, children (which, if true meant that Archie and Sholto were not even brothers, let alone twins) caused a public sensation. Further witnesses who had seen both children came forward to swear they had always believed one boy to be several months older, although these statements were countered by contradictory evidence given about the boys' likeness to each other and to both Lady Jean and Colonel Stewart.

Lawyers for the Duke of Hamilton also argued, of course, that at 50 years of age, Lady Jean was simply too old to have children. Evidence of what were thought to be miscarriages during the early years of her marriage was given. Also, witnesses who had known her and Colonel Stewart in 1748, but who had been unaware of their marriage or of her developing pregnancy, gave evidence. The odd, and rather furtive, behaviour of the couple around the time of the boys' births had been observed by a number of witnesses. In particular, the lengthy journey they undertook from Rheims, where they were well known, to Paris while Lady Jean was apparently heavily pregnant (and ill) was said to

23 This was stated in the Court of Session and, later, in the House of Lords. See, eg, *A Summary of the Speeches and Arguments,* pp 168–169.
24 *Archibald Douglas v Duke of Hamilton,* p 169.

be bizarre. They were also hidden as they travelled from boarding house to boarding house in Paris in the days immediately preceding the births of the boys. Le Brune's boarding house, at which Colonel Stewart swore the births had taken place, was never discovered. Nor was Monsieur La Marre, the male *accoucheur* (midwife) said to have delivered the children. Further, a handwriting expert gave evidence in court denouncing a series of forged letters between the "phantom" Monsieur La Marre and Colonel Stewart.[25]

15 JULY 1767: A DECISION THAT SATISFIED NO-ONE

After five years of hearing evidence and argument, the Court of Session proceedings concluded with a flamboyance characteristic of the whole cause. Closing submissions took 21 days in total and were made by 24 lawyers, each of whom had been instructed by one or other party. The 14 Court of Session judges who had heard the case took eight days to deliver their opinion. In the end, they were equally divided. In a move that was to cost him years of hard-earned popularity, the Lord President, Robert Dundas of Arniston, stepped in to cast the deciding vote. And, as at least some of the gamblers of the day had predicted, his vote was cast in favour of the Duke of Hamilton. Thus, on a majority of eight votes to seven, on 15 July 1767, the Lords of Session decided that Archie was not the lawful child of Lady Jean Douglas. Consequent upon that finding, the court set aside the jury's ruling of 1761 in the previous action to serve Archie as rightful Douglas heir.

The decision of the Court of Session in *Duke of Hamilton v Archibald Douglas of Douglas* was widely disparaged. The appearance of a court so clearly divided was a source of universal dissatisfaction. The great Dr Samuel Johnson, himself an ardent supporter of the Duke of Hamilton, observed that "a more dubious determination of any question cannot be imagined".[26] Indeed, such was the state of public unrest in Edinburgh following the judgment that troops were ordered into the city to restore calm (not before the windows of many of the judges' homes had been broken by the mob). The victory for the Duke of Hamilton was short-lived: an appeal against the decision of the

25 *A Summary of the Speeches and Arguments*, pp 120–121.
26 J Boswell, *The Life of Samuel Johnson* (1791), vol 2, p 236. The deeply-held differences in opinion over the Great Douglas Cause between Dr Johnson and his biographer, James Boswell, must have made for interesting discussion.

Court of Session was immediately made to the House of Lords, the highest appeal court in the Kingdom of Great Britain.

THE GREAT DOUGLAS CAUSE REACHES THE HOUSE OF LORDS

In the House of Lords, the case was reported as *(Archibald) Douglas v Duke of Hamilton*. The parties' names were reversed and Archie, as the appellant, was merely known as "Archibald Douglas" since, by the judgment of the Court of Session, he had been divested of his title, "Douglas of Douglas".

The parties to the Great Douglas Cause found a very different audience in the House of Lords in London. In the Court of Session, in Edinburgh, the cause had been a prolonged and painstakingly thorough affair, but it seems that London was keen to expedite matters. Counsel for each party was heard during January 1769 and the judgment of the House of Lords was issued at the end of February the same year. By that stage, the litigation had cost the modern-day equivalent of tens of millions of pounds.[27]

Just like his late mother, Lady Jean, it seems that Archie's life was prone to unexpected twists and turns of fate. On this occasion, Archie had his mother to thank for the great stroke of luck he encountered in the form of Lord Mansfield, one of the judges sitting in the House of Lords. For it was the same Lord Mansfield who, in his former role as Solicitor General for England and Wales, had been approached by the near-destitute Lady Jean in 1750 when she had begged for a pension from the King. In the House of Lords judgment, Lord Mansfield described Lady Jean as a "lady of the strictest honour and integrity [having] the deepest sense of the grandeur of [her] family … a race who had always been eminently loyal".[28] He observed in the opening sentence of his judgment:

> I must own that this cause before us, is the greatest and most important that occurs to me; it is no less than an attack upon the virtue and honour of a lady of the first quality in order to dispossess a young man of an

27 The total cost of litigation in 1769 was said to be £52,000. See J I Robertson, "The Douglas Cause", *Scots Magazine*, Issue 50, p 38 (April 2010). A variety of estimates as to the modern-day equivalent of this sum have been made in recent decades.

28 *Archibald Douglas v Duke of Hamilton*, p 174.

eminent fortune, reduce him to beggary, strip him of his birthright, declare him an alien and a foundling.[29]

Lord Mansfield ruled that Archie was the rightful Douglas heir. His judicial brethren, Lord Sandwich (a lay judge) and the Lord Chancellor (Camden), followed suit. The judgment of the House of Lords, delivered on 27 February 1769, was unanimous in Archie's favour, and the decision of the Court of Session was reversed. It is likely that, in its unanimity, the House of Lords sought to circumvent the public unrest that followed the previous decision of the lower court.

What, though, of the purchased (or, indeed, stolen) babies in Paris? The forged letters from the missing male midwife? Or the suspicious circumstances surrounding Archie's birth? The Duke of Hamilton's agent, Andrew Stuart, was strongly criticised for his part in discovering and advising the French witnesses who attested to baby-trading and theft. The House of Lords simply overlooked the other factual peculiarities and discrepancies. It might be said that the story of the Great Douglas Cause ends where it all began: with the extraordinary character of Lady Jean Douglas. The House of Lords was persuaded of the core truth of her claims and swayed by her maternal tenderness towards Archie and Sholto. Thus, she secured Archie his place in the great Douglas family.

CONCLUSION:
THE MOTHER OF THE MODERN CAUSE CELEBRE

And what of Archie himself? It would be interesting to know what he made of the cause, raised and in the end won through the efforts of dozens of great personalities and commentators (and, of course, lawyers). The litigation, which must have consumed his life entirely from the start of his teenage years until he reached the age of 21, made him an international celebrity. What were his own thoughts on his pedigree? History tells us that Archie Douglas of Douglas went on to become, if not an exceptional, then at least a worthy aristocrat. He inherited great wealth and vast lands. He was an improving landlord and took an interest in public affairs, eventually becoming a Member of Parliament. Although the Dukedom of Douglas had been extinguished on the death of his uncle Archibald, Archie was eventually given a peerage and created Baron Douglas of Douglas in

29 *Archibald Douglas v Duke of Hamilton*, pp 172–173.

1790.[30] Archie lived until he was almost 80 years old, married twice and had nine children. However, nothing in the later life of Lady Jean's son ever equalled his role as the youthful protagonist in the Great Douglas Cause – the mother of all modern *causes célèbres*.

30 J Burke, *A General and Heraldic Dictionary of the Peerage and Baronetage of the British Empire* (4th edn, 1938), p 381. This title, the original Barony of Douglas, became extinct following the death of Archie's youngest son in 1857.

The Good, the Mad and the Wealthy: The Insanity of Gordon Kinloch

Claire McDiarmid

Crime fiction may have developed considerably since Agatha Christie's heyday in the mid-20th century but she, and many of her successors, would have been pleased if they had been able to invent the cast of real characters, and the country-house setting, which surrounded the shooting, in the early hours of Wednesday, 15 April 1795, of Sir Francis Kinloch of Gilmerton. Indeed, all that the story lacks is the "whodunit" element, but it is attended by so many other layers of intrigue that this may not even be missed. From the inherent repellence of fratricide, through the, unexpectedly sophisticated, *fin de* (18th) *siècle* understanding of mental disorder to the blurred concept of motive which emerges, the levels of interest run deep.[1] It is a tale ripe for a 21st-century re-telling, starting and ending in the baronial family residence, Gilmerton House, in the Parish of Athelstaneford and the County of Haddington.

Today the building is strikingly attractive – a stone-built, well-proportioned, Georgian mansion operating as an exclusive venue for corporate events and weddings. In the second week of April in 1795, it was positively bustling, with servants, family members, visitors, doctors, messengers and lawyers coming and going, at all hours, literally, of day and night. While, no doubt, the business of the Gilmerton Estate continued apace, the focal point of much of the rest of this activity was one of the two main protagonists in the fatal event: Major Archibald Gordon Kinloch, known to his family as Gordon. His mental state, and the increasingly erratic behaviour which it had occasioned, was causing deep unease to his close family. It is important, first of all, to have some sense of who they were.

---

1 In what follows, page references in brackets are to *The Trial of Sir Archibald Gordon Kinloch* (Edinburgh: Elder & Robinson, 1795); and column references in brackets are to T B and T J Howell, *A Complete Collection of State Trials from the Earliest Period to 1783 and then to the Present Time* (1816), vol XXV.

THE MAIN PLAYERS: THE KINLOCH FAMILY

Sir David Kinloch, patriarch of the six surviving Kinloch children, had died only two months earlier on 19 February 1795. His eldest son, Francis, inherited the title, the house and the estate. It appears that he was then around 47 or 48 years of age and unmarried. Quite a clear picture emerges of Francis from the testimony given at Gordon's trial. He is portrayed as a pragmatist. We know, for example, that, on discovering that his father had a tendency towards hoarding, he had an archive containing almost every single paper his father had ever received reviewed and had all but those of clear, continuing significance destroyed by burning. He is the person most frequently informed by others, even during his father's life, of Gordon's strange behaviours and, in relation thereto, he comes across as, at various times, exasperated, alarmed and despairing but, almost always, solicitous and caring towards his brother as he sought mechanisms to contain and manage him.

The third brother, Alexander or Sandy, is a much more shadowy figure – partly because he did not give evidence at the trial. He appears most often somewhere between his brothers. There is evidence that he and Gordon disputed with Francis the settlements which their father had made for them on his death causing Francis to take legal advice. We also encounter Sandy doing his best, with many others, to contain Gordon in the two or three days leading up to the fatal incident.

There were three sisters: Mary, the wife of Sir Thomas Ashe; Janet, spinster of the parish of Athelstaneford; and Harriet, who, having been, in her time, a noted Edinburgh beauty for whom a piece of fiddle music "Miss Kinloch of Gilmerton" was written, was now married to Sir Foster Cunliffe. The case report notes that he, together with a cousin-german of the Kinlochs (James Wilkie) attended Gordon in the dock at the outset of the trial. Harriet and Foster were the parents of ten children, some of whom were present in the house on the night of the shooting.

Janet, because of her unmarried status, does not even always figure in lists of Kinloch family members compiled for the purposes of peerage records. Paradoxically, of the three sisters, it is she who is the major player in the dramatic events attending the death of her brother, displaying good sense and sound instincts in her attitude to Gordon as he became increasingly unpredictable. She locked her bedroom door in Gilmerton because of her fear that he would, otherwise, commit suicide in front of her. She discussed her anxiety about him openly with those who might be able to offer assistance, going so far as to summon George Somner (the family's surgeon, resident in Haddington) to Gilmerton on the afternoon of the shooting because of her concerns about the state of Gordon's mind. It is therefore rather disappointing to find her portrayed, within the court process, as fearful, shaking and emotional, requiring special concessions to enable her to give evidence at all. There is a mismatch between the perception of this woman as sensitive to the point of inertia and the evidence of her actions which suggests someone sensible and practical, if, understandably, unnerved by Gordon's behaviour.

The detail in the report of the proceedings of the trial in the High Court of Justiciary allows us an insight, which would be missing from contemporary criminal cases, into some of the dynamics of this large, apparently close, aristocratic family struggling to contain a brother, once a highly respected major in the British army, with mental health problems.

THE ORIGINS OF GORDON'S MENTAL INSTABILITY: THE ST LUCIA FEVER

In his time as an army officer, Gordon Kinloch had seen something of the world beyond East Lothian, though details of his activities in these years are scant. He joined up as an ensign in Cork, Ireland, in 1767 where he first met his friend Major John Mackay. He is placed by another army comrade, Captain Henry Miller, in Nova Scotia at some time in the early 1770s. On being offered a promotion to major, with another regiment, Gordon sailed to the West Indies in 1780. Unfortunately, along with a large proportion of the men who travelled with him, he contracted a terrible fever in St Lucia. It was of such potency that, in the throes of the delirium which it induced, he had to be held down by two soldiers. Indeed, in the end, 1,800 soldiers out of 5,000 detailed to the Caribbean island died. A 1781 painting exists, by Dominic Serres, of a British squadron off St Lucia on 25 March 1780. Around two dozen high-masted vessels are shown anchored or sailing in a sea the colour of mud. The squared shape of the wooden living areas of the ships is such that not much is required of the imagination to perceive how easily a virulent illness would spread in the confined space.

Gordon was eventually transported by sea to Barbados, as the air there was regarded as the only possible way to save his life. En route, his servant caught the disease and, in the grip of one of its spasms, threw himself off the ship to his death (by drowning). It appears that the illness was yellow fever or this, at least, is what is stated in Sir Frederick Treves's *The Cradle of the Deep*, published in 1908. (The book tells of the author's own travels in the West Indies, but it also contains accounts of certain events from the islands' history.) Today, it is recognised that the yellow fever vaccine may cause a severe neurological illness in a small percentage of those who receive it. Yellow fever's possible effects on the brain in the late 18th century are not documented though, within the evidence presented in the case, there is no doubt, even from prosecution witnesses, that Gordon had mental health problems and that these stemmed from his Caribbean illness. In any event, together with the accumulated evidence of Gordon's bizarre behaviour in the years following his return to Scotland, the strange manner of his servant's death is offered as proof of the madness, or furiosity, which that illness left in its wake – a matter which assumes importance as the plot strands tighten and draw together in early April 1795.

THE ANTECEDENT EVENTS

The best murder mysteries commence with the event causing the death and, moving back from that, tease out the means and the possible motives. This is, in the end, neither a murder nor a mystery, but it will still adhere to the formula. Gordon shot Francis with one of a pair of pistols which he had brandished, increasingly erratically, in the presence of a number of witnesses in the hours before the incident. He did this around 3.30 in the morning, yet Gilmerton House seems to have been alive with wakeful people, each in varying levels of alarm and readiness for his next unorthodox act.

In the dining-room on the ground floor, Francis, Janet, Sandy, Somner (the family surgeon) and Duncan McMillan, an Edinburgh lawyer who seems to have been on intimate terms with the Kinloch family and its legal affairs, had, until very shortly before, been at supper, which had commenced at 11 pm and drawn to a final close around 3 am. It is not quite clear which of them were still present and which had retired to bed. All evening, Gordon was in his room upstairs, though emerging from there at regular intervals, unable to remain still and far from at peace in his own company.

In the butler's parlour were George Douglas (servant to Janet), Alexander Campbell (Gilmerton "postilion" – the coach-driver who rode on one of the horses rather than the carriage itself), Walter Gibson (servant to Francis) and Alexander Menie (Francis's butler). It is not known whether gentry routinely lingered over supper until these hours, requiring attendance from servants who would presumably have to rise only a few hours later, or if this was yet another oddity arising from the anxiety surrounding Gordon. Elsewhere in the house, a nurse who sometimes cared for the insane was present, having been brought by Somner, as he and the family witnessed Gordon's condition worsening. A number of other farm-men had, prematurely as it would turn out, been sent away shortly before, as Gordon's state of mind was perceived to have calmed. There is a real sense of portentousness pervading the house. The enormous reluctance to confine one's brother in a straitjacket is evident and understandable, yet the fear of what he might do – clearly a fatality was anticipated – is palpable.

As far as we can tell, Gordon had not slept since the night of Sunday, 12 April though, in fact, there is no evidence that he was asleep even then. In his summing-up to the jury, his defence counsel, Mr Hope, also suggested that he had probably not eaten in that period either – and, certainly, the accounts which we have from the Reverend Mr George Goldie, the parish minister of Athelstaneford, and from those who encountered Gordon on the Monday, are of a man who is shaking so much that he is all but unable to put a glass of water to his lips and who attempts to eat but seems unable to swallow even the tiniest morsel.

Gordon arrived in Haddington by chaise on the Monday evening and went directly to Somner's professional premises. Somner, who was dining nearby, at a Mrs Fairbairn's, with Sandy and McMillan, saw and recognised the chaise as Gordon's and went out to meet him. He persuaded him to join the dining party but Gordon was distinctly ill at ease. After unsuccessful attempts to convince and assist him to eat, the three men ordered two chaises to return them all to Gilmerton. Gordon, travelling with Somner, ordered his chaise to stop en route however, and got down from it, giving the excuse that he had to "make water" (p 11). Instead, he disappeared into the night. He told the chaise's postilion, who was sent to intercept him, that he was going back to Haddington where he would spend the night, but no trace was found there when inquiry was made the next morning. Somner, Sandy and McMillan finally arrived back at Gilmerton around 10 pm.

Gordon, in fact, spent the Monday night wandering in the woods of Beanston, an adjoining farm tenanted by John Walker. He told another witness that, whilst there, much like Moses in the Bible, he had had a light from heaven and had seen a burning bush which was not consumed. He passed the day of the shooting, until around 5 pm, barricaded into a bedroom which Mr Walker and his family had kindly made available to him in their farmhouse, recognising that he was not himself. Walker thought that he slept. Hope, in his summing-up to the jury at the trial, thought this unlikely. Gordon had frightened Walker by cocking a pistol in his presence. He had similarly scared William Reid, the gardener at Gilmerton and a man of 26 years' service to the Kinloch family. We have vivid accounts of the fear caused to both men when Gordon interviewed them in, or even merely at the door of, the borrowed bedroom in Beanston farmhouse with the pistols ready to fire. Reid's evidence also strongly suggests that, at some point during that day (the Tuesday), Gordon had ingested a vial of laudanum, the effects of which, on his condition, might not have been beneficial.

Eventually, Gordon followed Walker off his farm, the latter being acutely aware that a loaded gun was pointed at his back. As Hope commented to the jury "I am sure [the evidence of Walker and Reid] made a sufficient impression on you, and I think I may venture to say, that not one of you would have changed places with them, to be Lord of the British Empire" (p 146).

Reid, in fact, had a number of encounters with Gordon back at Gilmerton over the course of that long night. Francis requested that he try to find the pistols in Gordon's room, a task which he finally agreed, with both reluctance and trepidation, to perform. He was surprised and relieved to find Gordon civil and quiet. We discover that every door in the house had been locked against Gordon's entry, as Reid follows him round the house. Menie, the butler, was forced to make an untruthful excuse about the rooms having been newly washed in an attempt to pacify Gordon. Gordon has Reid vouch for him to Reid's own daughter who was at Gilmerton babysitting the Cunliffe children. On her father's say-so, Reid's daughter unlocks the door, but Reid has to intervene to beg Gordon not to awaken the young people.

THE FATAL INCIDENT

As far as can be gathered, the shooting occurred when Gordon, restless to the point of frenzy, had, once again, left his bedroom and stumbled downstairs to the dining-room. He left almost immediately and Francis, anxious as ever about his mental state, followed. It seems that Francis finally, at that moment, took the decision (which he had been putting off) physically to restrain Gordon in the strait-waistcoat. He caught up with Gordon on the main staircase as he was returning to his room. Francis reached for Gordon who, with one of the pistols he had hidden in his clothing, fired directly into Francis' body as the brothers grappled with each other. Both men were standing on the same stair and were therefore level with each other as Gordon fired. All others present in the house were already tense as to what Gordon might do and those who heard the shot arrived on the scene immediately thereafter. Gordon, for some reason by this time in the dining-room, was restrained and disarmed and Francis was helped to his room.

The medical evidence as to the cause of Francis's death is clear, and stated as might be expected in any murder trial. The weapons were small. Francis was killed by a shot from one of a pair of pocket firearms inscribed "H W Mortimer, London, gunmaker to his majesty". The pistol ball entered his body about three or four inches below the sternum on the right-hand side. The day after, it was found and removed by Benjamin Bell, a surgeon from Edinburgh who had been sent for immediately following the shooting. The ball had lodged towards Francis's backbone. Dr Bell felt for it with his hand and it was extracted. The accounts of witnesses who attended Francis between the shooting and his death, the next day, are consistent as to the severe pain which the injury caused him. They also attest that there was never any doubt that the wound would prove fatal relatively fast. Sir Francis Kinloch's last hours then were passed in pain, in the certainty of death and in the knowledge that his brother had caused his misfortune yet, in relation to Gordon, he said only "God Almighty help that poor unhappy man" (col 903).

THE ACCUSED'S JUSTIFICATION

Gordon's own explanation of his actions could, given the instability of his mental state, almost be regarded as cogent. He certainly held to it consistently both immediately before and after the attack. We know, from the evidence of Somner, that Gordon appeared (at least) twice in the dining-room during supper. On the first occasion, he complained of severe pains in his bowels. He attributed these to pills which had been given to him by Francis. The case report states that these were almost certainly analeptic tablets. This is far from being a term in common use today, but it is defined by the *Collins English Dictionary* to mean "restorative or invigorating". Medical dictionaries offer a second, more technical meaning – that the word relates to a drug which acts to stimulate the central nervous system such as caffeine. The effect of giving such a drug to someone in Gordon's already unstable mental state should surely have seemed, at the very least, alarmingly unpredictable – but Francis was increasingly desperate. We can only speculate as to how such medication might have interacted with the laudanum which Gordon self-administered at Beanston.

Gordon seems to have been convinced that these pills were a deliberate attempt by his brother to poison him. Immediately following the shooting, he offered the servants sent to restrain him £100 each if they would only let him live one hour, so certain did he appear to be that he was to die soon. It is not entirely clear, however, if he anticipated his demise coming at the hand of those who restrained him or from the tablets he had ingested. He told George Douglas, Janet's servant, that Francis had poisoned him, otherwise he would not have done what he did. He gave a similar account to the Reverend Goldie when he came to Gordon's room between 8 and 9 in the morning of the Wednesday, some five or six hours after the shooting. Gordon was, by then, in a supreme example of closing the stable door after the horse had bolted, confined in a strait-waistcoat and appeared to be "in a very distracted state" (col 924). In answer to a question by Goldie, he asserted vehemently that he was not horrified by what he had done to Francis. He stated that there had been a "deliberate plan formed to destroy" him (col 924) and that the pills provided to him by Francis had "already deprived [him] of the use of all the lower parts of [his] body" (col 924).

Self-defence, if successfully pled, results in acquittal. Citizens are allowed to respond to life-threatening violence in kind. Indeed, then as now, the defence could still operate if an accused person had acted even in the wholly *mistaken* belief that his life was being endangered, provided that this was "also a reasonable apprehension, and well grounded in the circumstances of the situation".[2] Knowing what we do of Francis's solicitous care of his brother, we can agree with the Reverend Goldie that any such pills would have been "given [Gordon] with a view to do him good, not to hurt him" (col 924).

Observing them on the stairs as the shooting took place, one who knew the two would have disregarded the possibility that Francis

---

2 D Hume, *Commentaries on the Law of Scotland, Respecting Crimes*, vol i, 224 (Edinburgh: The Law Society of Scotland, 1986 reprint (1844)).

sought to kill his brother; one who did not would still have taken into account that Francis was unarmed and that Gordon shot him. Gordon, then, did not have a *reasonable* belief that life-threatening violence was being offered against him. His belief arose largely from his own mental condition. His eminent defence team did not even trouble the court with the suggestion that his retaliation was justified. They, like us, were considerably more interested in his rationality – or lack of it.

THE ACTUAL DEFENCE: INSANITY

The real story here, then, both legally and from the narrative perspective, is the extent and manifestation of Gordon's mental illness. He pled insanity and he pled it to a cast of legal characters whose fame and standing within the milieu of criminal law remains high even today, 218 years later. For his defence, he had had engaged on his behalf, among others, David Hume and Charles Hope, the latter becoming the Lord Justice-Clerk in 1804, a post which he held until 1811 when he was promoted to Lord Justice-General, the highest position in the Scottish criminal justice system. Two years after Gordon's trial, his other counsel, David Hume, published the first edition of his *Commentaries on the Law of Scotland, Respecting Crimes*, unarguably the most influential work ever written on the criminal law of Scotland.

On the prosecution side, both the Lord Advocate and the Solicitor-General – in other words, those holding the highest positions in the Crown Office – appeared, as did John Burnet, advocate, who also wrote a (rather less) influential work: *A Treatise on Various Branches of the Criminal Law of Scotland*, published posthumously in 1811. Five judges sat on the bench, led by the then Lord Justice-Clerk, Robert Macqueen of Braxfield, who had already acquired notoriety and a sobriquet – "the Hanging Judge". He appears elsewhere in this volume sentencing Deacon Brodie to death. Given his reputation for cruelty and easy resort to the death penalty, it is rather surprising that he seems simply to have accepted the validity of the insanity plea which must have been, at the time, of some novelty.

The fact of the manner of Francis's death was not disputed: Gordon shot him at point-blank range. The essential legal question was very much in issue however: could Gordon be held criminally responsible for the killing? If, at the key moment, when he pulled the trigger, he had lost all rational control over his actions, then, even in 1795, he could not. The prosecution therefore sought evidence as to whether, even in the grip of mental disorder, Gordon retained the ability to distinguish right from wrong. The defence presented him as a generally disturbed soul whose mental health had deteriorated markedly, possibly as a result of his father's death.

The evidence of Gordon's altered mental state is strong. There is testimony from two former army colleagues as to the transformation in his personality. If it is to be taken at face value then, before the fever, according to Lieutenant Colonel Samuel Twentyman, "no officer was more universally esteemed and beloved than [Gordon] was throughout the whole line, by both officers and men; his generosity, good temper, sociability, and general good conduct made him very popular both in his own and other regiments" (p 69). Captain Miller expressed similar sentiments.

Following his return to Britain, however, accounts of encounters with Gordon show him to be much changed. The evidence, until the period immediately preceding the fatal incident, is led in an episodic fashion so that snapshots of Gordon's life are presented revealing a necessarily partial image of his mental state through his relationships with others.

The clearest overall picture is provided by the Lord Advocate and by Hope, in their closing speeches to the jury. It is accepted that Gordon often absented himself from Gilmerton in the 15 years between his return from the Caribbean and the fatal incident. This seems to have been his mechanism for coping with periods where his mental state was poor. Both prosecution and defence called witnesses to speak to his mindset. This provides a rich seam of information on this point.

In general, the evidence of McMillan is not particularly expressed in Gordon's favour. When asked, however, he recounts to the court an incident which he can only date to "some years ago" (col 904) where Gordon had appeared at his bedside around 5 am to state that he was going to set out, there and then, to travel to Greenock. McMillan understood that Gordon had already been travelling all night, to get from Berwick to Edinburgh. He could not dissuade him from continuing his journey and could establish only that Gordon wished to go there to see Major Mackay. From this, McMillan formed the view, which he communicated to Francis, that Gordon was insane. Two hundred and eighteen years later, it is perhaps unwise to seek to comment on the propriety of such behaviour at the time. Nonetheless, it does seem at least unusual for an individual to present himself at the bedside of an acquaintance during the hours of night merely to report that he felt impelled to continue on a journey, for which, in itself, he could offer no clear explanation.

Major John Mackay recounts the culmination of the same incident in terms of Gordon's unexpected arrival in Greenock, though he is able to date these events more precisely to the summer of 1790. He was in the coffee room (presumably of a barracks) at Greenock when Gordon arrived, having posted, he explained, all night from Berwick. He had not slept. Mackay, reasonably, wished to know the nature of the business which had rendered such an exacting journey so urgently necessary. Gordon explained that he had been driven to communicate to his "most confidential friend" (p 76) some terrible ill-treatment to which he had been subjected by his family. He brandished a letter which he appeared to believe to contain the evidence of this. Mackay, in some trepidation, we might imagine, as to its contents, read it and found it to be almost directly the opposite of Gordon's description. It was from Sandy, advising of the death of a fourth Kinloch brother, Captain David. It recounted the extreme distress of the family. It also, presumably to Mackay's surprise given Gordon's demeanour and the strangeness of his journey, expressed deep affection for Gordon and entreated him to return to Gilmerton, at the personal request of his father, as soon as possible. Unprompted Mackay told the court that the only inference he could draw from this was that Gordon was "quite deranged in his mind" (p 76).

Perhaps 1790 was a particularly difficult year for Gordon – indeed, the death of his brother may explain this – but we also have a hearsay account from the Reverend Goldie of another incident in June that year, this time in Dunbar, where a Mr Lorimer, with whom Goldie lodged, had told him of odd behaviour there on Gordon's part. He described Gordon walking restlessly about the room, beating his head and chest and ordering a chaise for Gilmerton but taking it, instead, back into Dunbar. Lorimer also considered Gordon to be deranged.

Some of this behaviour seems to be what we might term, in its non-technical sense, paranoid. Gordon presents as ill at ease with himself to the extent that he cannot remain still. He is deeply suspicious of those close to him, forming utterly baseless views that they have, in some way, wronged or targeted him. At a house party in North Berwick in 1785, he alleged, out of the blue, that Major Mackay had gone out of his way to make him the butt of the company that evening, causing Mackay such embarrassment that he felt obliged to write to both Gordon and Francis thereafter, assuring them that he had done no such thing. It is interesting that there is no indication, ever, that Gordon himself felt compelled to apologise for any of his own strange, rude and sometimes wild behaviour.

Lieutenant Colonel Samuel Twentyman was latterly posted to Lincoln. Gordon came twice to see him, apparently around the mid-1790s. On the second occasion, Gordon sent a number of messages requesting that Twentyman attend at what is described as one of the "inferior inns" (p 71) in the town. He refused to send his name with the messages but insisted that the business was particular. Eventually, Twentyman's curiosity won the day and he went as asked. He was astounded to discover that the sender of the cryptic messages was, in fact, Gordon. Having checked that the door to his room in the inn was fastened, Gordon then told Twentyman a long and rambling tale apparently about various projects in which he was involved, "flying from one thing to another in the most incoherent manner" so that Twentyman found it all "totally unintelligible" (p 72). Gordon dined with Twentyman that evening and took an absolutely groundless exception to a fellow guest being, initially, rude and boisterous towards him. Perhaps the hapless man, a Colonel Gardiner, would have preferred that Gordon had simply continued in that way because, before the evening was over, Gordon leapt up from his place, threw his arms around Gardiner's neck and kissed him.

While it must be noted that both Mackay and Twentyman appeared for the defence, none of this appears like the behaviour of a rational person and even the prosecution did not seek to argue that it was. Its line was considerably more legal than that: it sought to ascertain whether Gordon, even in the midst of apparent derangement, was still able to discern good from evil and to understand that murder was a crime. The chief legal interest here, then, is the definition of insanity brought forth in 1795.

For 215 years, until June 2012, the definition of insanity in Scots law was as follows:

> the disorder must ... amount to an absolute alienation of reason ..., – such a disease as deprives the patient of the knowledge of the true aspect and position of things about him, – hinders him from distinguishing friend or foe, – and gives him up to the impulse of his own distempered fancy.[3]

This definition was written by Gordon's defence counsel, David Hume, and it is striking how closely it fits with the facts of the Kinloch case, particularly the inability to distinguish friend or foe. Francis was, in reality, Gordon's greatest friend but Gordon, unable to recognise this,

---

3 Hume, *Commentaries on the Law of Scotland, Respecting Crimes*, vol i, 37.

committed against him a crime, as one of the judges, Lord Eskgrove, stated, "of the deepest dye" (p 153).

Insanity was, and remains, a question for the jury to determine. Scotland, uniquely, employs a jury of 15. In 1795 they were all male – either landowners or businessmen. It is noticeable that the trial continued into the night. The Lord Advocate commenced his closing speech around 4.30 am. The jury returned its verdict about 7.35 am, after 35 minutes' deliberation: Gordon had killed Francis as set out in the indictment but, at the time he was "insane, and deprived of his reason" (p 152).

ASSESSING THE EVIDENCE

So what, then, are we to make of this strange, sad case? We can certainly lament, with Gordon himself, the well-intentioned indecision which continually drew back from restraining him in the strait-waistcoat and placing him under the care of the nurse, already ensconced at Gilmerton, who sometimes looked after mad people.

Those used to the structure of the modern-day crime drama might wish to examine more closely Gordon's actions in relation to his mindset and motives. At the moment of Francis's death, on Thursday, 16 April 1795, Gordon inherited the house and estate of Gilmerton and the title of 7th Baronet. Is there the faintest possibility that he somehow managed to simulate absolute alienation of his reason so that this could come to pass? The closest examination of the evidence suggests that this conclusion – and there are strong hints in Hume's opening address that plenty in Scotland held to it at the time – is unlikely. That Gordon's mental health was, at best, variable, in the years following his dreadful fever, is beyond question. Almost all who knew him seemed able to offer some example of paranoid, rude or simply bizarre behaviour. Even the prosecution accepted that, on at least one previous occasion, his mental health surrounding a suicide attempt (he had cut his wrist very deeply) did amount to total madness.

Bereavement affects those who are not otherwise afflicted in profound ways. For someone of a decidedly paranoid, melancholy disposition like Gordon, the death of his father, to whom he had been devoted, less than two months previously must have been all but unbearable. His behaviour, always odd, had become increasingly strange and disturbing in the days before the incident. Aristocratic families of the time were not in the habit of confining their members in straitjackets under the care of insanity nurses without demonstration of the most profound need. In Gordon's case, all of the evidence was there. It was not pieced together in time to save Francis's life, but it did, eventually, save Gordon's own.

THE FINAL DENOUEMENT

The matter was not settled even once the jurymen had returned the verdict however. Gordon was clearly found not guilty and emerged from the trial process, as a result, legally without a stain or blemish on his character. Nonetheless, the troublesome fact remained that he had killed his brother and that he had done so in the grip of insanity. There was, at least, a lingering risk that he might commit a similar act of violence at some time in the future. The legal process had no pretensions towards a therapeutic outcome, but it was concerned directly with the public safety issue thus arising. It is of interest that the solution adopted is not regarded as innovative. Lord Eskgrove, who first moots it, speaks of the "various adjudged cases standing in your records ... where the insanity of the perpetrator at the time of the act was found sufficient to excuse from punishment" (col 1000). In fact, however, the judgment delivered must surely have seemed punitive to Gordon. He was sentenced to be detained in the Tolbooth of Edinburgh "during all the days of his life" (col 1002) unless £10,000 caution was lodged. If that was done, Gordon could be released into the custody of the friend who vouched for him in this way. It is not a particularly straightforward exercise to establish the current equivalent value of such a sum, but the National Archives' currency converter indicates that £10,000 in 1790 would be worth about £560,300 (in 2005 terms). In 1800, the same sum (again in 2005) would be valued at £321,700. A very good friend would be required.

Sir Gordon Kinloch of Gilmerton had such a friend. He may have had many, but the surviving record lists only the one who took responsibility for him, for his parlous mental state and for the risk of commission by him of a further erratic and fatal action of the type of which he had, so tragically, proved himself capable. This friend was the doctor who had attended him in his previous derangement on the occasion when he had attempted to take his own life by lacerating his wrist: Dr William Farquharson, surgeon in Edinburgh. Part of his undertaking was to keep Gordon properly confined for the rest of his life. In the event, that period was short. Gordon died five years later, in 1800.

The Sheriff in the Heather:
Beaton v Ivory

Elspeth Reid*

The case of *Beaton v Ivory*[1] comes from one of the most remote locations in the Scottish law reports – the township of Herbusta in the Kilmuir Estate on the north-western tip of the Isle of Skye. Against the dramatic backdrop of the Trotternish ridge, Herbusta looks west over the Minch towards the mountains of Harris. Immediately to the north is the windswept Kilmuir graveyard where Skye's most famous daughter, Flora Macdonald, lies buried. Today, Herbusta is extraordinarily tranquil, but on 27 October 1886 the scene was very different. On that day, Sheriff William Ivory led a force of 70 police and troops into the township, bent on rounding up the ringleaders of a riot that had taken place two days previously. On failing to locate the rioters, he ordered the arrest of John Beaton, one of the very few men left in Herbusta that afternoon. After being imprisoned for three days and released without charge, Beaton made an unsuccessful claim against Ivory for wrongful arrest. It was a litigation in which the backgrounds of the parties could not have been more different. Beaton was the cowherd for this remote community; Ivory, on the other hand, was, as Sheriff of Inverness, Elgin and Nairn, the most senior judge presiding over the courts in this area.[2] *Beaton v Ivory* became one of the leading Scots cases in this area of law, but, although it has been cited regularly in the courts right up into the 21st century,[3] scant regard has been paid to the significance of the troubled times in which it was set.

* The author wishes to express her thanks to the staff of the Skye and Lochalsh Archive Centre, Portree for their kind assistance.

1 (1887) 14 R 1057.
2 Also son of Lord Ivory, Court of Session judge, and father of James, accountant and founder of Ivory and Sime investment managers, and Holmes, prominent Edinburgh lawyer.
3 Eg *Mckie v Orr* 2003 SC 317.

THE CROFTERS' WAR IN SKYE

The 1880s were the period of the "Crofters' War" in Skye.[4] The fundamental source of grievance for the crofter-fishermen of the north-west was that, despite emigration, land distribution was increasingly inadequate. The subdivision of crofting land between families reduced its quality and diminished its capacity to sustain the population and its livestock. At the same time, rents continued to rise, even although much of the better land had been lost to create larger farms, often to graze sheep, or in some cases to create lucrative shooting tenancies.[5] As the *Glasgow Herald* "special correspondent" reported from Kilmuir: "The pitiable condition of the people – the hovels in which they are housed, the sterile soil from which, with much toil, they scrape a scanty sustenance – combined with the gradual limitation of privileges ... which they formerly enjoyed, have reduced the crofters almost to despair."[6] And while the Irish had their Land Reform Act in 1881, legislative intervention was not yet promised in Scotland. Indeed it seems plausible to link growing unrest in Scotland to an awareness of progress on land issues elsewhere,[7] but Irish influence should not be overestimated.[8] Local causes for discontent in the Scottish crofting counties were ample and pressing and the proponents of reform found vocal support nearer to home.

The owner of the Kilmuir Estate, Captain William Fraser, had acquired a reputation for want of sympathy that marked him out even from the other Skye landlords. A revaluation of the land on his estate in 1876 had resulted in swingeing rent increases the following year. The tenants' opposition was vehement, and indeed when, in October 1877, a storm of biblical force devastated Uig Lodge, Fraser's Skye residence, *The Highlander* newspaper suggested divine retribution.[9] The publicity generated by this dispute led to the

---

4 I M M MacPhail, *The Crofters' War* (1989), pp 1–5.
5 A Mackenzie, *The Isle of Skye in 1882–1883* (1883).
6 *Glasgow Herald*, 22 April 1882, p 5.
7 See MacPhail, *The Crofters' War*, p 5.
8 On "willingness to see malign Irish hands behind every unwelcome development", see E Cameron, "Communication or Separation? Reactions to Irish Land Agitation and Legislation in the Highlands of Scotland, c. 1870–1910" (2005) vol CXX, no 487, *English Historical Review* 633 at 665.
9 On Fraser's action for verbal injury, see *The Scotsman*, 12 April 1878; the defender's account is at J Hunter (ed), *For the People's Cause: From the Writings of John Murdoch* (1986), pp 156–158.

formation of the "Skye Vigilance Committee" in Glasgow in May 1881, pledged to "watch the future dealings of Captain Fraser".[10]

But there was unrest too in other areas of the island. In Glendale, grievances over grazing land escalated into more serious disturbances towards the end of 1882.[11] And perhaps the most famous incident in the Crofters' War was the so-called "Battle of Braes", fought on the Braes peninsula not far from Portree. The immediate *casus belli* was a dispute with the landlord, Lord MacDonald, concerning common pasturage turned over to sheep-farming. When the aggrieved tenants withheld rent, a sheriff officer was sent in to serve summons to remove them. He was met by a crowd who seized the summonses and burned them, then sent him and his colleagues back to Portree, unharmed, but in little doubt as to the contempt in which these legal documents were held. In response, Sheriff Ivory requested reinforcements for the local constabulary, and an additional 50 officers were drafted into Skye from Glasgow and Inverness. On 19 April 1882, this brigade marched on Braes, through torrential rain, to arrest the ring-leaders of the earlier disturbance. Five crofters so identified were arrested,[12] but the local populace swiftly assembled, and attempted, with sticks and stones, to resist the prisoners' removal. The ensuing stramash, resulting in several serious injuries although no fatalities, was widely reported,[13] and came to be regarded as one of the defining moments of the crofters' campaign.[14]

10 Fraser ultimately conceded errors in the 1876 valuation: MacPhail, *The Crofters' War*, p 33; D W Crowley, "The 'Crofters' Party', 1885–1892" (1956) 35 *Scottish Historical Review* 110 at 112.

11 See *MacLeod's Trustees v Macpherson* (1883) 10 R 792. The crofters defied an interdict excluding them from the disputed ground and forced the retreat of police sent to restore order. Five ring-leaders eventually served two months' imprisonment for breach of interdict, but met a heroes' welcome on release from Edinburgh's Calton Jail (*The Scotsman*, 16 May 1883, p 10). One of the "Glendale Martyrs", John MacPherson, continued campaigning eloquently for land reform: for his evidence to the Napier Commission (n 21 below), see vol 1, paras 6500–6814.

12 For a transcript of their trial, see A Mackenzie, *The Isle of Skye in 1882–1883*, pp 36–89; *The Scotsman*, 12 May 1882, p 6. All were convicted, although on a charge of simple assault, with trifling penalties, not the serious charge of deforcement.

13 A Mackenzie, *The Isle of Skye in 1882–1883*, pp 32–33. Various newspaper correspondents followed the expedition: see, eg *Glasgow Herald*, 20 April 1882, p 5; *The Times*, 20 April 1882, p 6.

14 See J Hunter, "The Scottish Land Court's Revolutionary Origins" in *No Ordinary Court: 100 Years of the Scottish Land Court* (2012) 1 at 10, tracing the Court's origins to this "Battle"; also the Court's website at http://www.scottish-land-court.org.uk/centenary.html.

An important feature of the Battle of Braes was that the force was commanded on the ground by the intrepid Sheriff Ivory himself. From a modern perspective, the propriety of a sheriff placing himself at the head of a combined police and military force might seem questionable, but, aside from his judicial functions, superintending the local police force was one of the regular administrative duties of the sheriff of that era. The Police Scotland Act 1857 provided that chief constables directed their forces subject to the sheriff's orders,[15] and sheriffs also had common law powers to preserve order by calling in military force.[16] Indeed, it was they who were empowered to "read" the Riot Act of 1714, still in force at this time. Sheriff Ivory could not therefore be regarded as having exceeded his powers simply by virtue of leading the march across the heather to Braes. Nonetheless, it was highly unusual by the 1880s for sheriffs to adopt such an active role in quelling unrest,[17] and Sheriff Ivory's behaviour could hardly be regarded as conciliatory in the tense situation then overtaking Skye.

The Napier Commission

By the early 1880s the troubles in Skye were capturing headlines not only locally but in the national press,[18] and on the mainland the Highland Land Law Reform Association was campaigning vigorously for the crofting cause.[19] Finally, the Home Secretary, Sir William Harcourt, announced on 19 March 1883 the appointment of a Royal Commission, chaired by Lord Napier, "To inquire into the condition of the crofters and cottars in the Highlands and Islands of Scotland".[20]

---

15 S VI. (Cf Police and Fire Reform (Scotland) Act 2012, s 17(3).)

16 J C Dove Wilson, "Sheriff; Sheriff Court" in J Chisholm (ed), *Green's Encyclopaedia of the Law of Scotland* (1st edn), vol 11 (1899), 305 at 324.

17 A notable 19th-century example was Archibald Alison, Sheriff of Lanarkshire, summoning the cavalry in 1835 to control sectarian violence, and in 1837 to assist during a general strike, himself heading the force that arrested the ringleaders: A Alison, *Some Account of My Life and Writings: An Autobiography* (Lady Alison (ed) 1883) vol 1, pp 359–361, 369–385.

18 Eg *The Times*, 24 April 1882, p 11 (Editorial): "Even should we hear no more of riots in Skye, the disturbances which have occurred ought not to be forgotten ... we have had a sharp lesson as to the impolicy of allowing such evils to accumulate."

19 For its 1884 manifesto, see MacPhail, *The Crofters' War*, p 97.

20 Hansard HC 19 April 1883, 3rd series, vol 277, cols 796–797. Lord Napier was a Borders landowner and former diplomat. The Commission's other members were Sir Kenneth Mackenzie, Lord Lieutenant of Ross and Cromarty, Donald Cameron of Lochiel, former diplomat and Tory MP for Inverness, Charles

Over the ensuing months, the members of the Napier Commission toured the crofting counties hearing evidence from over 700 witnesses and producing a 4,000-word report,[21] but the sentiments of the very first witness, Angus Stewart from Braes,[22] were echoed by most of those crofters who followed:[23]

> The smallness of our holdings and the inferior quality of the land is what has caused our poverty; and the way in which the poor crofters are huddled together, and the best part of the land devoted to deer forests and big farms. If we had plenty of land there would be no poverty in our country. We are willing and able to work it.

The testimony from the Kilmuir estate underlined similar concerns: the essential problem was the insufficiency of crofting land, both in extent and in quality.[24]

The Napier Commission reported in 1884, although not unanimously.[25] Its recommendations – to create greater security of tenure and community management of the townships – were criticised by the landowners as too radical,[26] and by the crofting lobby as falling short of what had been achieved in Ireland. The result was political stalemate.[27] Disappointed expectations and impatience at government inaction led to renewed agitation in the crofting community, withholding of rent, and appropriation of grazing. In November 1884, in the face of growing lawlessness across the island, including in

Fraser Mackintosh, MP for the Inverness Burghs, Sheriff Nicolson, Skyeman and Sheriff at Kirkcudbright, and Donald MacKinnon, Professor of Celtic at Edinburgh University.

21 Report of Her Majesty's Commissioners of Inquiry into the Condition of the Crofters and Cottars in the Highlands and Islands of Scotland C.3980-I, C.3980-II, C.3980-III, C.3980-IV, vols XXXII.1, XXXIII.1, XXXIV.1, XXXV.1, XXXVI.1 (1884).

22 Stewart's croft became, much later, the home of the poet, Sorley MacLean: J Hunter (n 14 supra) at p 6.

23 Note 21 above, "Minutes of Evidence", para 23.

24 Donald Beaton from Herbusta argued for security against evictions and rent increases, land valuation by the Government, and access to hill pasture. Despite loss of pasture his rent increased from £5/15/- in 1864 to £8/10/- in 1880, and only one of the eight Herbusta families had paid the previous year's rent in full (Napier Commission, n 21 above, "Minutes of Evidence", paras 2188–2243).

25 Mackenzie and Cameron dissented on issues of land management (n 21 above, vol I, pp 113 and 119).

26 See, eg, Duke of Argyll, "A Corrected Picture of the Highlands" (1884) 16 *Nineteenth Century* 681.

27 For analysis, see E Cameron, *Land for the People* (1996), pp 17–28; J A Cameron, "Storm Clouds in the Highlands" (1884) 16 *Nineteenth Century* 379.

particular on the Kilmuir Estate, Sheriff Ivory succeeded in persuading the Lord Advocate, Sir John Balfour, that two gunboats and 350 marines should be sent to Skye.[28] This expedition was attended by a press corps of sixteen reporters and two newspaper artists;[29] the crofting disturbances of this period, as well as Sheriff Ivory's response thereto, were increasingly the focus of a highly visible media campaign.

After some weeks, the military departed Skye without significant confrontation, but without resolution of the problems that had brought them there.[30] It was not until 25 June 1886 that the Crofters' Holdings (Scotland) Act 1886 was passed,[31] providing for a degree of security of tenure, compensation for improvements made by the tenant, and limited possibilities for groups of crofters to extend holdings.[32] Very importantly, it also established the Crofters' Commission, empowered to fix fair rents and to adjust arrears.[33] The Crofters' Commission was rapidly constituted, chaired by Sheriff David Brand of Ayr, and in future years it was to reduce rent and arrears by significant amounts,[34] but its procedures could not be initiated immediately, and it was not scheduled to reach Skye until March 1887.[35] In the closing months of 1886, therefore, the situation on the island remained fraught.

Continuing unrest on the Kilmuir Estate

While in 1880 the level of bad debt on the Kilmuir Estate was negligible, by the mid-1880s widespread default on rent was creating serious problems. In June 1880, rent arrears stood at £63/3/7½, with only £2/12/6 marked as bad debt.[36] By March 1885, the estate manager

28 Papers relating to Despatch of Government Force to Skye (C 1257, 1884).
29 MacPhail, *The Crofters' War*, p 117.
30 John MacKenzie, Kilmuir Estate manager, reported the crofters would "pay no Rents at present until a Bill is brought in to Parliament on their behalf" (letter to Fraser of 7 March 1885). By 12 September 1885, MacKenzie could not "convince them to pay a penny", especially with "agitators making out to the tenants Government will pay the arrears for them as was done in Ireland" (Skye and Lochalsh Archive, Christie & Ferguson papers, GB3219/D123/2).
31 On the making of the 1886 Act, see Cameron, *Land for the People*, pp 28–39.
32 Sections 1–2, 8–9 and 11–13 respectively.
33 Sections 6 and 17.
34 In 1887, the Commission reduced Kilmuir rents by one-third and cancelled two-thirds of arrears (I M M MacPhail, *The Crofters' War*, p 199).
35 MacPhail, *The Crofters War*, pp 178–180.
36 Statement by Fraser to Crofters' Commission 20 April 1887, Skye and Lochalsh Archive, Inverness County Council Records, SL/D123/37.

had listed 72 tenants to receive a summons for non-payment of rent,[37] and, by early 1887, arrears totalled £10,000, with only £16 paid for the last quarter.[38] Meanwhile, as a result of this diminishing cash flow, Fraser, like other landlords, was himself being pursued for unpaid rates and tax bills, and since, increasingly, neither crofters nor landlords were paying rates, the funds were drying up for public services such as schools and poor relief. The archive of the Kilmuir factor, Alexander Macdonald, contains letters of demand from the Inland Revenue during this period, as well as increasingly urgent correspondence regarding collection of rent arrears[39] in anticipation that, when it eventually arrived in Skye, the Crofters' Commission might adjust the amount owed.[40] But increasingly, not only were the tenants resisting the service of summonses or notices to quit, the sheriff officers themselves were refusing to go into the townships where they feared for their personal safety.[41]

A general election in July 1886 resulted in the defeat of the Gladstone administration and the return of a Conservative government. While Sheriff Ivory's renewed requests for military support had earlier met a dusty response, the incoming Secretary of State for Scotland, Arthur Balfour, immediately declared his commitment "to restore to something like law and order the disturbed districts of the Western Highlands and Islands".[42] Almost as soon as he took office he authorised 250 marines and 50 police to be sent to Tiree, and in October 1886 a further contingent of marines was despatched to Skye.

EVENTS OF 27 OCTOBER 1886

Official intransigence, and determined resistance in the crofting community, thus form the background to the events of 27 October 1886. Two days previously, a sheriff officer supported by police had

---

37 Christie & Ferguson papers, GB3219/D123/2.
38 Statement to the Crofters' Commission 20 April 1887.
39 Christie & Ferguson papers, GB3219/D123/2. There was also discussion of a dispute over grazing at Garrafad. Interdict against the tenants and their minister was refused in the local sheriff court, but Sheriff Ivory and the Court of Session found for the landlord on appeal: *Macleod v Davidson* (1886) 14 R 92.
40 See *Fraser v Macdonald* (1886) 14 R 181: ordinary courts' jurisdiction to grant decree against tenants for non-payment of rent not suspended by tenant's application to the Crofters' Commission to fix a fair rent and adjudicate arrears.
41 J Hunter, *The Making of the Crofting Community* (rev edn, 2010), p 213.
42 Hansard HC 31 August 1886, 3rd series, vol 308, col 955.

been sent to the township of Bornaskitaig, adjacent to Herbusta, to serve summonses on various crofters for non-payment of rent. They met with vigorous resistance from a large jeering crowd throwing missiles and clods of manure, although no significant injury was inflicted. It was only by summoning the marines, who advanced with fixed bayonets, that the party was able to retreat, taking with them six of the ringleaders of the affray. Meanwhile, across the moor in Herbusta, Sheriff Officer Alexander Macdonald[43] had met with similar opposition in attempting to serve summonses for non-payment of rates.

In response, a combined force of 70 police and military personnel was mustered to round up those responsible, and once again it was led in person by Sheriff Ivory. No arrest warrants had been prepared because Macdonald had not been able to put a name to the miscreants two days previously, but he was in attendance, confident that he would recognise the faces of suspects. The party left Portree at 7 in the morning of 27 October on the gunboat, *Seahorse*, sailing round the Trotternish peninsula in clear weather, so that, by the time that it reached shore in Duntulm Bay, sentinels posted along the hills had given the local residents generous warning of its arrival. In the account of the *Glasgow Herald* reporter,[44] the force made a leisurely pace across the moor, going first to Bornaskitaig which it found deserted. All the men had taken to the hills, leaving only women and children in the village, mostly behind closed doors. Herbusta was similarly abandoned. The party found neither the suspected rioters nor anyone who could assist in ascertaining their whereabouts. As the troop paused to consider, a lone figure was spotted on the hillside. This was John Beaton, then in his late forties,[45] who as the local herdsman remained to mind the cattle. Sheriff Ivory, in exasperation, ordered that Beaton should be brought down from the hill, and that "every blessed place"[46] in the township was to be searched. Beaton offered no resistance, but his explanation that he had not been present at the riot was corroborated by other witnesses. For a further two hours, Sheriff Ivory ordered his men to comb the township. As an incentive, he produced one of the special medals[47] that he personally had commissioned earlier

---

43 Sheriff Officer Macdonald later achieved notoriety for poinding a cradle, with infant occupant, as a job lot valued at 6d: see *Glasgow Herald*, 26 November 1886, p 7.
44 *Glasgow Herald*, 28 October 1886, p 7.
45 Census of 1881 gives his age as 43.
46 *Glasgow Herald*, 28 October 1886, p 7.
47 With the inscription: "For zeal and activity. From Sheriff Ivory".

that year to reward police officers who arrested rioting crofters, promising that this would be awarded to any arresting officer that day. Despite this inducement, the only other arrest made was of a young woman, whom Macdonald pointed out as a rioter, although she strenuously denied involvement. Beaton meantime calmly smoked his pipe, accepted from his wife a change of clothes to go to Portree, and called out as he was led away that someone should mind the cows.[48]

Having taken just two prisoners – one middle-aged man and one young woman – the 70-man detachment then set off again in the late afternoon, stopping, just in case, at the Kilmuir graveyard to search (in vain) among the tombstones for stragglers. The prisoners were marched down to the shore to the *Seahorse*, and taken to Portree. Other arrests were made later and charges were brought against the Bornaskitaig and the Herbusta rioters,[49] but Beaton himself was questioned briefly by the sheriff-substitute, detained in Portree Prison for three days, then released without charge and without explanation.

Before setting out to walk the 25 miles home to Herbusta, however, Beaton apparently made enquiries in Portree on obtaining compensation. Although a local law agent reportedly counselled him that "he had better leave matters as they are",[50] others further afield plainly advised him differently. The Skye disturbances had been extensively reported locally and nationally, and various funds had been established to assist the crofters with the legal costs of the Crofters' War. In particular, the *North British Daily Mail*, owned by Dr Charles Cameron, a Liberal MP, launched a "Crofters Rights Vindication Fund" in November 1886, and a specific appeal for the fund was published in the issue of 12 March 1887. It seems likely, therefore, that Beaton received not only funds but advice and support from this quarter.

PROCEEDINGS IN BEATON v IVORY

So it was that John Beaton raised an action in the Court of Session against William Ivory claiming £500 in damages for wrongful arrest

---

48 *Glasgow Herald*, 28 October 1886, p 7.
49 The Herbusta accused included Donald Beaton, Napier Commission witness (n 24 above). Their trial, on charges of mobbing, rioting and deforcing a sheriff officer, is reported in *The Scotsman*, 4 January 1887, p 7. The jury found them guilty but, given "no excess of violence", requested "utmost leniency".
50 *Glasgow Herald*, 1 November 1886, p 7.

and detention. Beaton had engaged John Comrie Thomson as his advocate.[51] Ivory attempted unsuccessfully to persuade first the Lord Advocate and then the Solicitor General to conduct his defence in the case, but was eventually represented by William Mackintosh, Dean of the Faculty of Advocates.[52] The case was heard on the Procedure Roll before Lord Fraser in the Outer House on 19 May 1887 for preliminary discussion on the relevancy of its legal issues.[53] The defence was that, even without a written warrant, no wrong was committed by Ivory in ordering Beaton's arrest where he had "probable cause" to suspect that an offence had been committed and he had acted without "malice". Probable cause, counsel argued, was suggested by the disturbances two days previously, and personal malice was contradicted by the non-specific nature of the sheriff's instructions to round up all men found in Herbusta. The pursuer, on the other hand, doubted it could be "right that because a crime had been committed in a certain township policemen were to scour the country and bring in any man that they saw": the defender was obliged "to use his official powers with discretion".[54]

Lord Fraser ruled that want of probable cause and malice were both essential requirements in a case of this nature. Malice, in his interpretation, could not be established if, as accepted by both sides, the defender had issued "general instructions" to apprehend all in the township, "unless indeed it be meant to be averred that the Sheriff had malice against the whole population of crofters". The action was therefore dismissed as irrelevant, with Lord Fraser reflecting that "If the chief magistrate of a county ... were to lie under the threat of actions of damages for what he did in the bona fide execution of his duty, the result would be that his powers to quash tumult and insurrection would be altogether paralysed."[55]

Beaton appealed to the Inner House. On the matter of probable cause, his counsel's argument was that if, as here, an arrest was ordered without a warrant:[56]

51 Comrie Thomson was to have a highly successful practice. One of his best-known cases was *HM Advocate v Monson* (1893) 21 R (J) 5, the "Ardlamont murder", in which his defence secured a verdict of not proven, notwithstanding apparently damning circumstantial evidence.
52 Later to become Lord Kyllachy.
53 See *The Scotsman*, 20 May 1887, p 7. Arguments were also heard on the relevancy of the defamation action by Norman Stewart of Valtos claiming Ivory had dubbed him the Skye "Parnell". That action was held relevant but settled on Stewart accepting Ivory's tender of £25: *The Scotsman*, 1 July 1887, p 8.
54 Report at *The Scotsman*, 20 May 1887, p 7.
55 (1887) 14 R 1057 at 1059.
56 At pp 1059–1060.

[I]t must be because the person to be apprehended had been seen in the act of committing a crime, or there was reasonable ground for believing that he had committed a crime. But a general order to apprehend all persons in a locality was very different. There was therefore a *prima facie* case for an issue of this kind, viz, whether the pursuer was apprehended by order of the defender wrongfully and illegally given.

On the question of malice he reasoned that:[57]

[I]t was not necessary to aver or prove personal malice. If a reckless disregard of the rights and liberties of others was proved, that was enough. What was done here by the defender was in itself illegal. If it had been legal, but carried out in a harsh and oppressive way, then no doubt the pursuer would have been obliged to take an issue of malice, and facts must have been averred from which to deduce the malice.

The appeal was nonetheless unsuccessful. Lord President Inglis recognised "a kind of recklessness ... about an order that everybody in a locality should be apprehended".[58] But the sticking point, as in the Outer House, was the court's insistence that it was necessary to prove *both* want of probable cause *and* malice, and, reflecting on the meaning of malice in this context, Lord President Inglis stated:[59]

The presumption in favour of a public officer that he is doing no more than his duty, and doing it honestly and *bona fide*, is a very strong one, and certainly ought not to be overcome by the simple use of the word "malice". I think the duty of the pursuer in a case of this kind is to aver facts and circumstances, from which the Court or a jury may legitimately infer that the defender was not acting in the ordinary discharge of his duty, but from an improper or malicious motive.

Again, the agreed circumstance that Ivory had ordered the arrest of everyone in sight in Herbusta was inconsistent with personal malice in this sense. In effect, the indiscriminate nature of the sheriff's orders – the aspect of his conduct most problematic to modern eyes – was the very quality that put it beyond challenge and precluded further enquiry into its reasonableness or proportionality.

Moreover, in legal usage "malice in fact" has traditionally been distinguished from "malice in law"; the former takes the literal sense of being motivated by "ill will against a person", whereas the latter is inferred from "a wrongful act, done intentionally, without just cause or excuse" – in effect collapsing into the general notion of deliberate

57 At p 1060.
58 At p 1061.
59 At p 1061.

conduct normally understood in all the intentional delicts.[60] The Lord President's judgment emphasised the need for malice in this more pointed first sense – that the defender was inspired by malicious motive against the pursuer in particular. In practice, this conferred a near-absolute degree of privilege on the defender. Cases of this type typically arise between strangers, as in *Beaton*, so that any question of personal animosity is often absurd, but in any event it is extraordinarily difficult to prove subjective motivation even on the part of individuals with whom one has a prior acquaintance.[61] The malice requirement thus formulated was therefore to present an insurmountable hurdle not only for Beaton but also for future litigants referred to Lord President Inglis' dictum.

But should malice have been insisted upon, and if so, was malice correctly understood?

MALICE AND WRONGFUL ARREST

Then as now, in intentional wrongs against the person, such as assault or deprivation of liberty, malice in a general sense was most often inferred without specific enquiry.[62] The requirement specifically to prove malice reasserted itself only in circumstances which were somehow privileged, the context of law enforcement being a prime example. In the 19th century, as in the 20th, malice was thus a necessary ingredient in civil wrongs that constituted abuse of process, such as malicious prosecution or malicious use of diligence,[63] and the court in *Beaton* had taken note of several cases of this type.[64] The court also observed that malice was an essential element in judicial slander,[65] as well as in reparation cases brought against members of the public

---

60 *Bromage v Prosser* (1825) 4 B & C 247 at 255 per Bayley J; *Ferguson v Earl of Kinnoul* (1842) 1 Bell 662 at 730 per Lord Campbell; *Shields v Shearer* 1914 SC (HL) 33 at 35 per Lord Dunedin; G Fridman, "Malice in the Law of Torts" (1958) 21 MLR 484.
61 See eg *Mckie v Orr* 2003 SC 317 for problems of establishing malice on the part of former colleagues.
62 Bell, Principles, § 2044; R H Maconochie, "Malice", in Lord Dunedin (ed), *Encyclopaedia of the Laws of Scotland*, vol 9 (1930) 361 at 363; F Pollock, *The Law of Torts* (1st edn, 1887) p 236.
63 In English law too, abuse of process was one of the "few" torts requiring proof of malice: Pollock, *The Law of Torts*, p 264.
64 *Arbuckle v Taylor* (1815) 3 Dow 160 (second defender); *Rae v Linton* (1875) 2 R 669. Cf *Craig v Peebles* (1876) 3 R 441 (notwithstanding malice, action must fail where there *had* been probable cause).
65 *Scott v Turnbull* (1884) 11 R 1131.

whose complaints to the police had resulted in an innocent person being detained.[66] Public order required that individuals should be able to report suspected crime without undue fear of litigation. An analogy could be drawn therefore with cases of alleged defamation, which were protected by privilege where the individual had a social duty to report information and the recipient had an interest to receive it.[67] But the circumstances of *Beaton v Ivory* did not fall into any of these specific privileged categories.

Beaton v Ivory presented a case of alleged wrongful arrest without a warrant – not slander, nor malicious or wrongful prosecution, since no proceedings had been brought against Beaton. The basic rule in relation to arrest was simply stated in the Scots textbooks of the period: "where the [arrest] warrant is legal and regular, the party cannot claim damages, unless he avers and puts in issue malice and want of probable cause; but … he will not be obliged to do this where there was no warrant, or the warrant was illegal."[68] This was essentially the same general rule to be found in the contemporary English commentaries. Arrests might be made without warrant only where there was "probable cause" to suspect that an offence had been or was about to be committed, and any questions of wrongful intention were subsumed into the enquiry as to cause.[69] Without "probable cause", the arresting officer's actions could not be regarded as privileged, and the arrest was prima facie actionable, although very considerable latitude might be allowed in determining what constituted "probable cause".[70] There is nothing in the Scots case law cited in *Beaton v Ivory* to suggest that the Scots practice up until that point had been significantly different.

---

66 *Arbuckle v Taylor* (1815) 3 Dow 160 (first defender); (1880) 8 R 31; *Denholm v Thomson* (1880) 8 R 31; *Hassan v Paterson* (1885) 12 R 1164.

67 *M'Murchy v Campbell* (1887) 14 R 725; *Bayne v Macgregor* (1863) 1 M 615; *Urquhart v Grigor* (1864) 3 M 283; *Cameron v Hamilton* (1856) 18 D 423.

68 J Badenach Nicolson in his 1871 edition of Erskine, *Institute*, 4.4.31, note (a); also Bell, *Principles*, §§ 2036–2040. As noted by Lord Fraser at 1059, sheriffs witnessing an offence had common law powers to have the offender arrested, or could do so on receiving a report of an offence, where there was "certain knowledge of the fact, and the person of the offender" and a likelihood of escape (David Hume, *Commentaries on the Criminal Law of Scotland* (3rd edn, 1829), vol 2, 75). But Ivory had not seen Beaton offending, there was no "certain knowledge" linking him to the riots, and Beaton showed no inclination to abscond.

69 See eg C G Addison, *Addison on Torts: A Treatise on Wrongs and their Remedies* (6th edn by H Smith, 1887), p 151.

70 Pollock, *The Law of Torts*, pp 192–193; *Hogg v Ward* (1858) 3 H & N 417, 157 ER 533.

In short, therefore, the assertion by the court of a malice requirement in cases of arrest without probable cause was not clearly supported by the earlier cases to which the court referred. And there was no authority for a rule of general application, beyond the contexts already noted, insisting that malice be proved in all claims brought against "public officers" purporting to do their "duty" even if acting recklessly.

Even if it were accepted that malice was an essential element, it is doubtful that this should have been understood in the exacting sense of "malice in fact", as distinct from "malice in law". The authorities cited in *Beaton v Ivory* had pointed to the latter meaning in this context.[71] In a recent case, malice had been understood as "not necessarily personal hostility or ill-will, but ... a thing done against duty, with a reckless disregard of an individual's interests or feelings will, in the sense of the law, be a thing done maliciously".[72] This meant that it was "necessary for the party aggrieved to shew that the act complained of was maliciously done – in other words, with undue disregard to the rights of persons".[73]

It is of course by no means self-evident that Beaton's claim would have succeeded had the court not demanded that malice be present and had the case been allowed to turn on the question of probable cause for the sheriff's actions. The court clearly viewed the earlier riots as "of a very serious character",[74] and there was considerable sympathy for providing a "shield" for public officials in such circumstances.[75] Nonetheless, at a time when the founder of the Irish Land League was addressing the disaffected crofters of Skye,[76] and controversy surrounding Ivory's conduct was growing, it was certainly convenient that insistence upon "malice in fact" effectively eliminated the need for further examination of the reasonableness of his conduct.

71 See eg *Hassan v Paterson* (1885) 12 R 1164.
72 *Urquhart v Dick* (1865) 3 M 932 at 934 per Lord Kinloch; also *Cameron v Hamilton* (1856) 18 D 423 at 427 per Lord Deas: "Actual malice – that is personal enmity ... – is not necessary. Gross recklessness and culpa lata are enough. The want of probable cause goes deep into the question of malice as thus defined."
73 *Denholm v Thomson* (1880) 8 R 31 at 33, per Lord Moncreiff.
74 Lord President Inglis at 1061.
75 Lord Shand at 1063.
76 Michael Davitt addressed a rally in Portree on 2 May 1887 and thereafter toured the island.

LEGAL LEGACY

The malice requirement in claims brought against "public officers", as formulated by Lord President Inglis,[77] hardened into a general rule that continued regularly to be cited for a century or more in Scottish cases – invariably without reflection upon the extraordinary circumstances on the Herbusta hillside, or the equivocal nature of the authorities cited in *Beaton v Ivory*. This dictum found its way into cases brought against the police not only in relation to wrongful detention but also other intentional wrongs such as defamation[78] or assault,[79] making them actionable only if "actuated by malice", as interpreted in the more exacting sense of "malice in fact".

Unsurprisingly, this rule is now tested by human rights considerations, as demonstrated by the decision of the European Court of Human Rights (ECtHR) in the English case of *Keegan v United Kingdom*.[80] In *Keegan*, the applicants' house had been searched by the police on the authority of a warrant procured without malice, but in reliance upon mistaken information. In the English courts, a claim for damages against the Chief Constable failed in the absence of malice.[81] The ECtHR held, however, that insistence upon proving malice, without regard to proportionality and reasonableness, presented an unreasonable barrier to compensation and that "a limitation of actions for damages to cases of malice is [not] necessary to protect the police in their vital functions of investigating crime".[82] Accordingly, the domestic courts had offered inadequate redress for interference with the applicants' rights under article 8 of the European Convention on Human Rights.

If it is disproportionate to look for malice in determining liability for wrongful procurement of a warrant to search premises, it cannot be regarded as less so in cases involving infringement of liberty. The ECtHR in *Keegan* made no specific suggestions as to what should replace the malice criterion in determining the boundaries of privilege for public officials. The appropriate test will require further judicial elaboration in the domestic courts, but at the very least it must now involve proportionality, and turn upon objectively-verifiable standards, rather than the personal motivation of the defender. In

---

77 Text at n 59 above.
78 *Robertson v Keith* 1936 SC 29.
79 *Mckie v Orr* 2003 SC 317 at para 12 per Lord Kirkwood.
80 (2007) 44 EHRR 33.
81 [2003] EWCA Civ 936, [2003] 1 WLR 2187.
82 At para 34.

short, Lord President Inglis' dictum can no longer be accepted as representing the modern law.

POSTSCRIPT

While Beaton had his legal expenses paid by public subscription, Ivory was faced with a long battle to obtain public funding to meet his costs. It was not until March 1888 that he eventually secured a Treasury payment of £151/15/6 to his agents to reimburse them for the expenses that he plainly would not recover from Beaton.[83] And while Ivory avoided legal liability, his conduct in Skye had nonetheless made him the target of widespread criticism. By the autumn of 1886, he had already become embroiled in a bitter dispute with the Chief Constable and the Convener of the County regarding the command of the Inverness police.[84] He had also been criticised by the Lord Advocate, Lord Kingsburgh (whose grandfather was from Skye), because of his reluctance to censure Sheriff Officer Macdonald for his strong-arm tactics.[85] In December 1886, a public meeting in London, chaired by Charles Fraser Mackintosh MP, member of the Napier Commission, agreed on a memorial to be sent to the Queen requesting fair treatment for the crofters and an end to the "intolerable conduct" of Sheriff Ivory.[86] Questions were placed in parliament in early 1887, asking Balfour, the Scottish Secretary, whether Ivory had been reprimanded for his handling of the Skye disturbances.[87] Indeed, by 1887, Ivory was so much the target of vitriol that he had to employ

---

83 "*Stewart and Beaton v Ivory.* Copy of correspondence respecting the payment from public funds of certain expenses incurred by Sheriff Ivory in connection with actions brought against him by Norman Stewart and John Beaton" 1888 (446) *House of Commons Papers* vol LXXXI 545. Controversy continued regarding public funding for Ivory's expenses in the defamation action by Stewart (n 53 above): Hansard HC 18 March 1889, 3rd series, vol 334, cols 58–93.

84 See, eg, letter from Ivory to James Anderson, Procurator Fiscal, of 5 January 1887, complaining that "the fight" forced upon him had "been so distasteful"; letter from Scottish Under-Secretary Hugh Davidson of Cantray, Convener of the County to Sir Francis Sandford, of 29 October 1886, urging that "no time should be lost in making some enquiry by some influential person into the actions and conduct of Sheriff Ivory" (both Skye and Lochalsh Archive, Inverness County Council Records, CI 1/9/6/3).

85 N Macdonald, *Sir John Macdonald Lord Kingsburgh* (2010), pp 111–112.

86 *The Times*, 9 December 1886, p 6.

87 The response was a guarded negative, Hansard HC 15 February 1887, 3rd series, vol 310, cols 1571–1648.

personal bodyguards. Nonetheless, Ivory remained in office until 1900, holding the position of sheriff for nearly 40 years.

By the time of the 1891 census, John Beaton was no longer living in Herbusta, and it has not proved possible to trace what became of him. When Ivory died at the age of 90 in 1915, having survived a shipwreck off the Mull of Kintyre in 1895,[88] he had become the "father" (most senior member) of the Faculty of Advocates. *The Scotsman* glossed over the controversies of a long and active professional life with an unusually lukewarm obituary, pointing out that "as the son of a Judge with an influential Whig connection, preferment did not fail him", but that "Mr Ivory, although a learned lawyer and endowed with a vigorous mind, had not the peculiar gifts which bring forensic success".[89] A more colourful, if thoroughly scurrilous, epitaph came from the Skye bard, Mary MacPherson, composed prematurely in 1886 on false intelligence that Ivory had drowned in the bog at Trotternish:[90]

> A grey stone will certainly be placed above you
> Which will record every one of your iniquitous bribes
> And how you sold your entire reputation
> for a little booty
> for the sake of your corrupt ground ...

88 See http://www.nlb.org.uk/LighthouseLibrary/Lighthouse/Sanda/ (Ivory was one of the Commissioners of the Northern Lighthouses).
89 *The Scotsman*, 21 October 1915, p 6.
90 Translation of *Oran Cumha an Ibhirich* in D Meek (ed), *Tuath is Tighearna: Tenants and Landlords* (1995), p 267 (original at p 167).

The War of the Booksellers:
Hinton v Donaldson

Hector MacQueen

On 27 July 1773, the Court of Session in Edinburgh pronounced its decision in the case of *Hinton v Donaldson and others*.[1] The case was between book publishers (or "booksellers", as they were known in the 18th century). It concerned the "literary property" or "copy-right" (the latter term was only gradually emerging at the time) in *The New History of the Holy Bible*, a well-known and popular book by the Reverend Thomas Stackhouse (1681/82–1752) which had been first published in London in 1733. The rights in Stackhouse's book were claimed by the pursuer, John Hinton, a highly successful and prominent bookseller based in London. Stackhouse had sold the rights in his *History* to the publisher, Stephen Austen, in 1740. Austen died in 1750, bequeathing the rights to his widow, Elizabeth; and her subsequent marriage with Hinton transferred them to him. The defenders – Alexander Donaldson, John Wood and James Meurose – were all Scottish booksellers, based in Edinburgh or (in the case of Meurose) Kilmarnock. Hinton's claim was that these three had each printed, published and sold editions of Stackhouse's *History* without his permission and so had infringed his exclusive rights.

But in a decision of the greatest importance for copyright law, both at the time and, in some ways, still today, the Court of Session held against Hinton and in favour of the Scottish booksellers' liberty to publish. In doing so, the judges decided expressly in opposition to the view of the law which then prevailed in the English courts. Seven months later, their decision was instrumental in persuading the House

1 *Hinton v Donaldson* 1773 Mor 8307; more fully at 5 Br Supp 508; and most fully of all at 5 Pat 505 and in J Boswell, *The Decision of the Court of Session upon the Question of Literary Property in the Cause John Hinton of London, bookseller, against Alexander Donaldson and John Wood, booksellers in Edinburgh and James Meurose, bookseller in Kilmarnock* (Edinburgh, 1774). The case process is in the National Records of Scotland, CS 231/H/2/4.

of Lords in another case decided on 21 February 1774 to overturn the previous English approach.[2] The outcome was thus the reverse of the usual view of the House of Lords imposing an English solution upon a reluctant Scotland. Alexander Donaldson was to the fore again in this second case, first as losing defendant and then as triumphant appellant. The law was henceforth settled in both Scotland and England: copyright in published works depended on the relevant statute, and not on the common (or judge-made) law. The courts could not extend the basic exclusive right beyond what Parliament laid down.

In 1773–74, the statute in force was the so-called Statute of Anne, introduced to Parliament in its 1709–10 session and gaining its nickname from the then Queen. But the Statute also came not long after, and at least partly as a result of, the Anglo-Scottish Union of 1707. Before the Union, the Scottish "copyright" system had been based upon government grants to publishers, underpinned by the royal prerogative, of exclusive privileges to print and import particular works.[3] Authors too could apply for such privileges. The Scottish Privy Council provided both the granting body to which application for privileges was made and the forum in which disputes about the scope of the privileges were determined. The grants were increasingly in standardised forms, and typically provided for a 19-year period of exclusivity as well as search powers for the right-holder to root out infringing copies. This system was however undermined as an immediate consequence of the 1707 Union, when the separate Scottish Privy Council was abolished by statute from 1 May 1708. In terms of Article XVIII of the Union Agreement, which purported to regulate the parliamentary power to alter Scots law, some form of exclusivity to replace what had just been lost was for the "evident utility" of Scottish authors and publishers if it was not actually a matter of "public right" to make the grant of literary privilege uniform throughout the newly united kingdom. But the pre-Union English Privy Council had had no role in licensing publishing activities. Something different was needed in the new dispensation.

The Statute of Anne accordingly introduced a novel system for the whole kingdom. An author or a bookseller could gain an exclusive right to publish a book so long as its title was registered at Stationers' Hall (the headquarters of the London booksellers' guild, near St Paul's Cathedral) prior to publication. The right lasted for 14 years, with authors (but not booksellers) being entitled to a further 14 years of

2 *Donaldson v Beckett* (1774) 4 Burr 2408, 2 Bro PC 129.
3 A Mann, *The Scottish Book Trade 1500–1720* (2000), ch 4.

exclusive right after the expiry of the initial period of protection. The Statute further provided penal monetary sanctions for infringement of these rights, half payable to the Crown and the other half to the person with the relevant exclusive right. A requirement of "legal deposit" of published works in certain libraries was also established along with a system to regulate the price of books. The Scottish dimension was specifically provided for in the Statute. The Court of Session was given jurisdiction "if any person or persons incur the penalties contained in this Act, in that part of Great Britain called Scotland"; the deposit of copies of registered works was required in the libraries of the Faculty of Advocates and the Scottish universities via the Stationers' Company; and book price regulatory powers in Scotland were given to the Lord President of the Court of Session, the Lord Justice-General, the Lord Chief Baron of the Scottish Exchequer and the Rector of the College (ie University) of Edinburgh.

Although the Statute's requirement of registration far away in London might have made life more difficult for Scottish publishers and authors, in practice Scottish publications seem to have been frequently entered in the register throughout the 18th century, so the barrier of distance was not insuperable, at least for those with resources and good prospects of literary success.[4] In the mid-18th century, however, London and Scottish publishers and booksellers fell into conflict over a number of issues about literary property. The conflict has become known as "The Battle of the Booksellers" – but in some ways it was more like a war, lasting for over thirty years and involving not just court battles but other forms of struggle. *Hinton v Donaldson* was the penultimate battle of the booksellers' war, and the forerunner of the eventual triumph, not only of the Scottish booksellers, but also of the Scottish judiciary's view of the law.

The issues arose from the making and sale in Scotland by its booksellers of cheap reprints of works with subsisting registrations in Stationers' Hall, along with the export of these reprints to England and, indeed, to North America and Continental Europe. The London booksellers, led by the formidable (and Scots-born) Andrew Millar, first began to take legal action against such reprints in the late 1730s.

---

4 Mann, *The Scottish Book Trade 1500–1720*, pp 123–124. See further, R B Sher, *The Enlightenment and the Book: Scottish Authors and their Publishers in Eighteenth-Century Britain, Ireland, and America* (2006), pp 243–244; W McDougall, 'Copyright litigation in the Court of Session, 1738–1749, and the rise of the Scottish book trade' (1971–87) 5 *Transactions of the Edinburgh Bibliographical Society*, pp 2–31, 26–29. I have drawn extensively on these pieces in what follows.

The initial question to be debated in the campaign was whether the Statute's very limited sanctions against infringement – forfeiture of the infringing publications and payment of one penny for every infringing sheet, with only half the money going to the person suing – could be supplemented by other remedies available generally from the courts. After some equivocation, the answer given to this question by the Court of Session differed fundamentally from that of the English judiciary.

Well before 1740, the Court of Chancery had been persuaded that, provided the party bringing the action first waived his claim to the penalties provided by the Statute of Anne, it could grant the equitable remedies of injunctions (orders prohibiting the continuation of infringing activities) and requiring infringers to hand their profits over to the right-holders by way of damages.[5] These entitlements were seen to arise because the rights infringed were ones of property. The Scottish judges, on the other hand, ultimately refused to supplement the Statute of Anne in this way in 1748 in the case reported as *Midwinter v Hamilton*.[6] In fact, it involved a number of leading London booksellers (including Daniel Midwinter but led by Millar) and an even larger number of Edinburgh and Glasgow booksellers (including Gavin Hamilton as well as other prominent names such as Alexander Kincaid and Robert Foulis). An appeal to the House of Lords against the decision of the Court of Session failed in 1751, although not by upholding the court below, but rather through a technical finding that the action "was improperly and inconsistently brought". The appellant booksellers had illegitimately cumulated non-statutory with statutory remedies as well as suing several defenders in one action when the points at issue against each were about separate and distinct books and rights therein. The case was remitted back to the Court of Session, but no further litigation ensued there.

Henry Home, counsel for the Scottish booksellers in *Midwinter* and later raised to the Court of Session bench as Lord Kames, referred to his past triumph at the bar in his monumental book, *Principles of Equity* (first published in 1760 by Alexander Kincaid, one of the

---

5 See R Deazley, *On the Origin of the Right to Copy: Charting the Movement of Copyright Law in Eighteenth-century Britain (1695–1775)* (2004), pp 57–69, 137–138.

6 *Midwinter v Hamilton* 1748 Mor 8295; McDougall, "Copyright litigation in the Court of Session, 1738–1749, and the rise of the Scottish book trade", pp 5–8; R S Tompson, "Scottish judges and the birth of British copyright" 1992 JR 18 at 19–22; M Rose, *Authors and Owners: The Invention of Copyright* (1993), pp 69–71; Deazley, *On the Origin of the Right to Copy*, pp 116–132.

defenders in the case as already noted). Kames implicitly criticised the handling of the Statute of Anne by the English equity courts when he argued that "monopolies or personal privileges cannot be extended by a court of equity; because that court may prevent mischief, but has no power to do any act for enriching any person, or making him *locupletior*, as termed in the Roman law".[7] It was an important point that in England there was a dual system of courts, with the Court of King's Bench administering the law and the Court of Chancery equity, the latter in complex ways supplementing the jurisdiction of the former and providing remedies to deal with cases beyond the scope of the general law. No such division existed in Scotland, where it was usually said that the Court of Session administered law and equity together, or that law and equity were fused.[8] The significance of Kames' remark about Chancery's role in the copyright debate is that, while in general he favoured the expansion of the equitable aspects of the Court of Session's jurisdiction, he also thought that equity should operate within certain limits.[9]

After their disappointment in *Midwinter v Hamilton*, the London booksellers seem to have abandoned the tactic of suing in Scotland, choosing rather to mount actions in England or the English courts against those English provincial booksellers who also sold the cheap Scottish reprints. There was also the "Conspiracy of the London Booksellers", tagged as "one of the most successful propaganda campaigns in the history of restraint of trade" by Ernest Mossner in his biography of the great Scottish philosopher-historian, David Hume:

> Using every means at hand to reduce the success of books which they did not own, they developed a highly efficient communication system. It extended to provincial booksellers, to whom riders brought news of books – which to push, which to pass by. It often included direct threat of trade retaliation. It sometimes involved an offer to buy entire stocks (for which "correct editions" would be substituted). It nearly always relied upon a determined and damaging criticism of the books to be curtailed.

7 Kames, *Principles of Equity* (1st edn, 1760), p 185. The statement, or something close to it, reappears in subsequent editions (2nd edn, 1767, pp 265–266; 3rd edn, 1778 (last prepared by Kames himself), vol 2, p 126. See also *ibid*, vol 1, p 352 for this criticism expressly directed against the English copyright cases before *Donaldson v Becket*.

8 Stair, *Institutions*, IV, iii, 1–2; Bankton, *Institute*, IV, vii, 23–28; Erskine, *Institute*, I, iii, 22. See too, Deazley, *On the Origin of the Right to Copy*, p 117.

9 See further a paper by Andreas Rahmatian accessible at http://ssrn.com/abstract=1918046.

Mossner highlights this story because the "Conspiracy" ultimately compelled Hume to abandon Gavin Hamilton, the Edinburgh bookseller who published the first volume of his *History of England* in 1754, and to switch for the five remaining volumes to Andrew Millar of London, in whose hands the *History* became one of the great success stories of 18th-century publishing.[10]

Alexander Donaldson, the defender in *Hinton v Donaldson*, first came to prominence in the 1750s when in partnership with Alexander Kincaid, who had by then become the King's Printer in Scotland. At this time, their firm published some of the most significant works of the Scottish Enlightenment in philosophy, medicine and law. They also reprinted literary works previously published in England, such as the poetry of Milton. It has been suggested that Donaldson's initial move into cheap reprints was prompted by a realisation of the business opportunity that had been created by the failure of the London booksellers to make any headway with their mid-century litigations in Scotland. The truth of the matter seems to be, however, that reprinting of works previously published in England was widespread in Scotland throughout the 1750s; it was only when Donaldson left his partnership with Kincaid in May 1758 and then set up with a new partner, John Reid, in 1760, that reprinting became his primary activity. This business was carried on at premises on the south side of Castlehill (the street leading up to Edinburgh Castle from the Lawnmarket), but Donaldson also had a bookshop in the High Street under a sign bearing an image of the head of Alexander Pope, the famous English poet.

Donaldson made himself a weapon of potential mass destruction in the booksellers' war when, in April 1763, he set up business inside enemy territory on the Strand, centre of the world of London booksellers.[11] Joining initially in a partnership with his brother John (who had been established in bookselling at 195 Strand, at Arundel Street, since 1756), he there set about developing still further his very successful business of making and selling cheap reprints. There can be little doubt that Donaldson's move was a direct challenge to the "Conspiracy of the London booksellers". The Strand office became known as "the shop for cheap books", and later he marketed his stock as "Books Sold Cheap", with his prices "thirty to fifty per cent cheaper

---

10   E C Mossner, *The Life of David Hume* (2nd edn, 1980), pp 312–316 (quotations at pp 313–314).

11   See J Raven, *The Business of Books: Booksellers and the English Book Trade 1450–1850* (2007), pp 158–161.

than the usual London prices".[12] Moreover, within a year of his arrival on the Strand, Donaldson published a pamphlet exposing damning evidence of the combination of the London booksellers against Scottish reprints.[13]

Unsurprisingly, the response to all this was hostile, with (Donaldson later claimed) eleven actions apparently being raised against him in the Court of Chancery by around 100 London booksellers.[14] He also attracted the disfavour of the great Dr Samuel Johnson, as recorded in James Boswell's *Life*:

> He was loud and violent against Mr Donaldson. "He is a fellow who takes advantage of the law to injure his brethren; for, notwithstanding that the statute secures only fourteen years of exclusive right, it has always been understood by *the trade* that he, who buys the copy-right of a book from the author, obtains a perpetual property; and upon that belief, numberless bargains are made to transfer that property after expiration of the statutory term. Now Donaldson, I say, takes advantage here of people who have really an equitable title from usage."

When someone else said that, "Donaldson, Sir, is anxious for the encouragement of literature. He reduces the price of books, so that poor students may buy them", Johnson retorted, "Well, Sir, allowing that to be his motive, he is no better than Robin Hood, who robbed the rich in order to give to the poor."[15]

Back in Edinburgh, however, Donaldson had many friends and supporters, not least amongst them the lawyers in Parliament House, home of the Court of Session. He had patronised young advocates with literary pretensions such as James Boswell. Donaldson not only published Boswell's poetry,[16] but also feasted him at his house at the foot of the West Bow. In December 1761, Boswell wrote to his fellow versifier, Andrew Erskine:

> Notwithstanding your affecting elegy on the death of two pigs, I am just now returning from eating a most excellent one with the most magnificent Donaldson. ... His dinners are the most eloquent addresses

12 Raven, *The Business of Books*, p 183.
13 *Some Thoughts on the State of Literary Property, Humbly Submitted to the Consideration of the Public* (London, 1764).
14 A Donaldson, "Petition", in *Petitions and Papers Relating to the Bill of the Booksellers now before the House of Commons* (London, 1774), p 10.
15 G B Hill and L F Powell (eds), *Boswell's Life of Johnson*, vol 1 (1934; reprinted 1971), p 438 (all quotations).
16 See T Blacklock, *A Collection of Original Poems by Scotch Gentlemen* (1762), pp 68–91.

imaginable. For my own part, I am never a sharer in one of his copious repasts, but I feel my heart warm to the landlord.[17]

Donaldson also published in 1767 a pamphlet by another advocate, John MacLaurin. The content is evident enough from its title: *Considerations on the Origin and Nature of Literary Property, wherein that species of property is clearly proved to subsist for no longer than the terms fixed by the statute 8vo Anne*. The argument thus supported Donaldson's business model with much legal learning. The pamphlet was reprinted the following year along with an appendix containing "a letter to Robert Taylor, bookseller, in Berwick", Taylor being also the printer on this occasion. Sitting only just inside England's northernmost bounds, Taylor's interest was exactly the same as Donaldson's. He seems to have been an active reprinter and reseller of reprints in both England and Scotland.[18] He had already been sued twice in the Court of Chancery by London booksellers in 1765: once for reprinting "several thousand copies" of the poet Edward Young's collection, *Night Thoughts*, and exchanging 150 of them for books from Donaldson; the other for selling Donaldson's allegedly infringing 1767 edition of James Thomson's poem, *The Seasons*. In both cases, Taylor had been subjected to an injunction, but new legal issues had been raised by the one relating to *The Seasons*. On these, the opinion of the judges of the King's Bench (ie the court of law as distinct from the equity of Chancery) had been sought and in 1768 was still awaited. The reprint of MacLaurin's pamphlet in England was thus clearly connected to events there rather than in his home jurisdiction.

The issue for the King's Bench was not one of equitable remedies but of whether there were any rights at all to be protected. Thomson's *Seasons* had first been published in parts between 1726 and 1730, the complete set being finally published together in the latter year, and Thomson had died in 1748. The maximum period of protection for the work under the Statute of Anne – 28 years from first publication – had thus clearly elapsed. Even if there were rights outside the statute, were they not the author's rather than the publisher's, and could they survive him? The King's Bench decision in *Millar v Taylor* was finally handed down on 20 April 1769.[19] The four judges were not unanimous, but the majority, led by the Scots-born Lord Chief Justice Mansfield, were firm for the view that there was indeed a common

17 *Letters between the Honourable Andrew Erskine, and James Boswell, Esq* (1763), pp 28–29.
18 Sher, *The Enlightenment and the Book*, p 512, n 18.
19 *Millar v Taylor* (1769) 4 Burr 2303.

law right to literary property, which vested in authors pre-publication and revived after the expiry of the privileges conferred by the Statute of Anne. The common law right could be assigned to the author's publishers and so continue to be used by them even after the author died.

Alexander Donaldson responded to *Millar v Taylor* with another pamphlet, dated 8 May 1769, arguing once more the case against any literary property beyond the Statute of Anne.[20] His friend James Boswell owned a copy of the pamphlet, which Donaldson may have presented to him. But the law having been determined by the King's Bench, the case returned to Chancery, which in July 1770 granted a perpetual injunction against Taylor and ordered him to account for all the illicit copies of *The Seasons* that he had sold. Just three months later, the London booksellers renewed their legal campaign in Scotland by raising their action in the Court of Session against Alexander Donaldson and the two other Scottish booksellers who had reproduced Stackhouse's *History*. Early in 1771, Thomas Becket, one of the London booksellers who had succeeded to Andrew Millar's titles upon the latter's death in 1768, filed a bill in the Court of Chancery against both Donaldson brothers, seeking both an injunction against their further reprinting of Thomson's *Seasons* and an account of profits from the sales already made. The war of the booksellers was moving towards its climax, and it may have been in realisation of this, and with a view to hedging against the financial risks of defeat in court, that the Donaldson brothers dissolved their partnership in June 1773. John continued business on his own account in the Strand, while Alexander moved to larger premises at 48 St Paul's Churchyard, still very much in the heartland of London publishing at the time, and only a very short walk away from Stationers' Hall.[21]

The issue in the Scottish case against Donaldson was exactly the same as the one in England with Thomson's *Seasons*. The statutory rights in the *History* had expired some time earlier, and Stackhouse himself had been dead for nearly 20 years. The case came first before a single judge in the Outer House (Lord Coalston) in July 1771, for him to decide how it should proceed. Alexander Donaldson's advocate was John MacLaurin, who raised initial issues about the identity of the un-named "wife" in Stephen Austen's will and about whether the

20 *A Letter from a Gentleman in Edinburgh, to his Friend in London; concerning Literary Property* (no place of publication given, 1769).
21 Raven, *The Business of Books*, pp 168–185.

property that the will purported to bequeath to her automatically passed to any subsequently acquired husband. On these points, Lord Coalston directed parties to seek the opinion of English counsel. That opinion having been obtained, confirming the identity of Austen's widow as now Hinton's wife, and that the copyrights she had owned did indeed pass in English law to her new husband, Lord Coalston next ordered the parties to prepare and submit to the court written memorials on the merits of the cause. Although that order was made on 16 November 1771, the memorials were considered by the court only on 5 August 1772, whereupon the matter was referred to the Inner House for consideration by all the judges. Counsel prepared and submitted printed informations which are each dated 2 January 1773 and appeared on the Inner House rolls on 12 January.[22] It was already more than two years since the action had begun; the wheels of 18th-century Scottish legal process turned scarcely more quickly than they do today. But this does not suggest that the parties were pressing the matter as one of urgency either. Nor does the pursuer bookseller, John Hinton, seem to have travelled north to be present during the litigation in the Court of Session. His side of the case was managed as attorney by Alexander Mackonochie, a writer (ie solicitor) in Edinburgh. But overall pressure certainly intensified during 1772: a number of other Court of Session actions were raised by London booksellers against Edinburgh counterparts in respect of various alleged infringements of the Statute of Anne. Meantime, in London, the Court of Chancery had granted a perpetual injunction in *Becket v Donaldson* in November 1772, and the Donaldsons had lodged an appeal to the House of Lords the following month.[23]

The oral debate on the written pleadings in *Hinton v Donaldson* began before 11 of the 13 Inner House judges on Tuesday 20 July 1773, and lasted for the rest of the week. The "fund of learning, ingenuity and acuteness" displayed in the oral pleadings attracted much contemporary interest.[24] Certainly, the parties were represented by some of the cream of the contemporary Scottish bar. Three counsel spoke on each side. For Hinton, there appeared Allan Maconochie (a future Professor of Public Law and the Law of Nature and Nations at

---

22 See Advocates Library Session Papers (henceforth "ALSP"), Pitfour Collection, vol 54, no 9, Arniston Collection, vol 3, no 17, and Campbell Collection, vol 23, nos 8–9.

23 Deazley, *On the Origin of the Right to Copy*, pp 180–182, 191–192.

24 The quotation is from the *Caledonian Mercury*, 24 July 1773. See also the issues of 17 and 28 July.

Edinburgh University and also, as the first Lord Meadowbank, a Court of Session judge), Alexander Murray (also later a judge, as Lord Henderland), and David Rae (who had written the informations on this side and who too was to become a judge as Lord Eskgrove). Alexander Donaldson and his colleagues were represented by his friends and clients, James Boswell and John MacLaurin, as well as a future Lord President in Ilay Campbell. Campbell was the author of the closely-reasoned written informations for the Donaldson side; but rather remarkably he had already appeared for Hinton when the proceedings were before Lord Coalston in the Outer House in 1771. MacLaurin, who would later be raised to the bench as Lord Dreghorn, was already well known as a defender of liberty, in particular of the liberty of the press. In 1778, he would gain further prominence as advocate for the slave Joseph Knight in the great case of *Knight v Wedderburn* which declared that Scots law did not recognise the status of slavery.[25] MacLaurin's advocacy powers owed more to knowledge of the law than eloquence, however: "His voice, though not strong, was agreeable; but, from the want of teeth, rendered rather monotonous" was one verdict not long after his death in 1796.[26] Boswell then was the only one of the six counsel involved in *Hinton v Donaldson* who did not eventually reach the Court of Session bench. But so long as he continued in regular practice, he was a much more effective advocate than he has tended to be given credit for by posterity.[27] It probably did his side no harm, however, that his father, Lord Auchinleck, was amongst the judges listening to the pleadings in the *Hinton* case.

The work of the Donaldson team, oral and written, carried the day with the court. After a long weekend's reflection on the debate they had heard, 10 of the judges declared that literary property, or copyright, had no existence in relation to published works except under the Statute of Anne. There was no such thing as copyright at common law in Scotland. The court refused to follow *Millar v Taylor*. Only the famously eccentric Lord Monboddo dissented. As Ronan Deazley has pointed out, however, the style of argument supporting the majority decision in *Hinton v Donaldson* has a flavour quite distinct from those in the earlier English case law, flowing from the powerful Civilian

25 *Knight v Wedderburn* 1778 Mor 14545.
26 Anon (ed), *The Works of John MacLaurin Esq of Dreghorn , one of the Senators of the College of Justice and FRS Edinburgh* (1798), vol 1, xvi.
27 See H M Milne, *The Legal Papers of James Boswell* (Stair Society vol 60, 2013), vol 1, introduction, xlv–lv, lxvii–xviii.

influence on Scottish legal thinking which had little parallel in England. Professor Deazley draws attention to "three central tenets" in the opinions of the Court of Session judges: "a common law copyright was deemed to have no foundation either in the law of nature, or the law of nations, nor was any vestige of such a right to be found in the law of Scotland".[28]

In an as yet unpublished paper, Professor John Cairns has, however, elaborated and reshaped Professor Deazley's point in so far as it distinguishes between the law of Scotland and the law of nature or the law of nations.[29] Professor Cairns points out that for the Scots lawyer the "common law" was closely linked to European ideas of the *ius commune* as the *ius gentium*, Roman law and, ultimately, the *ius naturale*. Natural law was not something separate from, but was rather the foundation of, Scots law.[30] Its content was to be determined by looking at what men in general understood and accepted as well as the laws of other peoples and nations – the *ius gentium*. As Lord Gardenstone put it: "[t]he most substantial and convincing evidence of what is really just and rational, in a matter of public concern to all countries, is the concurring sense of nations."[31] For this purpose, the law of England could of course be considered, but if that law was the only system to recognise a right of literary property outside statutory provision or the grant of a special privilege, then it was not very powerful support for the existence of such a right in Scots law. Certainly, the mere fact that the English courts had held that such a right existed was not decisive for the Scottish courts. Lord Auchinleck noted that the laws of England were "in many particulars special to itself", while Lord Hailes commented that "English law, as to us, is foreign law; foreign law is matter of fact", ie it was not law in Scotland.

The absence of any previous reference to a general right of literary property in Scots law was also evidence that it was not a natural right, readily comprehended by all; indeed, in Lord Gardenstone's words again, "property, when applied to ideas, or literary and intellectual compositions, is perfectly new and surprising". A further point of significance in the *Hinton* opinions is a distinction previously drawn

28 Deazley, *On the Origin of the Right to Copy*, p 185.
29 J W Cairns, "Natural Law and copyright in eighteenth-century Scotland", unpublished draft.
30 Stair, *Institutions*, I,1 is the best-known exposition of this approach, also perceptible in diluted form in Bankton, *Institute*, I,1; Erskine, *Institutes*, I,1.
31 All quotations from the *Hinton* opinions are to be found in Boswell, *Decision* (n 1 *supra*).

by contemporary jurists such as Adam Smith and Lord Bankton, and stated again a little later by David Hume, Professor of Scots Law at Edinburgh University from 1786 to 1822, and nephew of the great philosopher:[32] one between the real right of property – outright ownership – and the real right of exclusive privilege, also good against the world, but not to be regarded so much as property as the product of policy. In essence, this came down to saying that literary property (and indeed patents for inventions) were grants of special privilege made by the Crown in the exercise of the royal prerogative. The monopolies were created for specific periods designed to encourage and reward useful or beneficial activity in a way that the market, left to itself, would not. While the rights conferred were good against the world while they lasted, they were not to be likened at all to the ownership of land or goods.

Several of the judges in *Hinton v Donaldson* refer to this distinction. Thus, Lord Auchinleck distinguished prerogative from property and criticised "blending the notions arising from privileges and patents with a common-law right, which is quite erroneous". The Lord Justice-Clerk, Thomas Miller of Barskimming (later Lord Glenlee), recognised that "every civilized state in modern times has introduced exclusive privileges for authors"; but, he said:

> [T]his suggests no idea of an original property in the author; on the contrary, it is inconsistent with it: for if such property previously existed in the author, how should it have occurred to sovereigns, meaning to encourage authors, to limit the endurance of the author's right to a certain term of years; which is the case of all letters patent known in the different states of Europe.

For Lord Kames, "the meaning of property, in the laws of all nations, is a right to some corporeal subject, that can be possessed, that can be transferred from hand to hand, that goes to heirs, that may be stolen or robbed, and that may be demanded by a real action, termed *rei vindicatio*". But the right claimed by the pursuer was not to any corpus that could be possessed or stolen. He continued:

> *Ergo*, it is not property. Taking it in all views, no more can be made of it than to be a privilege or monopoly, which intitles the claimant to the

---

32 See further my "Intellectual property and the common law in Scotland c1700–c1850" in C W Ng et al (eds), *The Common Law of Intellectual Property* (2010), pp 21–43, 29–33; also, for the philosopher, my "Law and economics, David Hume and intellectual property" in N Kuenssberg (ed), *Argument amongst Friends: Twenty-five years of Sceptical Enquiry* (2011), pp 9–14.

commerce of a certain book, and excludes all others from making money by it. The important question then is, from what source is this monopoly derived, a monopoly that endures for ever, and is effectual against all the world? The act of Queen Anne bestows this monopoly upon authors for a limited time upon certain conditions. But our legislature, far from acknowledging a perpetual monopoly at common law, declares that it shall last no longer than a limited time.

Lord Gardenstone thought that the "concurring sense of nations" showed that the nature of an author's right was "no more than a temporary privilege" and not one of property. Lord Alva's opinion is also to be understood as distinguishing privilege, resting upon public interest grounds, from property:

By the common law of this country, or any other country, where there is not a restriction upon natural liberty understood, either *tacito populi suffragio*, or by express statute, there is no antecedent property vested in an author, or his heirs, or assigns, further than what relates to the *ipsum corpus* of the MS: that this property, in so far as it exists, is merely a creature of civil society and refined policy, and consequently will go no further than it is expressly established by custom or statute: but we have no custom or common law for it here; and therefore it can go no further with us than it is carried by the statute.

Another way in which the judicial arguments draw upon the idea of exclusive privilege to reject the claim of property is in their observation that the author of a book might be analogised with the inventor of a useful machine who, however, had no property right in his invention apart from the monopoly of a patent granted under the royal prerogative. Indeed, the existence of such a perpetual property right in inventors would be deeply damaging to society and commerce; Lord Kames commented darkly that "it would be in the power of inventors to deprive mankind of both food and raiment".

A final important feature of the opinions in *Hinton v Donaldson* is that most were careful to distinguish between unpublished and published books. With the former, the judges were much more ready to recognise the existence of a property right. So, for example, Lord Auchinleck: "It is agreed by all, that while the book is not published, whether the work be in the author's head or his cabinet, it is absolutely his, and no man can deprive him of it"; and similarly the Lord Justice-Clerk: "Before publication this copy-right in the author exists, and must have all the effects of property in every nation." As the sole dissentient judge, Lord Monboddo, pointed out, however, they did not explain what happened to this property right upon publication of the work. Lord Kames, Lord Gardenstone, Lord Coalston and Lord Alva also recognised a pre-publication property right, albeit on the basis of the ownership of the manuscript on which the work was recorded rather than anything more abstract or incorporeal. But the two latter judges also recognised what Lord Coalston termed "full power" and Lord Alva an "interest" over, respectively, one's "own ideas" or the "productions of [one's] own brain". In both cases, the judges were careful to distinguish this power or interest from property, but did not otherwise seek to define what if any legal effects arose from it. Further, to the eye of the modern copyright lawyer, they and their fellow judges failed in their discussion of property rights to distinguish adequately between ideas, forms of expression and the physical record of the work in question.

We have for the 18th century an unusually large amount of detail about the judges' opinions in *Hinton v Donaldson* because James Boswell took the trouble to gather and publish them in full text in a booklet of not quite 40 pages. The publication was not simply the product of a successful advocate's vanity. It appeared early in 1774, "printed by James Donaldson, for Alexander Donaldson, and sold at his Shop, No 48 St Paul's Churchyard, London, and Edinburgh; and by all the Booksellers in Scotland". It is thus clear, as Richard Tompson and Mark Rose have pointed out,[33] that this was part of Donaldson's preparation for his appeal to the House of Lords in *Donaldson v Beckett*, material that could be laid before the court for the Scottish judges' reasoning on the general question to be determined. Perhaps also, the publication would help demonstrate, through the judicial discussion of comparative law, that English law was alone if *Millar v Taylor* was correctly decided. Certainly, this latter point was picked up in the arguments for Donaldson in the House of Lords:

> [I]n Scotland the *jus gentium*, or laws and customs of other nations, were pleaded in the courts of that kingdom, and from a diligent search into the laws and customs of every nation, ancient or modern, the Scotch lawyers, when the question concerning literary property was lately agitated in that kingdom, found themselves justified in affirming that no such property ever existed or ever was claimed in any civilized nation, England excepted, under the canopy of heaven.[34]

---

33 Tompson, "Scottish judges and the birth of British copyright", p 29; Rose, *Authors and Owners: The Invention of Copyright*, pp 95–96.
34 W Cobbett (ed), *The Parliamentary History of England from the Earliest Period to the Year 1803*, vol 17 (1813), col 957.

The House of Lords' eventual decision in *Donaldson v Beckett*,[35] that there was no right of literary property outside the Statute of Anne, was greeted with "great rejoicings in Edinburgh ... bonfires and illuminations, ordered though by a mob, with drum and two pipes".[36] Boswell, describing the outcome as "great news", went to have "tea with Lord Monboddo to triumph over him".[37] He does not record Monboddo's reaction to either the news from London or the jubilant advocate's visit. But Alexander Donaldson for his part had clearly succeeded in commanding popular support for his cause in Scotland; in part, no doubt, because his struggle had been against London domination, but also because he enabled the rapidly growing class of readers to indulge their pleasures and intellectual interests at far less cost than would otherwise have been the case. His, of course, was not a wholly disinterested approach, driven by notions of the public good alone; he died a wealthy man in 1794 in retirement at his mansion, Broughton Hall, just to the north-east of Edinburgh. But his wealth also laid the basis for the fortune of his son, James, whose public benefactions included the endowment of Donaldson's Hospital for deaf and poor children in Edinburgh. It may finally be noted that, despite the loss of the rights he once thought he had, John Hinton too died a wealthy man, in 1781.[38]

Earlier, I anachronistically compared Alexander Donaldson to a weapon of mass destruction. A slightly more apt modern comparison for the war of the booksellers might however be with the Google Books saga, still unresolved in mid-2013, nearly a decade after it began. Like Donaldson, Google set out to make generally available books that the company took to be out of copyright; the accompanying rhetoric of putting all human knowledge in the hands of those who want it has grandiose echoes of Donaldson's "books sold cheap".

There were still legal issues which Donaldson's two cases left unresolved: for example, the status of unpublished works, and the availability of remedies against infringement of copyright beyond those in the Statute of Anne. These would be tackled in the courts over the next 30 years.

But Donaldson's energy, determination and entrepreneurship had led to a transformation in the understanding of copyright itself which

35 *Donaldson v Beckett* (1774) 4 Burr 2408, 2 Bro PC 129.
36 H Paton (ed), *The Lyon in Mourning* (1896), vol 3, p 294.
37 W K Wimsatt Jr and F A Pottle (eds), *Boswell for the Defence 1769–1774* (1960), p 215.
38 Raven, *The Business of Books*, p 217.

has lasted down to the present. Copyright is a creature of statute. While judges, lawyers and legal writers may work creatively with the statutory wording that happens to be in force, real expansion (or contraction) of copyright law is the job of the legislator, who is, perhaps, better placed (or at least has more legitimacy) than a court dealing with disputes between individuals to assess where the overall balance of interests should lie in law. It remains to be seen, however, whether that long-held view is now in turn about to be overthrown by the global market force that is Google.

Martyrs to Circumstance:
Longworth v Yelverton

Elaine E Sutherland

C hance encounters happen all the time and, while most are of no lasting significance, others change the course of our lives. When William Charles Yelverton retrieved the shawl dropped by Maria Theresa Longworth on a damp August evening in 1852 aboard the cross-Channel steamer from Boulogne, little could either of them have realised how firmly their meeting would fall into the latter category.[1] The fateful meeting and the relationship that developed between the two led to some eight years of litigation in the Scottish, English and Irish courts, eventually reaching the House of Lords. At its heart lay what Wilkie Collins, one of the many novelists to draw inspiration from the case,[2] described as "the scandalous uncertainty of the marriage laws of Scotland ... entirely without parallel in any other civilized country in Europe".[3] He was talking, of course, of Scottish irregular marriage.

The Victorians showed every bit as much prurient interest in the romantic adventures of others as do modern-day tabloid readers and Facebook devotees. This tale had the essential elements – love, sex, money and betrayal – and the couple's failed relationship offered so much to fuel partisan loyalty. The principal characters were both known by their middle names, but the disparities between them were

---

1 In addition to the law reports and Theresa's own publications, this account draws particularly on Duncan Crow, *Theresa: The Story of the Yelverton Case* (1966); William Roughead, "The Law and Mrs Yelverton" (1916) 28 JR 38 and Chloë Schrama, *Wild Romance: The Scandal That Shook Victorian Society* (2010).

2 J R O'Flanagan, *Gentle Blood, or the Secret Marriage* (1861); Cyrus Redding, *A Wife and Not a Wife* (1867). The extent to which Mrs Wood's *East Lynne* (1861) and Mary Elizabeth Braddon's *Lady Audley's Secret* (1862) drew inspiration from the case has been doubted, given the timing of their publication: Jeanne Fahnestock, "The Rise and Fall of a Convention" (1981) 36 *Nineteenth-Century Fiction* 47 at 53.

3 Wilkie Collins, *Man and Wife* (1870), p 522 in the 1995 Oxford World Classics edition.

rather more significant. Theresa was a motherless, Roman Catholic teenager who had emerged from a convent school only two years before they met. In contrast, Charles was a 28-year-old Royal Artillery officer, a man of the world, whose somewhat ambiguous religious commitment was to feature in the litigation. Then there was the matter of social class, another factor that became significant as events unfolded. Charles was a member of the Irish aristocracy, albeit an impoverished one, ultimately succeeding to the title Viscount Avonmore. As the youngest daughter of a Manchester silk manufacturer, Theresa had a distinct whiff of commerce about her.

Set against the backdrop of the Crimean war, our story has much to offer to the historian, while many of its themes resonate for the modern reader. The position of women in society and the importance of marriage, particularly for "respectable" women, are central to it. The concern voiced in some quarters over Scottish irregular marriage was tied to both the public interest in the institution and its essential role in the transmission of property across the generations. Debate over the public interest in marriage and its purpose is echoed today in the controversies over whether it should be available to same-sex couples and what, if any, legal consequences should flow from open, non-marital cohabitation.

Then there is the double standard that held women so much more morally accountable for their actions than it did men. Commenting in a law journal of the day, one observer referred to Theresa as showing,

> an utter recklessness of social laws, a disregard of feminine propriety, a nature violent in its passions and impulses, but not tender, gentle, or womanly, and an intellect of considerable force but ill-trained, and without discretion.[4]

Yet of Charles' conduct, the same commentator expressed "no wish to join the outcry against a person who, if seriously guilty, was not we think as bad as he has been described, and was led on by peculiar temptation".[5]

To describe Theresa as a complex character is something of an understatement. It may be tempting to view her, as did some contemporary commentators, as a wronged woman, a victim. The title of her first novel (and of this chapter), *Martyrs to Circumstance*, a gothic romance with autobiographical overtones published in 1861, may lend support to that view. As we learn more about her life,

---

4 Anonymous, "The Yelverton Marriage Case" (1861) 11 *Law Magazine and Law Review* or *Quarterly Journal of Jurisprudence* 215 at 227.

5 "The Yelverton Marriage Case", p 224.

however, we find a woman who showed initiative and tenacity and was anything but passive when faced with a challenge. Victorian society admired men who identified their goals and pursued them with determination and vigour, but women who displayed similar fortitude met with disapproval, if not hostility. Some might say little has changed – just ask Hillary Rodham Clinton.

SCOTS IRREGULAR MARRIAGE

It will be apparent that Scots irregular marriage is central to our tale and a brief account of the relevant law is offered by way of background. Nineteenth-century Scots law provided for the kind of formal marriage, complete with public notice and a ceremony, not so different from that with which a modern reader will be familiar. The benefit of that approach is the publicity surrounding the event and the record kept of it having taken place. Far more controversial, at least outside the country, was the Scottish option of irregular marriage, a concept that has its roots in the not unreasonable principle that the consent of the parties is fundamental to matrimony. That being the case, it is undesirable to place cumbersome legal formalities in the way of those wishing to marry.

Three kinds of irregular marriage were available and the first, marriage by declaration of present consent (*per verba de praesenti*), required nothing more than for the parties to exchange genuine consent, in Scotland, to immediate marriage. There was no need for a celebrant, nor for witnesses, although, as Theresa was to discover, the absence of the latter might prove problematic were a dispute to arise later. The second form, marriage by promise followed by sexual intercourse (*per verba de futuro subsequente copula*), required a serious promise of marriage, that promise being crystallised by sexual intercourse following in reliance on it, both events taking place in Scotland. The third form of irregular marriage, marriage by cohabitation with habit and repute, was more like what is known as "common law marriage" in many other jurisdictions. It required the parties to live together in Scotland for a sufficient, but unspecified, period of time and to be regarded in the community as a married couple.

Scots irregular marriage stood in stark contrast to the marriage laws of England where Lord Harwicke's Marriage Act of 1753 sought to get rid of clandestine marriages, viewed as a problem because of the danger they posed to later, formal marriages, by tightening up the legal formalities for marriage.[6] Having been proactive in the attempt to rid themselves of a perceived evil, it is little wonder that Scots irregular marriage engendered such hostility from our southern neighbours since geographic proximity meant that English men and women might find themselves embroiled in that very evil if they came to Scotland. Irregular marriage, however, had stout defenders amongst the Scottish legal fraternity with the advocate, John Campbell Smith, commending it for its "simplicity and security; simplicity in the entering into it, and facility in proving and enforcing it".[7] That characterisation was to prove unduly optimistic in Theresa's case and another advocate, John Ferguson McLennan, offered the more pragmatic justification, at least for the first two kinds of irregular marriage, that "wherever a secret marriage takes place, a union of a different nature would probably have been consummated, had the marriage in secret been impossible".[8]

A RELATIONSHIP OF SORTS DEVELOPS

Following their meeting on the steamer, Theresa and Charles were not to see each other again for some three years. After a period in England, Theresa travelled in southern Europe, settling in Naples for a time, before she was summoned home in 1854 to care for her dying father. After his leave was over, Charles returned to his regiment and was variously stationed in Malta and Turkey. They began corresponding when Theresa asked Charles to convey letters to her much-loved cousin, John Augustus Longworth, who was working in Montenegro. Whether this was a ruse to re-establish contact with the object of her youthful fantasies or a genuine request for help is a matter for debate, but it marked the beginning of an exchange of letters between Theresa and Charles that was to feature in the

---

6 Scottish irregular marriages and the case of *Campbell v Cochran* (1747) Mor 10456 contributed to the drive to pass the Act. See, Leah Leneman, "The Scottish Case that Led to Hardwicke's Marriage Act" (1999) 17 *Law and History Review* 161.
7 John Campbell Smith, *The Marriage Laws of England, Scotland and Ireland* (1864) p 8.
8 John Ferguson McLennan, "Marriage and Divorce – The Laws of England and Scotland" (1861) 35 *North British Review* 187 at 199.

subsequent litigation. There is little doubt that Theresa was the more enthusiastic correspondent and their early letters suggest she attached greater romantic significance to the relationship than did Charles whose tone was often somewhat casual and distant. However, over time, their pet names for each other, "Carlo" and "Carissima", entered the correspondence.

After the death of her father, Theresa joined the *Soeurs de Charité* as a civilian nurse (a *vivandière*), serving in the Crimea. Whether she chose that path to be near to Charles is another unanswered question, but she clearly experienced the horrors of war first-hand and was seriously committed to her work tending wounded soldiers at the hospital in Galata.

When the two finally met again in 1855, whatever attraction Charles felt for Theresa was rekindled and she claimed he proposed that they be married right away by the local Greek Orthodox bishop. As a Catholic, that option was unacceptable to her and, besides, she wanted to continue her nursing work. How serious Charles was about marriage is questionable given the speed with which his ardour cooled when he again returned to his regiment. Nonetheless, after a truce was declared in the Crimea in 1856, the couple met again at the home, near Sevastopol, of Theresa's friends, Colonel and Mrs Straubenzee, who later confirmed that Charles introduced himself as her fiancé.

After the war, Theresa moved to Bebek while Charles remained at Sevastopol and, again, his affections seemed to fade. It was at this point that he spun a somewhat incredible tale about being financially dependent on an allowance from his uncle whose generosity would only continue as long as Charles remained unmarried and childless, the uncle hoping that his own son would inherit the Avonmore title. Given that Charles had an elder brother who was in line for that position, it was little wonder that the uncle dismissed the story years later as a fabrication and, to be fair, even Theresa seemed to have doubted its veracity at the time.

Their correspondence continued, but with a desperation on Theresa's part that makes her letters painful to read. Saddest of all is that she was well aware of how pathetic she sounded and was wracked with self-loathing and thoughts of suicide. Charles responded, quite unequivocally, "I cannot counsel you to wait for me." Whatever he lacked in terms of sensitivity, he was at least being honest and he made his way from the Crimea to Vienna, via the Danube, to avoid meeting up with her in Bebek. Meanwhile, Theresa was unaware of Charles' whereabouts and travelled to Malta in a fruitless search for him, before returning to England.

LOVE IN THE ATHENS OF THE NORTH

On her return, Theresa found two letters from Charles waiting for her, one of which informed her that he was stationed in Leith, near Edinburgh, and containing the words, "Be welcome". Accompanied by an old friend from convent school, Arabella MacFarlane, she headed for Edinburgh, taking rooms with a Mrs Gemble in St Vincent Street in the city's respectable New Town.

The point of Theresa's relocation was, of course, to see Charles and the couple began meeting almost daily, often at Theresa's apartment with Arabella present. They also rode out together in the city, Charles accompanied Arabella to church when Theresa was singing in the choir and Theresa visited him at his barracks after a fall from his horse rendered him temporarily immobile. It seemed almost as if her feelings for him were finally being reciprocated.

According to Theresa's version of events, it was on 12 April 1857 that the couple exchanged consent to marriage: something that, it will be remembered, would be enough to seal the bond of matrimony under Scots law. They were alone in her sitting room and Arabella's Church of England prayer book was lying on a table when they solemnly exchanged consent to marriage, later reading through the marriage ceremony from the prayer book. What actually happened came down very much to "he said, she said", because there was no witness, Arabella being absent or out of earshot; and Charles denied later that the incident had taken place. But he went one better, alleging that the couple engaged in sexual intercourse in February 1857, something Theresa denied. If sex had preceded any promise, then the case for marriage by promise *followed* by sexual intercourse would be cast into doubt. If Theresa is to be believed, he continued to press his advances after the exchange of marital consent but, as a Catholic, she preferred to delay consummation until after a priest had blessed the union. Accordingly, she removed herself from temptation and went to stay with her friends, the Thelwalls, in Hull, and Charles later went to visit his family in Ireland.

THE IRISH MARRIAGE

During their separation, the couple's correspondence continued, following the all-too-familiar pattern of greater enthusiasm on her part than on his. Charles appears to have instructed Theresa to keep quiet about the Scottish marriage, the very marriage he later denied, but he did buy a wedding ring from a jeweller in Dublin. Theresa finally travelled to Waterford in Ireland in July 1857, where Charles left her waiting for several days before whisking her off to less populated parts of the country. They stayed at hotels in Malahide, Newry and Rostrevor, taking suites of rooms, and Theresa was adamant that they slept separately during this time, albeit hotel staff regarded them as husband and wife.

At Rostrevor, Theresa consulted a priest, the Reverend Bernard Mooney, about her marriage and he confirmed that no ceremony was necessary since they were already married in Scotland, something confirmed by his bishop. However, Charles urged him to comply with Theresa's wishes for a Catholic ceremony. The priest asked Charles if he was a Catholic, to which Charles replied, "I am a Protestant Catholic." That was no idle question because, at the time, peculiarly anti-Catholic legislation provided that a marriage performed by a priest between a Catholic and a Protestant in Ireland was void.[9] There is every likelihood that Charles knew of the statute because his grandfather had escaped a union years before by relying on it. On 15 August 1857, the couple knelt before the altar in the chapel of Killowan and the priest repeated the marriage ceremony, omitting only the benediction.

After the ceremony, the couple travelled extensively in Ireland, Scotland and England, visiting the Thelwalls in Hull. On numerous occasions, Charles referred to Theresa as his wife. Arabella, John Thelwall and others gave evidence to that effect, although all seemed to be aware that the marriage had to be kept secret from Charles' family. Charles obtained a passport for Theresa in the name "Mrs Theresa Yelverton" and they travelled in France where Theresa, who was pregnant by this time, became ill. Charles had to return to his regiment in Leith and it fell to her landlady to care for Theresa when she miscarried. Meanwhile, Charles had turned his attentions to Emily Forbes, of whom more presently.

LOVE LOST

The couple's final meeting took place in Leith on 25 June 1858 when Charles urged Theresa to go to Glasgow, thence to New Zealand to stay with her brother, Jack, repeating his request in a letter the following day and indicating that his brother would call upon her to

9 19 Geo II, c 13.

explain. Charles' conduct was distinctly disingenuous: on 26 June, he married Emily Marianne Forbes at Trinity Episcopal Church in Edinburgh. Emily was the widow of the renowned Edinburgh University naturalist, Professor Edward Forbes, and, while she had some independent means, she was not particularly wealthy. Thus, a desire for financial security hardly explains Charles' urgency in marrying her. Of greater significance may be the fact that their eldest child, Barry Nugent Yelverton, was born some seven and a half months after the marriage.[10]

Whether Charles' brother, the Honourable George Frederick William Yelverton, actually broke the news of the wedding to Theresa is unclear, but he repeated the request that she go to New Zealand. Far from leaving quietly, Theresa went on the offensive, raising her first court action in August 1858 in which she sought declarator in the Court of Session, recognising her marriage to Charles as valid. That action was abandoned and a civil suit, raised in England in February 1861, failed on jurisdictional grounds. Meanwhile, the Irish courts became involved and Theresa raised a fresh action in Scotland where she pursued her cause relentlessly. Information was also passed to the procurator fiscal in Edinburgh, leading to Charles' arrest on a charge of bigamy, albeit no prosecution followed.

THE IRISH COURT

It was an Irish court that addressed the validity of the marriage first and it came to do so somewhat tangentially and by a rather circuitous route. At the time, a husband was obliged to support his wife and anyone who supplied a wife with items necessary to sustain her could sue the husband for payment. It will be remembered that Theresa had stayed with her friends, the Thelwalls in Hull, and John Thelwall raised an action against Charles for some £260, being the cost of board and lodgings for Theresa and her maid. There is no doubt that Thelwall's primary purpose was not to recover money for something he had provided gladly but, rather, it was to give Theresa the opportunity to air her case publicly. Procedural restrictions prevented the parties to a consistorial (family law) action in the Scottish courts from giving evidence, but no such constraints applied to an action for debt in Ireland. Both Theresa and Charles gave evidence before

10 He was born on 11 February 1859.

Lord Chief Justice Monahan and an all-male jury in the Court of Common Pleas in Dublin.[11]

What might have been a rather dull court action over a debt turned into nothing short of a public spectacle with the court filled to capacity, observers overflowing into the snowy street outside. Sergeant Sullivan led for Thelwall, while the equally-eminent Right Honourable Abraham Brewster appeared for Charles and the sole point at issue was whether Charles was, indeed, Theresa's husband and, thus, liable for her support. It was not only members of the public whose passions ran high throughout the proceedings, with cheers and jeers greeting the various witnesses. The Chief Justice himself repeatedly gave way to uncontrolled emotion and such was the fervour with which counsel approached their task that he was compelled to remind them that the court was not a bear garden. As a Scots lawyer observed, somewhat primly, later,

> The proceedings, which occupied ten days, were marked by a passionate display of Hibernian enthusiasm, amazing to those accustomed to the dignified decorum of our Scottish Courts.[12]

Theresa was at her most articulate and the favourable impression she created was undoubtedly helped by her beauty and charm. Charles, on the other hand, failed to impress, coming over as the callous cad that, one suspects, many observers had decided he was before the case began. In the event, the jury returned an unqualified verdict for Thelwall, finding Charles to be Catholic and the Scottish and Irish marriages to be valid. The court "rang with enthusiastic and prolonged applause" and "members of the Bar stood up and joined heartily in the public manifestations of delight; many of them actually took off their wigs and waved them with energy".[13] There was no doubt where popular sentiment lay, with a contemporary observer noting:

> One of the greatest demonstrations of popular enthusiasm that perhaps was ever witnessed in the city of Dublin, took place as the Honourable Mrs Yelverton proceeded from the Four Courts to the Gresham Hotel. ... Over fifty thousand people frantic with joy proceeded to bid her welcome as she issued from the hall.[14]

---

11 *Report of the Trial in the Case of Thelwall v Yelverton: Before the Chief Justice and a Special Jury, on 21st February, 1861, Containing the Letters, Speeches of Counsel, Judge"s Charge, and Finding of the Jury* (1861).
12 Roughead, "The Law and Mrs Yelverton", p 55.
13 Roughead, "The Law and Mrs Yelverton", p 56.
14 *Report of the Trial in the Case of Thelwall v Yelverton*, p 130.

THE SCOTTISH COURTS

While the Irish proceedings must have given Theresa a much-needed sense of vindication, litigation addressing the validity of the marriage was underway in the Scottish courts. It had been triggered by Charles seeking declarator of freedom and putting to silence,[15] essentially asking the court to confirm that he was not married to Theresa and to order her to stop claiming that he was. Theresa responded by instituting fresh proceedings for declarator of marriage, relying on all three kinds of irregular marriage under Scots law. The two actions were conjoined and came before Lord Ardmillan in the Outer House of the Court of Session in Edinburgh. Again, the case attracted the finest legal minds of the day with counsel for both parties later holding judicial office. In a lengthy and detailed opinion, his Lordship found against Theresa on both the facts and the points of law argued by her eminent legal team.[16]

Theresa did what unhappy litigants the world over do, she appealed, in this case to the Inner House. She abandoned her claim based on marriage by cohabitation with habit and repute, but succeeded in convincing Lords Curriehill and Deas that she and Charles were married by declaration of present consent and by promise followed by sexual intercourse, the Lord President (McNeill) dissenting.[17] It was then Charles' turn to appeal and the case reached the House of Lords where the bench again split on the matter, with the Lord Chancellor (Westbury) and Lord Brougham affirming the decision of the Inner House, while Lords Wensleydale, Chelmsford and Kingsdown preferred Lord Ardmillan's conclusion.[18] Taking a head count of the judges in the Scottish case – and, of course, that is not how these things work – Theresa had lost by one vote.

Later proceedings before the Scottish courts proved fruitless[19] and the result of the years of litigation was that Theresa was a single woman while Charles was married to Emily and had narrowly avoided a trial for bigamy. In short, the courts had finished with the matter. Writing of the case some years later, McDonnell Bodkin KC noted of Theresa

---

15 Such actions remained competent in Scotland until they were abolished by the Family Law (Scotland) Act 2006, s 42.
16 *Longworth v Yelverton* (1862) 24 D 696.
17 *Longworth v Yelverton* (1862) 1 M 161.
18 *Yelverton v Longworth* (1864) 2 M (HL) 49.
19 *Longworth v Yelverton* (1865) 3 M 645; *Longworth v Yelverton* (1867) 5 M (HL) 144; *Longworth v Yelverton* (1868) 7 M 70.

that, "the unhappy lady lapsed into a miserable obscurity from which no corner of the curtain has ever been raised".[20] The learned silk could not have been more wrong.

THE AFTERMATH

Charles may have won in the courts, but the case was not without its consequences for him. He was suspended from military duties following the Irish trial, later being placed on half pay and eventually being removed from the list of the Royal Regiment of Artillery: not exactly drummed out of the regiment, but the message was clear.[21] He went on to become the fourth Viscount Avonmore in 1870, his elder brother having predeceased their father. Charles and Emily had four children, two of whom died in infancy. He himself died in Biarritz, France, on 1 April 1883 and the Avonmore title passed to his son, Barry Nugent Yelverton.[22]

What did single life mean for Theresa? Her always-delicate health continued to trouble her, but her more immediate problem was money since the costly litigation had exhausted her limited resources. It is a reflection of the sympathy and support she engendered that friends took up a collection for her in her native Manchester. If she had shown resourcefulness in pursuing her goals thus far, that was nothing compared to her response to this difficulty since, putting pen to paper, she published three volumes drawing on the case.[23] While these works were undoubtedly prompted by financial necessity, they reflect the extent to which she remained firmly convinced of the rightness of her cause. Despite losing in the courts, she never flinched from her conviction about where justice lay, styling herself Theresa Yelverton and, from 1870, Viscountess Avonmore. For a woman of less than pristine reputation, however, opportunities in Victorian Britain were limited. The New World offered something of a fresh start and in 1867 she set off for America with plans to write a travel book.

---

20 M McDonnell Bodkin, *Famous Irish Trials* (1918), p 78.
21 Roughead, "The Law and Mrs Yelverton", p 61.
22 Hellena Kelleher Kahn is mistaken in claiming that Charles had no heirs and the title died with him: "The Yelverton Affair: A Nineteenth Century Sensation" (2005) 13 *History Ireland* 21 at 25.
23 *Martyrs to Circumstances* (1861); *The Yelverton Correspondence* (1863); and *A Woman's Trials* (1867).

TERESINA IN AMERICA

Theresa was not the first British woman to travel in America and write about her experiences. Frances Trollope is widely regarded as the founder of the genre, with the publication, in 1832, of *Domestic Manners of the Americans*, and others followed in her footsteps.[24] The attraction is not difficult to fathom since, alongside novelty and adventure, there was a degree of freedom from familiar social constraints. As Isabella Bird, another intrepid traveller, put it, "Travellers are privileged to do the most improper things with perfect propriety; that is one of the charms of travelling."[25] The country Theresa found was still reeling from the Civil War which had ended in 1865 and amongst the many changes that came with the post-bellum era were new opportunities for women. It is no surprise, perhaps, that women seizing this liberating prospect met with disapproval in some quarters, with Lord Curzon describing this "genus of female globetrotters" as "one of the horrors of the latter half of the nineteenth century".[26]

If Theresa hoped that America would offer an escape the publicity that had surrounded her in Britain she was mistaken since the first person who contacted her when she arrived in New York was Horace Greenly, editor of the *New York Tribune*, who wanted to meet her precisely because of the interest she had generated in the British press. Her world may have been free from the easy communication of the Internet, but news still travelled and the *New York Times* had been less than kind in assessing her final performance before the House of Lords, warning that it presaged

> what we shall have in Congress when women's suffrage is fairly established ... the language is arabesque – the ideas are confused and ladylike. The point is to crowd as many poetical quotations and images into a given space as human ingenuity is capable of'.[27]

Theresa's travels, running to over 20,000 miles, were to take her from the east coast cities, where conventional comforts were readily available, to southern states experiencing post-war privations, through the mid-West and, ultimately, to San Francisco and Yosemite. During that time, she had her share of adventures. In Bainbridge, Georgia, her presence

---

24 See Harriet Martineau, *Retrospect of Western Travel* (1838) and Isabella Bird, *A Lady's Life in the Rocky Mountains* (1879).
25 Quoted in Dea Birkett, *Spinsters Abroad: Victorian Lady Explorers* (1989) p 115.
26 Quoted in Shirley Foster, *Across the New World: Nineteenth Century Women Travellers and Their Writings* (1990) p 6.
27 "Minor Topics", *New York Times*, 23 July 1867.

inadvertently fuelled tensions between former Confederate soldiers and the local garrison commander, armed men swarmed her hotel and it was surrounded by an angry crowd, it being rumoured that she was a Union spy. In the event, the matter was resolved amicably, with Theresa receiving an apology from three of the armed men and enjoying mint juleps and sherry cobbler with them.[28] In Yosemite, she became separated from her party and was caught in a snowstorm, sheltering overnight alongside her horse in a hollow tree, only to find herself face to face with a bear the following morning.[29]

A degree of ingenuity was required of all travellers at the time and Theresa was clearly up to the challenge. Leaving New York for South Carolina, she packed her dresses in a coffin to prevent them from wrinkling. In addition to the coffin and a long-handled coffee pot that she was never without, she was accompanied by a male secretary. Little is known of him, but she called him "Domine Tinglethumb" in her travel books and he appears to have been a Scot who had studied for the ministry and had also read Scots law. Almost certainly, there was no romantic connection between the two and, indeed, Theresa thought him rather pompous, often pedantic, and something of a prig. He had an "admiration for antique art and a hatred of all discomforts and bad dinners".[30]

Theresa's reflections on her travels offer further insights into the complexity of her character. On occasion, she joined other writers in rather mocking observations on the peculiarities of American life, and the American penchant for drinking iced water provided her with ample ammunition, prompting the observation:

> Drinking ice-water is an American mania, an anti-hydrophobia sort of disease, and it is quite probable that if there is not a good supply of ice-water in heaven they will all petition St Peter to be allowed to return to New York.[31]

Yet she was quick to distance herself from the narrowness of some of her fellow English travellers, observing that many

> remain too short a time, and are too strictly enclosed by the conventionalities of visiting and organised sight-seeing, to be able to take a comprehensive and unprejudiced view of the vast and varied field of American character.[32]

28 *Teresina in America* (1875) vol 1, p 182.
29 *Teresina in America*, vol 1, p 89.
30 Crow, *Theresa*, p 260.
31 Crow, *Theresa*, p 257
32 Crow, *Theresa*, p 255

One facet of that character to impress itself upon her particularly was the social mobility that was the hallmark of the country and she noted that, "If a man is dissatisfied with the station he occupies in the world, there is no place like America for changing it."[33]

It is hardly surprising that Theresa would be a keen observer of marriage laws in America. What struck her most was the fluidity of the institution and she observed that trains passing through Chicago stopped "for *twenty minutes* for divorces and for the performance of the marriage ceremony".[34] Her impression of the matrimonial regime in Indiana was no more favourable and she described it as "the Gretna Green of the West",[35] something that she can hardly have intended as a compliment in the light of her own experience of Scots marriage law.

Rather more surprising was Theresa's reaction to the Mormon practice of polygamy or, more correctly, polygyny, which permitted a man to have multiple wives simultaneously, but extended no similar latitude to women. Long a rich seam for travel writers, Theresa had the opportunity to observe polygynous marriage first-hand in the Utah territory, talking with numerous wives, meeting Brigham Young and dancing with one of his sons at a ball.[36] While not blind to its limitations, she was impressed by the domestic harmony and efficiency of the arrangement. It may have been the honesty with which it was embraced that led her to mount a strong defence of the practice later in *Teresina Peregrina*. That said, she clearly did not see it as an option for herself, commenting that she was fortunate to leave the territory without the "matrimonial noose being cast over me".[37]

In Philadelphia, she heard Anna Dickinson, a leading activist in the growing women's rights movement, addressing a crowd running into the hundreds. This prompted Theresa to expand in print on her own views and she clearly found common ground with the cause, expressing disquiet over the way in which women were encouraged to espouse helplessness and, thereby, forced into manipulative behaviour within marriage.[38] Where she parted company with the movement was over its somewhat androgynous dress code and penchant for short hair.

33   *Teresina in America*, vol 2, p 240.
34   *Teresina in America*, vol 2, p 189.
35   *Teresina in America*, vol 2, p 192.
36   Crow, *Theresa*, pp 263–264; Schrama, *Wild Romance*, pp 140–142.
37   *Teresina Peregrina or Fifty Thousand Miles of Travel Round the World* (1874) vol 2, p 45.
38   *Teresina Peregrina*, vol 2, pp 138–139.

Like all complex characters, Theresa had the capacity to disappoint and nowhere is that clearer than on the issue of race. In Charleston, South Carolina, she met a former slave-owner and, while not expressing support for slavery itself, she was moved by his ruin. That, perhaps, is no more than an illustration of her human compassion, but her observations on the newly-freed slaves stand out in stark contrast. Precisely what she said will not be repeated here because it is so utterly offensive, but she likened African-American children to "little pups" or "little pigs", distinguishing them from the "angelic sweetness" of white infants, and referred to their parents as "savage adults".[39] It would be all too easy to excuse her observations as fairly usual for the time, but she was not a person to accept received wisdom without question. Given her own experience of discrimination – remember her Irish marriage was ultimately held by the House of Lords to be invalid because of anti-Catholic legislation – one might have expected her to spot prejudice when she saw it.

Undoubtedly, her final months in America were the happiest for Theresa. After a brief spell in San Francisco and Sausalito, where the poet and author Charles Warren Stoddart sought, unsuccessfully, to revive her career giving public readings, she settled in the small community in the Yosemite Valley, becoming friendly with the Hutchings family whose hotel was something of a magnet for the many urban visitors drawn to the wilderness. Theresa charmed her companions, with one noting that "her conversational powers were wonderful"[40] and another describing her as "the most interesting woman I ever knew".[41]

It was there that she met the noted entomologist Harry Edwards who showed her how to collect butterflies and beetles, a hobby she continued to enjoy later in Hong Kong. But perhaps the most famous friendship she established at Yosemite was with John Muir, founder of the Sierra Club and hero of the American wilderness.[42] Commentators differ on the nature of their relationship with some presenting Theresa as a rather pathetic figure, yet again experiencing

---

39 *Teresina in America*, vol 1, pp 49 and 60.
40 Sanborn, Preface to *Zanita*, p xxiii.
41 Mary Viola Lawrence, "Summer with a Countess" (1871) 7 *Overland Monthly* 474.
42 Recently, Muir's heroic reputation has undergone something of a revision, largely due to his emphasis on a "pristine" wilderness where the Native Americans, who had lived there for centuries, had no place. See, Carolyn Merchant, "Shades of Darkness: Race and Environmental History" (2003) 8 *J Env Hist* 380.

unrequited love, while others dismiss such a scenario as insulting to these two strong individuals.[43] In any event, Muir was to provide the model for the character Kenmuir in her novel *Zanita*.[44] Meanwhile, she continued to write for various newspapers and travel magazines and to work on both the novel and *Teresina in America*. After a brief flirtation with farming, she left America in 1871 and set sail for Hong Kong.

THERESA THE PILGRIM

Theresa travelled to Hong Kong, via Hawaii, where the last king, Kamehameha V tried to tempt her to stay with the promise of a thousand acres of land. Having already discovered that farming did not suit her, she continued on her way to Hong Kong, spending the next three years travelling in Asia and India, visiting what are now Borneo, Cambodia, Malaysia and Singapore.

It was amongst the Chinese community in Hong Kong that she again encountered polygyny and, again, she saw much to recommend it.[45] However, that was nothing compared to her delight when she discovered that polyandry – a woman having multiple husbands simultaneously – had been practised in Sri Lanka until the "horrid British" had sought to abolish it a few years earlier. "There's masculine tyranny for you!", she observed.[46]

When it was time to return to Britain, Theresa chose to travel via Gibraltar and Spain, undaunted by the fact that the country was in the midst of a civil war. Finally, she arrived in Edinburgh again and, this time, her companion was a young Sinhalese boy whom she had adopted on her travels, money having changed hands with his parents. After a time devoted to writing and the publication of *Teresina in America*, she again set sail for Sri Lanka with the goal of returning her young companion to his home.

She charts much of this time in *Teresina Peregrina or Fifty Thousand Miles of Travel Round the World*, published in 1874, the title drawing on the Spanish word for a wanderer or pilgrim, *peregrino*. Reactions to the book ran the gamut of reactions to Theresa herself but the fact that it was reviewed in a number of leading journals of the day suggests

43 Sanborn, Preface to *Zanita*, p xxvi.
44 *Zanita: A Tale of Yo-semite* (1872).
45 *Teresina Peregrina*, vol 1, p 150.
46 *Teresina Peregrina*, vol 2, p 287.

that it certainly had an impact. Some reviewers were clearly impressed by her courage and the range of her travels. The more negative reviewers focused on the unfeminine nature of her pursuits and the candour with which she discussed her experiences, with one commenting, "Most women, if they had lingered in a crowd among frescoes that were obscenely gross, would have preferred silence on the subject."[47] An author keen to sell copies of a book could not have asked for more.

THE FINAL CHAPTER

South Africa was to be Theresa's final destination. How she came to be there again reflects her indomitable spirit. Whilst in Sri Lanka, Theresa learned that the Empress Eugénie was *en route* to South Africa to visit the site where her beloved son, Prince Louis Napoleon, had met a less-than-glorious death in a skirmish with Zulu warriors. Scenting a story worthy of her journalistic talents, Theresa set off for Cape Town and followed the Empress' party for weeks in the attempt to gain an interview with the grieving mother. Whether Theresa had met the Empress previously, as she claimed, is doubtful, but she showed characteristic tenacity in pursuing her goal, on one occasion facing down a cordon of Zulu warriors engaged by the Empress' aides to keep her away. In the event, the determination of the Empress' retinue prevailed and the two never met, Theresa contenting herself with making a sketch of the cross marking the Prince's grave. She remained in South Africa and, adopting the *nom de plume* "Kate the Critic", continued her career as a journalist, writing sometimes-scathing pieces for the *Natal Witness* and becoming something of a thorn in the side of local officials and the more pompous community worthies.

It was in South Africa that Theresa was diagnosed with dropsy (oedema) and her friend, George Mason, moved her into his home where she was nursed through her final illness by his daughter. She died on 13 September 1881, aged forty-five, surrounded by friends, one of whom reported that "her mind was clear and vigorous up to the last moment".[48] The Reverend Joseph Rice, curate of St Paul's Cathedral, conducted the funeral service and she is buried in Pietermaritzburg Church of England cemetery in Natal.

47 "Teresina Peregrina", *Pall Mall Gazette*, 26 March 1874, p 11.
48 Sandborn, Preface to *Zanita*, p xxxvi.

PARTING THOUGHTS

What was the legal impact of *Longworth v Yelverton*? Undoubtedly, the publicity surrounding the case and its eventual outcome contributed to the campaign to repeal the anti-Catholic marriage legislation in Ireland.[49] As a result, a "mixed marriage" solemnised by a priest between a Catholic and a Protestant, like that of Theresa and Charles, became valid.[50]

Initially, it seemed that the case would have a similarly dramatic effect on Scots irregular marriage since a Royal Commission recommended abolition of all three forms in 1868.[51] However, nothing came of the recommendations, probably because, whatever the opprobrium with which it was viewed abroad, there was no real dissatisfaction with the practice in Scotland. The first two forms of irregular marriage – marriage by declaration of present consent and marriage by promise followed by sexual intercourse – remained until their eventual abolition by statute in 1939.[52] The third form – marriage by cohabitation with habit and repute – endured unaltered into the 21st century when it was severely curtailed by statute in 2006 amid considerable debate.[53] Plans to abolish it altogether a few years later were abandoned by the Scottish Government in the face of opposition.[54]

What of Theresa herself? Was she a victim or, to paraphrase her words, "martyr to circumstance"? Clearly, Charles treated her badly and the case left her impoverished and with her reputation somewhat tarnished at a time when such things mattered. But had she succeeded in establishing her marriage to him, what would her life have been like? At best, it would have been that of the wife of a none-too-wealthy Irish aristocrat – and one who had shown every sign of being utterly selfish. He might not have been able to shake off the bonds of matrimony, but that would not necessarily have restricted his conduct. Instead, "circumstances" forced Theresa to make her own living and to draw on her considerable inner resources in stretching herself. She travelled the world, meeting many of the leading lights of the day,

49 William O'Connor Morris, *Memories and Thoughts of a Life* (1895).
50 Marriage Causes and Marriage Law Amendment (Ireland) Acts 1870 and 1871.
51 Report of the Royal Commission on the Laws of Marriage (1868).
52 Marriage (Scotland) Act 1939, s 5.
53 Family Law (Scotland) Act 2006, s 3.
54 Policy Memorandum: Marriage and Civil Partnership (Scotland) Bill (2013), para 153.